THE SCOTTISH LABOUR PARTY

EDITED BY GERRY HASSAN

EDINBURGH UNIVERSITY PRESS

© in this edition Edinburgh University Press, 2004.
The copyright in the individual chapters is retained by the contributors.

Edinburgh University Press Ltd
22 George Square, Edinburgh

Typeset in Goudy by
Hewer Text Ltd, Edinburgh, and
printed and bound in Spain by
GraphyCems

A CIP record for this book is available from the British Library

ISBN 0 7486 1784 1 (paperback)

The right of the contributors to be identified as
authors of this work has been asserted in accordance
with the Copyright, Designs and Patents Act 1988.

THE SCOTTISH LABOUR PARTY

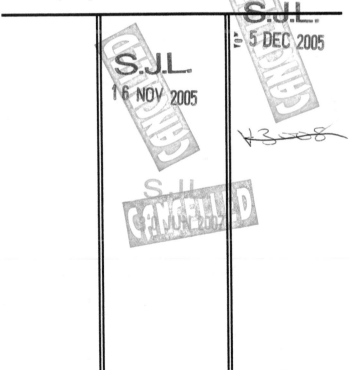

In memory of Henry Drucker (1942–2002)
Labour academic, thinker and inspiration

Contents

Notes on the Contributors   vii

1. The People's Party, Still?
   The Sociology of Scotland's Leading Party
   Gerry Hassan   1

I   Understanding Scottish Labour: History and Environment

2. The Labour Party in Scotland 1888–1945:
   Pragmatism and Principle
   Richard Finlay   21
3. Labour in Scotland since 1945: Myth and Reality
   Bob McLean   34
4. The Economic and Social Context of Scottish Labour
   Christopher Harvie   51

II   Scotland's Leading Party

5. The Scottish Electorate and Labour
   Paula Surridge   69
6. The Politics of Scottish Labour's Heartlands
   Jane Saren and James McCormick   86
7. Women and the Labour Party in Scotland
   Fiona Mackay   104

III   Scottish Labour, State, Nation and Autonomy

8. New Labour, New Parliament
   Douglas Fraser   127
9. Scottish Labour and British Politics
   Iain McLean   146

10. Pragmatic Nationalists?
    The Scottish Labour Party and Nationalism
    Nicola McEwen   160
11. The Autonomy and Organisation of Scottish Labour
    Peter Lynch and Steven Birrell   176

IV The Wider Movement, Scotland and Internationally

12. Labour's Journey from Socialism to Social Democracy:
    A Case Study of Gordon Brown's Political Thought
    Gerry Hassan   195
13. Scotland, Labour and the Trade Union Movement:
    Partners in Change or Uneasy Bedfellows?
    Mark Irvine   219
14. Socialism, Territory and the National Question
    Michael Keating   233

    Index   247

Notes on the Contributors

Steven Birrell is a freelance writer and postgraduate student at the University of Stirling where he has also taught part-time. His research focuses on political parties in Scotland post-devolution.

Richard Finlay is Director of the Research Centre in Scottish History at the University of Strathclyde. He is the author of *Independent and Free: Scottish Politics and the Origins of the SNP* (1994) and *A Partnership for Good? Scottish Politics and the Union Since 1880* (1997). His latest work is *Modern Scotland: 1914–2000* (2004).

Douglas Fraser has been Political Editor of the *Sunday Herald* since soon after its 1999 launch. Previously, he covered politics and other Scottish stories for *The Observer*, *The Sunday Times* and *The Irish Times*. He worked for *The Scotsman* from 1989 to 1997, as a news and feature writer on education, arts and the Highlands and Islands. He grew up in Edinburgh, was at university in Oxford, Cardiff and Harvard, and is co-author *of The Political Guide to Modern Scotland*, published in 2004.

Christopher Harvie has been Professor of British Studies at the University of Tübingen since 1980. His historical interests are wide and varied, and he is author of a number of books on Scotland including *Scotland and Nationalism: Scottish Society and Politics 1707–1997* (3rd edn 1998), *No Gods and Precious Few Heroes: Scotland in the Twentieth Century* (3rd edn 2000), *The Road to Home Rule* (2000) with Peter Jones, and *Scotland: a Short Story* (2002).

Gerry Hassan is a freelance writer, researcher and consultant, and has produced a number of books including *The Political Guide to Modern Scotland*, co-written with Douglas Fraser, *Anatomy of the New Scotland* and *Tomorrow's Scotland*. He has undertaken research in a wide range of areas, including social justice, public health and cities. He has worked with the Fabian Society, Social Market Foundation and Demos, is Associate

Editor of the Labour journal *Renewal* and is Honorary Research Fellow at Glasgow Caledonian University.

Mark Irvine is a writer, consultant and commentator, and a member of the National Union of Journalists. He is a former chair of the STUC Youth Committee and was NUPE's first ever winner of the TUC Youth Award in 1983 and operated at the highest levels of the trade union movement for twenty years working in London for most of the 1980s. He left full-time union work in 1999, having worked latterly as Unison's Head of Local Government and chief negotiator in Scotland.

Michael Keating is Professor of Regional Studies at the European University Institute, Florence, and Professor of Scottish Politics at the University of Aberdeen. He previously taught at the Universities of Western Ontario and Strathclyde. He has held visiting posts in the USA, England, France, Spain and Norway. He has published widely on urban and regional politics, nationalism and European politics.

Peter Lynch is Senior Lecturer in Politics at the University of Stirling. He is the author of *SNP: The History of the Scottish National Party* (2002) and *Scottish Government and Politics* (2001).

James McCormick has been Director of the Scottish Council Foundation, an independent think tank, since October 2002, having been Research Director from 1997. His main interests include welfare reform, the future of schools, public services and public involvement in decision-making. He has been involved in running various citizens' juries and visioning processes, including the *Possible Scotland* study (2002). He was also a member of the Treasury's Policy Action Team (PAT 14) on Access to Financial Services. Before joining the Foundation, he worked at the Institute for Public Policy Research as a Research Fellow with the Commission on Social Justice.

Nicola McEwen is a Lecturer in Politics at the University of Edinburgh, and Associate Director of the University's Institute of Governance. She obtained her Ph.D. from the University of Sheffield in 2001, after completing a doctoral thesis entitled 'State Welfare Nationalism: the territorial impact of welfare state development in Scotland and Quebec'. She has published work on Scottish politics, territorial politics, and inter-governmental relations in the UK and Canada.

Bob McLean works for the City of Edinburgh's Culture and Leisure Department. He writes and lectures on aspects of Irish and Scottish history, in particular the Irish War of Independence, the Irish Free State 1922–32 and the Scottish Labour and Home Rule movements. He is author of *Labour and Scottish Home Rule* and a number of articles and chapters.

Iain McLean is Professor of Politics, Oxford University, and a fellow of Nuffield College. He was educated in Edinburgh (Royal High School) and Oxford. His publications include *The Legend of Red Clydeside* (2nd edn 1999) and numerous academic articles from the 1970s to the present on devolution, finance and representation. He has recently completed a report for the Office of the Deputy Prime Minister on the regional distribution of public expenditure in England.

Fiona Mackay is a Senior Lecturer in Politics at the University of Edinburgh. Her broad research interests are in the areas of women and politics, gender and constitutional change in the UK, and gender and public policy. Recent publications include *Love and Politics: Women Politicians and the Ethics of Care* (2001) and the co-edited collections *Women and Contemporary Scottish Politics* (2001) and *The Changing Politics of Gender Equality* (2002).

Jane Saren is Business Manager of the Scottish Council Foundation, and a freelance consultant on management, public policy and communications. From 1996 to 2002 she was the founding managing director of the market-leading public affairs consultancy in Scotland. Prior to this she was a senior manager in local government. A native of Edinburgh, she has also lived and worked in Aberdeen, Liverpool and London.

Paula Surridge is Lecturer in Sociology at the University of Bristol. She began work on Scottish electoral behaviour as the research assistant to the 1992 Scottish Election Survey and has since been co-director of the 1997 Scottish Election Survey, the 1999 Scottish Parliament Election Survey and has worked closely on the Scottish Social Attitudes series.

CHAPTER I

The People's Party, Still?
The Sociology of Scotland's Leading Party

Gerry Hassan

The Scottish Labour Party has been one of the most important and defining institutions in the last 100 years plus of Scotland. It has contributed widely to Scottish society and politics, and played an important role in terms of ideas, policy, administration and government at a Scottish and UK level. This introductory chapter outlines some of the key issues on Scottish Labour. It examines the focus on historical studies of the party, key contemporary issues, and concludes with an overview of some of the major themes which emerge from the book.

REMEMBERING SCOTTISH LABOUR: MEMORIES AND MYTHS

Scottish Labour began its long history in April 1888 when Keir Hardie's legendary candidacy in the Mid-Lanark by-election resulted in him winning 617 votes, or 8.4 per cent. However, Hardie's campaign set off a chain of events which led four months later to the founding of the Scottish Labour Party (Harvie 1989: 10; McLean 1990: 10–12). Hardie's Scottish Labour Party had a brief existence, winding up one year after the forming of the Independent Labour Party (ILP) in 1893, but it left behind an important influence. A separate Scottish Workers' Parliamentary Committee was set up months before the Labour Representation Committee in 1900, which wound up in 1909. The incorporation of the Scottish party into British structures occurred with the establishment of the Scottish Advisory Council – a subordinate body – in 1915, and three years later, the party's constitution formalised the Scottish party's 'regional' status (Keating and Bleiman 1979: 56). However, on an informal level, the 'Scottish Labour Party' as an entity and idea continued to exist. While formal autonomy did not operate, and on one level it appeared like a branch line of the UK operation, on another, informally, the party retained

1

a degree of autonomy and discretion which mirrored the importance of formal and informal roles in Labour culture.

Scottish Labour first established itself as the leading party of Scotland in votes in 1923 and in seats in 1929, but this was not yet an uncontested dominance for all the myth of 'Red Clydeside'. Scottish Labour broke through in the 1920s in a three-party system between Labour, Conservatives and Liberals. When the Liberals collapsed in 1931, Scottish politics for the rest of the 1930s developed into a socialist/non-socialist divide from which the Conservatives (with their 'National' guise) benefited.

Scottish Labour did not really emerge as the uncontested leading party until well into the post-war era, winning the most seats in 1959 and votes in 1964. Its increasing dominance of Scottish politics began from this point forty years ago. And where for most of the initial post-war era, Conservative and Labour competed fairly equally for votes, seen in the small Labour lead of 3.8 per cent on average across the eight UK elections of 1945–70 (see table 1.1), this began to change with the slow decline of the Conservatives and the emergence of the SNP. From 1974 onwards, a four-party politics established itself which has reduced both the Labour and Conservative votes, but which led to a wider Labour lead over the Tories of 15 per cent in the period 1974–2001.

Given this contribution to Scottish public life, it is surprising that the main research and publications on Scottish Labour have focused exclusively on historical matters to the exclusion of contemporary analysis. In the last twenty-five years, a host of publications have looked at various aspects of the party's past. Some have addressed the party's entire history in chronological order, most notably the *Forward* centenary collection (Donnachie et al. 1989), while others have examined specific parts such as Labour and devolution, including Keating and Bleiman's *Labour and Scottish Nationalism* (1979) and Robert McLean's two-part *Labour and Scottish Home Rule* (1990, 1991). Others have shown fascination with 'Red Clydeside' and the role of the ILP, most notably Iain McLean's *The Legend of Red Clydeside* (1983) and McKinlay and Morris's *The ILP on Clydeside 1893–1932* (1991). Important ground was broken examining Labour and gender by feminist historians such as Eleanor Gordon in *Women and the Labour Movement in Scotland 1850–1914* (1991), an examination of women in work and trade union culture in Dundee. Several of the above Labour historians and writers have contributed to this volume: Bob McLean analysing politics post-1945; Christopher Harvie examining the socio-economic conditions which gave birth to Labour and the nature of 'the new society' Labour helped create; Iain McLean on Scottish and British political dynamics; and Michael Keating on wider issues of territorial politics.

Table 1.1   Party share of the vote by period for Westminster elections, 1918–2001

	1918–35	1945–70	1974–2001
Labour	34.8	47.3	40.0
Conservative	36.8	43.5	25.0
SNP	0.3	2.8	19.9
Liberal	23.3	5.0	13.9
Others	4.9	1.3	1.2

Source: F. W. S. Craig, British Electoral Facts 1832–1980; The British General Election series, 1983–2001.

Scottish Labour has also been covered in studies of the trade union movement in Scotland and STUC, via the anniversary works of Tuckett (1986) and Aitken (1997). Biographies can be seen as 'a sad sign of the general debasement of the political and civic culture: we all seem more interested in personality than in ideas' (Crick 2002: 101). Despite this, Labour movement biographies have long been a rich, specialist sub-section, and have provided one of the most fertile areas for looking at Scottish Labour. These range from William Knox's *Scottish Labour Leaders 1918–1939* (1984) to studies of individual politicians. Not surprisingly, the early years of Scottish Labour provide a richness of biographies with Keir Hardie (Morgan 1975), Ramsay MacDonald (Marquand 1977), James Maxton (Brown 1986; Knox 1987), Manny Shinwell (Slowe 1993) and many others. From the 'middle period' of Scottish Labour have come two biographies of Thomas Johnston, Secretary of State for Scotland in Churchill's wartime coalition (Walker 1988; Galbraith 1995). And Scottish Labour's popularity in the 1980s contributed a whole new series of studies, ranging from John Smith (McSmith 1994) and Gordon Brown (Routledge 1998) to Robin Cook (Kampfner 1998) and the maverick Tam Dalyell (Galbraith 2000). What unites all these studies is that while all the above politicians were undoubtedly Scottish Labour politicians, their success as British Labour politicians with respect and status at Westminster merited these volumes. The absence of a biography of Donald Dewar, the architect of Scottish home rule and First Minister from 1999 to 2000, speaks loudly for the biases of biography and harsh realities of the book trade.

The lack of analysis of the contemporary Scottish Labour Party needs to be addressed given the importance of the party in public life, and particularly so since the establishment of the Scottish Parliament. Two other inspirations for this book were my own research into Scottish Labour, and realising the dearth of contemporary material (Hassan 1998; 2002), and the development of other parallel studies looking at, for example, the historical and contemporary condition of the Labour Party in Wales (Tanner et al. 2000). This book aims to reflect the evolution of Scottish politics post-devolution – setting the historical context before addressing some of the key issues facing the party today, analysing different aspects of it, and situating this within wider UK, international and territorial politics.

This book does not aim to be the definitive study of the Scottish Labour Party, but by addressing some of the most important aspects and issues facing it, hopes to contribute to increasing understanding of Scottish Labour and its role in Scottish and UK politics. We have not attempted to impose a single editorial line, reflecting the diversity of contributors, their opinions and expertise. It also in no way attempts to be an 'official' or 'authorised' account of the party. Contributors have in many cases sought the views and opinions of a range of Labour members, officials and elected representatives, but this does not detract from the independence of the views expressed within this book.

ANATOMY OF SCOTTISH LABOUR

Scottish Labour is a different party in a number of ways from the rest of the British party: in membership, as an institutionalised party, and in its dominance of politics, and the implications that flow from that. First, the Scottish party has traditionally had a smaller membership than the British party. The Scottish party caught the upswing of the Blair honeymoon in opposition from 1994 to 1997 as British membership rose, seeing the party grow from a low of 19,708 in 1993 to a high of 30,770 in 1998 – an increase of 56 per cent. Since then membership has followed the British party downwards, falling to 22,153 at the end of 2002 – a fall of 28 per cent. Given the historically small Scottish membership, this is the recruitment base for the election of a whole swathe of the political classes; in the aftermath of the 2003 Scottish Parliament elections, Labour still elected 108 out of Scotland's 209 national representatives (MPs, MSPs, MEPs).

Second, Scottish Labour has become through its dominance of Scottish public life an institutionalised party – blurring the boundaries between party and state, particularly in the local state. In the last ten years, a number of Labour councils have been implicated in a series of scandals about corruption and malpractice. These have been predominantly, but not exclusively, in the West of Scotland: Monklands, Glasgow, Renfrewshire and the exception to the rule – the Fife 'Officegate' scandal which led to the resignation of the First Minister,

Henry McLeish. This has been called 'the West of Scotland Labour question' – which has risen to the fore under devolution as Labour's governing style in one-party states and cultures has come under more scrutiny (Hassan 1998: 125–8).[1]

Third, Scottish Labour has sought intellectual and cultural hegemony over progressive Scotland despite its minority status in terms of votes. This in part has been validated by the first-past-the-post (FPTP) electoral system at Westminster working so clearly in Labour's favour, so that in 2001 on 43 per cent of the vote the party won 78 per cent of seats. However, Labour's hegemonic instincts go much deeper than the mechanics of any electoral system, and are about how the party sees itself and the world. There has always been within Labour a traditional disdain for progressive opinion outside the party; in the UK this has been reflected in the way a large part of the party has viewed the Lib Dems as either an irrelevance or with hostility. Things are different in Scotland where the Lib Dems are not direct competitors to Labour electorally, but can be seen in the vitriol many Labour members feel towards the SNP.

Who are Scottish Labour Party members, the people who make up Scotland's leading party, and who contribute so disproportionately to the political classes? Are they similar or different to British Labour? Table 1.2 examines some of the main findings from Seyd and Whiteley's research (2002) into British party members, while using unpublished data from their research on Scottish members based on 371 interviews in 23 constituencies.[2]

What is striking are the similarities, rather than differences, between the two. Both parties are 61 per cent male, have few young members and in particular minuscule memberships under 25 years, have sizeable proportions over retirement age, and are predominantly middle class with the British party made up of 15 per cent working-class members and the Scottish party 18 per cent.

Labour Party members in both are nearly exclusively white, but even more so in Scotland, while there is no significant difference in religious beliefs, despite the sensitivities of the Scottish party leadership to the Catholic Church, 38 per cent of British members and 35 per cent of Scottish members having religious views. In household income, both the Scottish and British parties show significant patterns of inequality with each having one-quarter of their members with less than £10,000 per annum, and one-fifth with a household income of £40,000 and over. In this respect, party membership north and south of the border is a microcosm of Blair's Britain.

Table 1.2   Characteristics of British and Scottish Labour Party Members

	British	Scottish
Gender		
Male	61	61
Female	39	39
Age		
25 and under	4	5
26–35	13	11
36–45	20	22
46–55	24	21
56–65	16	17
66 and over	23	24
Occupational Status		
Salariat	64	59
Routine non-manual	12	12
Petty bourgeoisie	2	3
Foremen and technicians	7	8
Working class	15	18
Ethnic Origin		
White/European	95	98
Afro-Asian	3	0.3
Other	2	1.7
Religious		
Very religious	10	12
Somewhat religious	28	23
Not very religious	28	28
Not at all religious	34	36
Household Income		
Under £5,000	8	12
£5,000 to under £10,000	17	16
£10,000 to under £20,000	25	28
£20,000 to under £30,000	19	16
£30,000 to under £40,000	12	10
£40,000 plus	19	18

Source: British figures: Seyd and Whiteley, *New Labour's Grass Roots* (1997); Scottish figures, unpublished Seyd and Whiteley figures (1999).

A majority of party members (51.5 per cent) joined the Labour Party for ideological reasons – to create a just society (19.5 per cent), a more equal society (17.5 per cent), or to support socialism (14.5 per cent). Pragmatic reasons were identified as strong support for Labour (11.5 per cent), opposing the Tories (9.8 per cent), and getting Labour into power (9.2 per cent). A mere 5.6 per cent identified the appeal of Tony Blair or New Labour as a reason for joining Scottish Labour.

Levels of activism and contact in the party are not very high. Nearly half of party members (45.3 per cent) never attend a single party meeting during the course of a year, while 20.4 per cent attend one to two, 12.8 per cent three to five, and 21.5 per cent attend six or more. In relation to wider party activities, 31.4 per cent had no contact whatsoever with the party over a year, compared to 28.9 per cent having occasional contact and 39.7 per cent frequent contact; 71.5 per cent of members were satisfied with this degree of contact. These figures chime with other indicators of a relatively inactive, disconnected party membership such as the 27 per cent turnout of party members in the postal voting for the 2003 Scottish Parliament regional list rankings.[3] While political parties across the Western world are seeing memberships fall, reflecting economic, social and cultural change, with parties becoming 'empty vessels', there are particular peculiarities for Scottish Labour. This is the party which elects most of Scotland's MPs, MSPs, MEPs as well as 508 councillors. It is increasingly a top-heavy party dominated by elected politicians, paid workers and officials; a party shaped by professional politicians, rather than voluntary activists. It is this stratum of people who increasingly make up the backbone of Labour organisation and campaigns.

The Scottish party is not according to these findings New Labour or traditional socialist; the picture is more complex and contradictory. When asked if the party should adjust its policies to the middle ground, 46.0 per cent agreed and 36.7 per cent disagreed, but when asked if Labour had not moved away from its traditional values and principles, only 33.8 per cent agreed and 55.2 per cent disagreed.

There is evidence of significant anxiety over New Labour. Asked if Labour looks after working-class people, 78.9 per cent agreed, yet, when asked if Labour looks after the middle class, party members responded with 94.8 per cent agreement – a 16 per cent gap between the two. A similar picture emerges in relation to trade unions and big business: 60.7 per cent of party members feel the party looks after the interests of trade unions, while 80.8 per cent believe Labour looks after big business interests – a gap of 20 per cent. And a surprisingly large minority of party members – 45.7 per cent – think that Labour looks after the very rich (while 54.4 per cent disagree).

Do party members still hold traditional socialist views? On public owner-ship, the picture is a complex one, with 48.3 per cent supporting more nationalisation, 46.0 per cent for maintaining the status quo and 5.7 per cent more privatisation. However, on other indicators party members take a more traditionalist stand, supporting by large majorities opposition to trade unions losing power (75.7 per cent), redistribution of income and wealth (73.0 per cent) and 'tax and spend' (87.9 per cent). Seyd and Whiteley found similar evidence on policy with British party members, leading them to state that there was still 'grass roots support for collective intervention in the market' and this 'belies any notion of a successful New Labour take-over of the party' (Seyd and Whiteley 2002: 55).

Party members have mixed views of Tony Blair: 49.6 per cent saw him as right-wing, 39.0 per cent as neither left nor right, and 11.4 per cent as left-wing. However, sizeable majorities saw him as caring (79.2 per cent), likeable (69.0 per cent) and decisive (82.4 per cent). When asked who their choice of alternative leader was, respondents answered: Gordon Brown (33.4 per cent); John Prescott (25.5 per cent); and Robin Cook (24.4 per cent). Only two other figures gained noteworthy support, Margaret Beckett (3.7 per cent) and Tony Benn (3.4 per cent) – both David Blunkett and Jack Straw scored derisory levels of support (each 1.4 per cent).

Thus the overall picture provided by this survey of Scottish Labour Party members is of a party which is significantly disconnected, ageing, failing to recruit younger or new members, and which while it has accepted the need for Labour to shift to the centre ground to win, has never bought into the Blair agenda, and has maintained its support for traditional socialist policies in a number of areas. It is too easy from these findings to paint an Old Labour picture: members have instead retained a detached scepticism (sometimes to the point of leaving the party) of developments in the party in recent years.

UNDERSTANDING SCOTTISH LABOUR: THEMES, CULTURES AND FUTURES

From the range of contributions to this book a number of common threads emerge about the nature of Scottish Labour. First is the importance of Labour culture as a defining feature of the party. This makes a distinction between the formal policies and positions of a party – the programmatic details – and the informal feel, attitudes and culture. Henry Drucker in his influential book talked of the difference between 'doctrine and ethos' (1979) and this is examined further below.

Second, the politics of ideas and ideology has played a significant part in the evolution of Scottish Labour. The party, as Gordon Brown noted about the 1929 Scottish Labour group of MPs, was the 'voice of labour, not socialism' (Brown 1981: 484). Richard Finlay addresses this in his chapter on the party from its origins to 1945, and sees the balance between Labour as a party of interests and one of ideology as one fundamental to the party's existence. One of the defining narratives of Scottish Labour has been seeing itself as more radical, real and a more authentic expression of Labour politics than British Labour. In part, this was due to the socio-economic composition of the working class in the West of Scotland at the turn of the century, in part the coalescing of events around the mobilising myth of 'Red Clydeside', and in part the power of collectivist ideas and culture via state intervention which contributed towards a very different kind of Scottish Labour to the party south of the border.

Third, it is important to understand when we talk of 'Scottish Labour' that we are not talking about a uniform entity, but a party with different senses of itself across the different political geographies of Scotland. The party has gained different levels of support in differing parts of Scotland, breaking through at different points – in Glasgow in 1922 at parliamentary level and 1933 at council elections, but having to wait in Edinburgh until 1984 at a council level and 1987 at UK parliamentary level. And the nature of party competition has helped shape Labour: so in the West of Scotland Labour one-party citadels which emerged in the 1980s and 1990s, Labour politics were more driven by internal dynamics and factionalism than external pressures, the party more in hoc to producer interests, and opposed to proportional representation (PR) for local government. Elsewhere in Scotland, in Edinburgh, Dundee and Aberdeen, for example, the party has faced more competitive challenges, and subsequently has been more influenced by external pressures than internal party dynamics. And yet Scottish Labour has been shaped by its West of Scotland heartland to the exclusion of other Labour areas; it is here that the culture, norms and practices of Labour were formed and crowded out the other Labour Scotlands that undoubtedly exist. Saren and McCormick in their analysis of the politics of Labour's heartlands detect movement, but whether it can make the shift onto the level of how Scottish Labour understands itself is another question.

Fourth, there has been a changing relationship between economic and social conditions and political change. Scottish politics have never experienced a golden age of a homogeneous working class united in its behaviour and beliefs. Instead, class has been linked to a variety of socio-economic factors, and mediated through such things as status, skill, geography, gender, culture, and access to power whether at local government, Scottish or UK level. Much of Scotland's economic debate over the previous century has been driven by concerns over economic performance, Scotland's low growth rate and low rates of productivity, and since the 1930s the debate on this has been framed around managing Scotland's economic decline. The implications of this are studied by Christopher Harvie in his chapter, but what emerged was a politics of corporatist incorporation led by the Labour Party, but including until 1979 the Tory Party, trade unions and private industry. This 'negotiated order' (Moore and Booth 1989: 150) was challenged by Thatcherism, and has not been reconfigured by Scottish and UK Labour post-1997.

Fifth, we need to acknowledge that Scottish Labour is a party of contradictions – of conservatism and also of change. The party is a conservative organisation being the political establishment of much of Scotland, but is also capable of advocating change. One of the central paradoxes of Scottish Labour is why did this deeply conservative institution introduce such a radical change as devolution, with the potential to undermine its dominance (Hassan 2002)?

Devolution can be seen as the establishment of an intermediate tier of government below the Westminster Parliament which changes very little. This is the minimalist view of devolution which carries sizeable support in Scottish Labour (and certainly British Labour). An alternative view is to see devolution, as Douglas Fraser examines in his chapter on Labour and the politics of the Scottish Parliament, as a catalyst which can set off numerous changes: to local government, party politics, and political culture. And in other respects, such as introducing a PR-shaped Parliament and advancing gender equality in the previously macho culture of Scottish Labour, as Fiona Mackay in her contribution makes clear, the party has embraced far-reaching change.

Sixth, the Scottish party has had a sense of Scottish identity throughout its history. This should not necessarily be seen as synonymous with support for a Scottish Parliament which has become the expression of such a politics in the last thirty years. Instead, Scottish Labour's sense of Scottishness has been part of something much wider than constitutional change – about seeing the party as one that has a distinctive agenda north of the border, and a different history and culture. At points the party has emphasised its Scottish credentials through support for home rule, as it did in the 1979–97 period, but at other points, when the party has emphasised a politics of the British state as the best means of redistribution, it has still seen itself as Scottish. Nicola McEwen examines these different strands in her chapter, and analyses the tensions emerging post-devolution: the extent to which the party can continue to emphasise a distinct Scottish agenda while being in government north and south of the border.

Scottish Labour's sense of distinctiveness has been one of the most powerful narratives of the party from its earliest days. This has in recent years with the creation of New Labour seen an increasing divergence between the party north and south of the border. New Labour was a response to four successive electoral defeats by which the party aimed to win back ex-Labour voters who had supported Thatcher in the 1980s; Scottish Labour in a very different political climate had emerged as the unchallenged leading party in the same four elections, and did not have the same need to reach out and convert Tory or other parties' voters.

A number of powerful schools of thought have been articulated in relation to New Labour and Scottish politics. One account associated with emphasizing traditional Labour values and a commitment to socialist politics sees New Labour as an illegitimate capturing of the party by a *coup d'état* involving ex-SDPers and Communists. This view seems to present Labour pre-Blair as a golden era when left and right despite their differences shared a common agenda, and also appears sanguine about Labour's popular support in the 1980s arguing that the party did not need to renew or modernise. John McAllion gave voice to this view when he stated, 'Old Labour was never unelectable in Scotland. Even at the high tide of Thatcherism in 1983, Michael Foot's Labour won a majority of seats in Scotland.' (McAllion 1998) This is a politics of breathtaking complacency considering Labour won a majority of seats in 1983 on 35.1 per cent of the vote.

It also looks back with a sense of romanticism to the achievements of Labour Scotland: council housing, municipalism, the trade union link – and invokes a nostalgia for the collectivist certainties of 1950s Scotland. This politics has little understanding of Labour's lack of appeal to non-Labour Scotland, and is shaped by the values of Labour tribalism and chauvinism – celebrating the uniqueness of Labour as the party of organised labour, while dismissing other parties and opinions. If only Labour were to return to a politics of traditional Labour values and a re-emphasis of a simpler class politics, of 'them' and 'us', it would have more of a sense of principle and mission, and hold power with purpose. This perspective totally fails to understand the way society has changed in the last twenty-five or more years, is blind to the clientism of local Labour politics and that producer groups as much as any other organised group can be a 'vested interest'. This is a defensive, backward-looking politics with little positive to contribute, but a powerful sense of opposition to all things New Labour. As such it touches a wider Scottish consensus and collectivism which defined much of the debate up until 1997.

A second account is offered by New Labour modernisers. This presents the Scottish Labour Party as a party of producer and vested interests. What is needed is a Blairite New Labour politics of choice, competition and public sector reform. This view seems to be increasingly falling behind events, invoking a sense of 'Blairism' that either never existed in some accounts or is now proving increasingly problematic with Labour and the wider public. John McTernan has made the case for an unapologetic Blairism, noting that Labour won in Scotland in 2001 on a Blairite programme of 'social justice combined with low taxation; and increased public spending together with reforms to ensure higher quality and increased productivity', whereas McConnell won in 2003 with 'a commitment to higher public spending and social justice' (McTernan 2003: 97). In this analysis, McConnell has adopted some of Blairism's rhetoric and some of its programme by stealth, but to gain its full benefits he needs to embrace it unconditionally.

Jack McConnell seemed to agree with this when post-2003 election he addressed the party's reverse in the election which saw it lose six FPTP seats and its vote slump. According to McConnell, 'There are many people in Scotland who prefer London Labour to Scottish Labour, and we need to tackle that.' He went on, 'A 10 per cent gap worries me and I want to do something about it' (*The Scotsman*, 26 August 2003).[4] One motivation for McConnell might have been that he was trying to justify shifting to a more explicit Blairite position by pointing to the success of UK Labour at Westminster elections compared to Scottish Labour at devolved contests. This has been called 'the Pentlands question' whereby Lynda Clark held the seat in 2001 against Tory Malcolm Rifkind with a 1,742 majority, whereas Iain Gray lost to Scots Tory leader David McLetchie by 2,111 votes in 2003.

And yet if we look at the survey evidence on New Labour and Scottish Labour laid out by Paula Surridge in her chapter, it is clear that the latter is much more highly thought of. For example, considering which party is best seen as looking after Scottish interests at the time of the 2001 UK election, 40 per cent trusted New Labour (down from 42 per cent in 1999), while 68 per cent trusted Scottish Labour (up from 63 per cent in 1999): a 28 per cent widening difference between the two.

A different perspective from the simplicities of the hard left and Blairite true believers would acknowledge the complexities of the Scottish party. The Scottish party has many positive features and contributed richly to the life and politics of Scotland, but it does need to embrace a politics of renewal and modernisation. However, this should not be a 'Blairite' or even 'Brownite' politics, but one devised by the Scottish party itself to reflect Scottish conditions, political attitudes, culture and identity. Scottish Labour has significant advantages as the leading party, yet on another level its dominance may look vulnerable, winning the support as it did of only 34.6 per cent of voters in the 2003 Scottish Parliament election and a mere 29.6 per cent on the list vote – both performances worse than Labour even scored in 1983 or any other post-war election. However, in a six-party system shaped by fragmentation and diversity it does not take much of a plateau to dominate things. Scottish Labour has a core support across five surveys or 'waves' undertaken from 1997 to 2001 of 35 per cent of respondents, compared to a mere 12 per cent for Tories, 10 per cent SNP and 6 per cent for Lib Dems; 60 per cent of those surveyed have at least once over this period supported Labour (Paterson 2003). And yet, for all these undoubted advantages, Labour's vote is falling, and the size of their opponents' rising, and even if it is dispersing across a range of parties (Greens and Scottish Socialists) this can be contained in a PR-hybrid Parliament due to Labour's FPTP strength.

Henry Drucker's notion of 'doctrine and ethos' as the two dimensions of Labour ideology provide us with a way of analysing Scottish Labour. Doctrine is according to Drucker 'a more or less elaborate set of ideas about the character of (in this case) social, economic and political reality' which 'lead to a programme of action' (Drucker 1979: 8). Ethos are 'sets of values which spring from the experience of the British working class' and 'a shared past, a series of folk memories of shared exploitation, common struggle and gradually increased power.' (Drucker 1979: 9, 31) Doctrines are much more easy to understand, being formal, written and recordable, whereas ethos are nebulous and in a sense part of what the 'spirit of the party' is; doctrines are more open, aiming to attract new supporters and converts, whereas ethos are more closed and driven by inner dynamics.

Drucker's 'doctrine and ethos' allow us to make more sense of Scottish Labour, and its direction since 1979. Scottish Labour, doctrinally, has in policy terms, thinkers and ideas seen itself as to the left of the British party, as more radical, popular and connected to people. This manifests itself in the way Scottish Labour thinks of itself as the inheritor of a long Whig-like lineage of radical Scots opinion – from the legacy of the Highland Clearances to Crofters' radicalism, temperance, Gladstonian home rule, and Red Clydeside. In other ways, it articulates itself through its pride in its long history of 'socialist pioneers' from Hardie onward. Scottish Labour's ethos are very different, reinforcing an insular, inward-looking, defensive view of the world which by emphasising the party's uniqueness sees itself as the sole vehicle of progressive change, aiding a sense of Labour chauvinism and tribalism (see Drucker 1978: 141–3). Scottish Labour has tended to emphasise this sense of closedness more than openness, partly because it is Scotland's leading party, and partly because it has seen its interests as synonymous with Scotland's.

Scottish Labour in the 1980s contributed, perhaps reluctantly at points, to the Kinnockite modernisation of the party at the level of doctrine.

Policies were reviewed, positions changed. However, what did not alter was the party's innate sense of ethos, its 'spirit', and this had profound consequences. Ethos is what saved Labour in the 1980s from being replaced by the Alliance at a UK level, giving Labour an anchor and sense of self-preservation; but it has proven problematic in how Labour has historically spoken to non-Labour progressive Britain. Scottish Labour politicians could still in the 1980s talk the tribal language of 'our people' long after the rest of the party (Wales exempted) had abandoned it as patronising. The strength of Scottish Labour's ethos as well as being an asset has also been a hindrance. It enabled Labour to maintain its hold on its Scottish heartland, hold off the Bennite left, and contribute to the Kinnock revisionism, but it also made it difficult for Scottish Labour to respond to the more diverse and pluralist nature of Scottish society. And while Scottish Labour continued to win elections, it did so with a sense of complacency, and without the rethinking the party south of the border undertook. Scottish Labour has never understood non-Labour Scotland, particularly Nationalist Scotland, and this matters more and more in an increasingly pluralist politics.

The New Labour experiment created a number of tensions in Scottish and UK Labour. For example, there were fundamental ambiguities at the heart of what 'Blairism' stood for, which went to the heart of what 'the third way' stood for. Was it a renewed social democracy, an abandonment of even a centre-left politics for triangulation between Old Labour and New Right, or was it a distinct post-Thatcherite politics? Blairism stood for embracing Anglo-American capitalism instead of the Rhine model and a politics informed not only by the need to be pro-business, but informed by business sensibilities. 'Blairism', according to Finlayson, 'seeks to "modernise" the state by bringing it in line with business best practice' and its public-sector reform aims to 'make public services more like modern businesses' (2003: 89).

Where this leaves Scottish Labour is too early to tell. If Blairism is a permanent departure from a centre-left politics towards an Americanised 'catch-all' party and politics, clearly Scottish Labour is going to have difficulties. And yet it is possible to attempt to see the shift to New Labour in a wider picture whereby post-Thatcher, post-Communism social democrats had to adapt and review the political possibilities in an age of a resurgent capitalism and globalisation. There should be no argument here; social democrats have always had to renew and modernise, as Donald Sassoon made clear in his masterful study of the Western European experience (1996). However, different choices exist across the continent: from the Swedish Social Democrats, to German SPD, French Socialists and Italian Party of Democratic Socialism, and New Labour has departed from a European sense of centre-left politics.[5]

Scottish Labour has made a powerful contribution to British Labour over its existence, adapting and evolving to prevailing political conditions. The establishment of a Scottish Parliament has provided the opportunity for a new kind of politics to emerge, burying the corpse of centralist, uniform British state social democracy based on the central state as the means of authority and redistribution, and developing a new decentralist politics based on autonomy, localism and self-government. Two obstacles seem to block the articulation of this kind of politics. One is the characteristics of Blairism and New Labour, and the thought that any post-Blair politics may be shaped by the same political realities. Another, just as serious, is the nature of the British state, still, despite six years of Labour constitutional reform, relatively untouched and unreformed in terms of its structure, culture and who has power (Hassan 2003). The British state is still recognisably an *ancien régime* – an imperial state, with an Imperial Parliament – underwritten by the fact that Tony Blair has fought an unprecedented five wars in six years (Kampfner 2003). And British Labour has never given much time or thought to these issues, being content in arch Fabian gradualist style to see the British state as a neutral instrument capable of being used for progressive change (Jones and Keating 1985).

Scottish Labour has played an important part in all these and more debates, and contributed greatly to changing the lives of hundreds of thousands of Scots for the better. It has contributed immensely to the British party, providing the ballast and stability when the party was on the rocks in the 1980s. At some point in the future, the party will face profound questions and challenges beyond the serious mid-term difficulties of the UK Labour Government over Iraq and public service delivery, and the aftermath of the 2003 Scottish Parliament elections governing in coalition with the Lib Dems in a six-party system.

Scottish Labour will have to face questions about what kind of party it wants to be. How will it cope with a less sure dominance of Scottish politics? How can it develop a more distinctively Scottish agenda? What kind of relationship does it want to have with British Labour and the British state? And what happens to Scottish Labour, when, as is certain, it loses power – and there is a change of government – at Holyrood or Westminster? How will the party respond to losing power at a Scottish or British level? These challenges and more will shape Scottish Labour and Scottish politics for decades to come.

Notes

1. Renfrewshire and Fife councils, two of the examples provided where significant Labour scandals arose, actually have significant oppositions to Labour on their councils, in the

former the SNP, the latter the Lib Dems. However, in Renfrewshire the origin of significant SNP opposition to Labour occurred in the last ten years, leaving Labour as a party which had grown used to one-party rule, reacting to the arrival of a serious challenge in one of its strongholds. Fife council, which brought down Henry McLeish as First Minister in November 2001, and revealed 'the secret state' of networks by which party, council, trade unions and businesses worked together, had similarities to Labour one-party politics. However, it was unusual in having a sizeable Lib Dem opposition group; Labour actually lost overall majority of Fife council in the aftermath of 'Officegate'.

2. Many thanks to Patrick Seyd, University of Sheffield, and Paul Whiteley, University of Essex, for allowing the author access to their database of Labour Party members.

3. Information from party official, January 2003.

4. McConnell's citing of a 10 per cent gap refers to the difference between Labour's vote at the 2001 Westminster elections in Scotland and the 2003 Scottish Parliament first vote. However, the gap is not 10 per cent, but 8.6 per cent – a 2001 vote of 43.2 per cent and 2003 of 34.6 per cent. What is more, this difference has always been with us, the gap after the first Scottish Parliament elections being 7.5 per cent. And across the developed world, one finds similar differences in voting between devolved and national legislatures.

5. For a very different, and equally impressive, historical canvas to Sassoon, see Eley (2002) which takes a critical line on how Western European mainstream social democracy has evolved in the 1990s and early twenty-first century.

REFERENCES

Aitken, K. (1997), *The Bairns O' Adam: The Story of the STUC*, Polygon, Edinburgh.

Brown, G. (1981), *The Labour Party and Political Change in Scotland: 1918–1929: The Politics of Five Elections*, unpublished Ph.D., University of Edinburgh.

Brown, G. (1986), *James Maxton*, Mainstream, Edinburgh.

Crick, B. (2002), *Crossing Borders: Political Essays*, Continuum, London.

Donnachie, I., Harvie, C. and Wood, I. S. (eds) (1989), *Forward! Labour Politics in Scotland 1888–1988*, Polygon, Edinburgh.

Drucker, H. M. (1978), *Breakaway: The Scottish Labour Party*, Edinburgh University Student Publications Board, Edinburgh.

Drucker, H. M. (1979), *Doctrine and Ethos of the Labour Party*, Allen and Unwin, London.

Eley, G. (2002), *Forging Democracy: The History of the Left in Europe 1850–2000*, Oxford University Press, Oxford.

Finlayson, A. (2003), *Making Sense of New Labour*, Lawrence and Wishart, London.

Galbraith, R. (1995), *Without Quarter: A Biography of Tom Johnston*, Mainstream, Edinburgh.

Galbraith, R. (2000), *Inside Outside: A Biography of Tam Dalyell: The Man They Can't Gag*, Mainstream, Edinburgh.

Gordon, E. (1991), *Women and the Labour Movement in Scotland 1850–1914*, Clarendon Press, Oxford.

Harvie, C. (1989), 'Before the Breakthrough 1886–1922', in I. Donnachie, C. Harvie and I. S. Wood (eds), *Forward! Labour Politics in Scotland 1888–1988*, Polygon, Edinburgh, pp. 7–29.

Hassan, G. (1998), 'Caledonian Dreaming: The Challenge to Scottish Labour', in A. Coddington and M. Perryman (eds), *The Moderniser's Dilemma: Radical Politics in the Age of Blair*, Lawrence and Wishart, London, pp. 111–43.

Hassan, G. (2002), 'The Paradoxes of Scottish Labour: Devolution, Change and Conservatism', in G. Hassan and C. Warhurst (eds), *Tomorrow's Scotland*, Lawrence and Wishart, London, pp. 26–48.

Hassan, G. (2003), 'Talking About Devolution: A Decade of Constitutional Wish Fulfilment', *Renewal*, vol. 8, no. 1, pp. 46–53.

Jones, B. and Keating, M. (1985), *Labour and the British State*, Oxford University Press, Oxford.

Kampfner, J. (1998), *Robin Cook*, Victor Gollancz, London.

Kampfner, J. (2003), *Blair's Wars*, Free Press, London.

Keating, M. and Bleiman, D. (1979), *Labour and Scottish Nationalism*, Macmillan, Basingstoke.

Knox, W. (1987), *James Maxton*, Manchester University Press, Manchester.

Knox, W. (ed.) (1984), *Scottish Labour Leaders 1918–1939*, Mainstream, Edinburgh.

McAllion, J. (1998), 'Blair's modernisers want a party of the people, but up here the people want a party of the left', *The Observer*, 22 March 1998.

McKinlay, A. and Morris, R. J. (1991), *The ILP on Clydeside 1893–1932: From Foundation to Disintegration*, Manchester University Press, Manchester.

McLean, R. (1990), *Labour and Scottish Home Rule: Part One: Mid-Lanark to Majority Government*, Scottish Labour Action, Broxburn.

McLean, R. (1991), *Labour and Scottish Home Rule: Part Two: Unionist Complacency to Crisis Management 1945–1988*, Scottish Labour Action, Broxburn.

McLean, I. (1983), *The Legend of Red Clydeside*, John Donald, Edinburgh.

McSmith, A. (1994), *John Smith: A Life 1939–1994*, 2nd edn, Mandarin, London.

McTernan, J. (2003), 'Stands Scotland where it did?', *Renewal*, vol. 8, no. 3, pp. 93–9.

Marquand, D. (1977), *Ramsay MacDonald*, Jonathan Cape, London.

Moore, C. and Booth, S. (1989), *Managing Competition: Meso-corporatism, Pluralism and the Negotiated Order in Scotland*, Clarendon Press, Oxford.

Morgan, K. O. (1975), *Keir Hardie: Radical and Socialist*, Weidenfeld and Nicolson, London.

Paterson, L. (2003), *Attitudes to Scottish Independence and to the SNP*, paper to seminar to the SNP, Dunblane, 22 August 2003.

Routledge, P. (1998), *Gordon Brown: The Biography*, Simon and Schuster, London.

Sassoon, D. (1996), *One Hundred Years of Socialism: The West European Left in the Twentieth Century*, Tauris, London.

Seyd, P. and Whiteley, P. (2002), *New Labour's Grass Roots: The Transformation of Labour Party Membership*, Palgrave Macmillan, Basingstoke.

Slowe, P. (1993), *Manny Shinwell: An Authorised Biography*, Pluto Press, London.

Tanner, D., Williams, C. and Hopkin, D. (eds) (2000), *The Labour Party in Wales 1900–2000*, University of Wales Press, Cardiff.

Tuckett, A. (1986), *The Scottish Trades Union Congress: The First 80 Years: 1897–1977*, Mainstream, Edinburgh.

Walker, G. (1988), *Thomas Johnston*, Manchester University Press, Manchester.

I

Understanding Scottish Labour: History and Environment

CHAPTER 2

The Labour Party in Scotland 1888–1945: Pragmatism and Principle

Richard Finlay

A comprehensive study of the history of the Labour Party in Scotland during this period could not be squeezed into the space allotted in this volume.[1] Rather, this chapter will specifically examine the often competing roles of pragmatism and ideology in the development of the Labour movement in Scotland between 1888 and 1945. In many ways, this chimes in with much of the contemporary debate regarding the role of New Labour and to what extent it represents a fundamental break with not only the party's past, but also its mainstream ideology. As this chapter will argue, the debate as to whether Labour should be a party which represented a specific set of interests that were tied to its core constituency of the working class or whether it was an organisation that was guided by a set of principles or ideology which gave coherence to a wider political vision, has always been at the heart of Labour's historical development in Scotland, and for that matter, Britain too.

On the one hand, Labour sought to represent working-class interests and was dependent on working-class votes for its electability. This might be deemed the party's pragmatic side, as without this, the party would be unlikely to attain political power. On the other, Labour never represented itself as a purely sectarian class party and framed its appeal within a broader intellectual framework; namely socialism, however loosely defined. Socialism, it was argued, was the reconstruction of the whole of society based on rational principles that would ensure the greatest benefit for the greatest number. Early Labour pioneers, such as Keir Hardie and Ramsay MacDonald, believed that the middle class would come to recognise that socialism, as a rational ordering of society, would be in their own best interests. For others, this did not matter much as the working class constituted the majority in society and it was the interests of the majority that counted. It is the reconciliation of political ideology with the promotion of working-class interests, and the tensions which often arose between them, that is the main focus of this chapter.

BEFORE 1914

Before 1914, the Labour Party in Scotland was characterised by weakness in terms of its comparative performance with south of the border (Hutchison 1986: 218–77). On the eve of the First World War, Labour had only been able to win three parliamentary seats in Scotland and had made limited inroads in terms of local government and elections to school boards. This latter point was of significance in that it was often at the local level that proscriptive legislation, such as the 1908 Act governing the 'feeding of necessitous children', mattered most to working-class constituents. A number of features account for this. Firstly, the party had not been able to conclude a secret electoral agreement with the Liberals, as had happened in England (the MacDonald–Gladstone Pact of 1903). By the time of the negotiations in Scotland, the Conservative Party had helpfully shot itself in the foot over the issue of Tariff Reform and the Liberals believed that their position was strong enough north of the border not to need a progressive alliance. This effectively stopped the Labour Party in Scotland establishing itself in a number of potential marginal three-way seats in which the Liberals would have stood down and allowed a free run against the Tories had the pact been operational.

Secondly, the Labour Party faced a serious intellectual challenge from the Liberals, whose espousal of the 'New Liberalism' (known as Progressivism in Scotland) was effectively able to outbid Labour on issues of social reform. The Liberal Party put forward a barrage of claims on issues dealing with education, housing, land reform and temperance, all of which were part and parcel of Labour policy. For many working-class voters, it made more sense to stick with the party that had established itself locally and was likely to be elected to government. Finally, Labour had little direct access to working-class voters. Activists were drawn mainly from the lower middle class and had difficulty in converting the abstracts of socialism into a means which could readily be picked up and understood by ordinary people. Trade unions, while making encouraging noises about an independent workers' party, were more inclined to rely on the Liberal Party, and socialist activists waiting to espouse their message at the factory gates were inevitably bowled over by the stampeding horde anxious to get home for tea (Hutchison 1987: 120).

Before the advent of World War One, the Labour movement can be characterised as having a dichotomy of interests in that on the one hand there was a commitment to ethical socialism, held by party activists in the Independent Labour Party (ILP), and on the other a broader grouping which, while paying lip service to ideas of socialism, was motivated

22

primarily in terms of defending working-class interests. This can be seen in the fact that in none of the manifestos of the three successful Labour parliamentary candidates before 1914 does the word socialism appear. Furthermore, each stressed that they had good 'Liberal' connections and emphasised their trade union links and commitments. Indeed, there was a tendency before the First World War for radicals in the Liberal Party and members of the Fabian Society and ILP to share platforms on a whole range of issues. Many Liberal radicals regarded Labour not so much as an independent political movement, but as belonging to a broad progressive coalition (Finlay 1996: 64–72). It is more likely that Labour activists spent more time arguing with Liberal activists than among working-class voters.

Part of the reason that the Labour movement in Scotland developed an active political wing in the form of the ILP was due to the weakness of Scottish trade unions. Reflecting the structure of the specialist economy, unions were disparate, diffuse and small, and it was due to the apparent lack of industrial muscle that politics emerged as a way to take forward the promotion of working-class interests. Unlike England, where the 'New Unionism' resulted in powerful and united organisations that were able to wring concessions from employers for the benefit of members, Scottish trade unions tended to be more concerned about the protection of craft privileges at the expense of other unskilled workers (Knox 1990: 138–67). The idealism of ethical socialism was believed to be a way that would help create working-class unity, but it failed to capture the imagination of the working-class constituency. It is worth pointing out that the areas which did have most success in terms of Labour politics were issues such as John Wheatley's £10 cottages, because it could demonstrate in a tangible way the material benefits of socialism to the working class. The argument that capitalism was iniquitous and that socialism was rational may have struck a chord with many, but it was difficult to translate this into a medium that could be readily appreciated by the working class, hence Scottish socialism was informed more by Burns and the Bible (perhaps the two most important reference points in working-class culture) than Marx. As a political and economic system, socialism had many hurdles to overcome. Firstly, there was an inherent distrust of the state whose intrusion into working-class life was resented. Secondly, the Free Trade versus Tariff protection debate, which dominated the 1906 general election, was reduced to the 'big loaf versus little loaf' and found ready support among the working class who associated *laissez-faire* with cheap food. Finally, there was the fragmentation of the working class itself. Trade union politics was dominated by the desire to maintain craft differentials, the Scottish–Irish community was dominated by Irish home rule, and even socialist activists, such as Thomas Johnston, expressed disdain for the 40 per cent of the working men which still did not have the vote. He boasted that his socialist newspaper, *Forward*, was not read in slums. Ideologically, socialism seemed to pay little electoral dividends and in terms of pragmatic politics, the working class still turned to Liberalism as the best defender of their interests.

THE FIRST WORLD WAR

It took the impact of the Great War to change Labour's political fortunes in Scotland. Although politics were important in driving this development, it was the social and economic impact of war that was the deciding factor in bringing about Labour's electoral breakthrough. The war increased class tensions. Rising inflation, government intervention and worsening industrial relations conspired to bring the shop stewards in the Clydeside war industries to the fore in representing workers' rights. Similar developments also took place in Dundee and Edinburgh and through many smaller industrial and mining communities. Rapacious landlords also played their part in the Clyde by racking rents up to unacceptable levels which brought about communal action in what was known as the rent strike of 1915 (Melling 1983: 50–74). The fact that the Liberal government was seen to be on the side of the bosses, together with the fact that tenants and workers were able to utilise collective action to successfully protect their position, demonstrated in a practical way that their interests were best served by their own devices. The polarisation of class meant that the co-operative movement and the trade unions became increasingly politicised and the ILP stepped in to provide political leadership. By utilising the membership and organisational strengths of these institutions, Labour was able to promote its message to a wider and more receptive audience. Also, by providing meeting places and members, the trade unions allowed direct access for the ILP to the working class. In an environment of increasing class tensions, the rhetoric of socialism made sense to many in the working class. After all, the middle class and the bosses had used government repression to silence the strike leaders, the shell scandal of 1915 had exposed the principle of profits before patriotism among the arms manufacturers, and repression in Ireland made a sham of the Liberal commitment to Irish home rule.

At the end of the day it is difficult not to conclude that it was social and economic factors which lay at the heart of working-class demands for political change. The extent to which this was driven by the ideals of socialism are hard to gauge.[2] Certainly the rhetoric used by the leaders of the Labour movement was replete with socialist idealism, so much so that the middle class took it at face value and believed that this was the principle driving force behind working-class discontent. Part of the attraction of socialism was that it was delivered in an authentic working-class accent and led by working-class people. After all, the main experience of the war was that social and economic reform came as a result of their own actions and not through government regard for their best interests. The working class had flexed its political muscles and found them powerful enough to take on both employers and the state. Yet as Iain Hutchison and others have argued, too much cannot be read into the ideological apparatus which accompanied this development. Much of the industrial agitation was driven by the demand to preserve craft differentials. The call for welfare reform, education reform and improved housing were part and parcel of the Liberal staple before the war. Even demands for Scottish home rule, temperance reform and land reform demonstrate that there was a considerable degree of continuity in the radical tradition. One way to look at this development is to see Labour as ousting the Liberal Party from its position as the most credible champion of working-class interests (MacDonald 2000: 267–83). In other words, the interests and aspirations of the working-class constituency remained pretty much the same, it was just that they could be better delivered by Labour. Socialism was the new catch-all phrase to replace radicalism.

The drive towards pragmatic politics was further reinforced when the party opted to go down the 'gradualist' path to socialism, rather than revolution, as was advocated by the likes of John Maclean. The advocacy of a doctrinaire socialism was one that was not suited to Scottish Labour. The party was a broad church and had an amalgam of left and right, trade unionists and co-operative members, home rulers and former Liberals, supporters of the war and pacifists, and too much time spent on ideological definitions would inevitably lead to alienation from some of the groupings. A loose ideology was an aid to unity. In the general election of 1922, Labour with twenty-nine seats became the largest party in Scotland. Anti-socialism became the hallmark of Scottish politics, with formal co-operation between Liberals and Tories before 1922 which later existed informally in places in order to keep Labour out. However, the party emerged as a more than credible political force. This further reinforced the idea that socialism could be achieved by the parliamentary route because if Labour continued its electoral advance, it would be within striking distance of forming a government. In 1924, the party formed a minority government for a mere nine months until it was brought down by its Liberal partners. The government was significant in two respects. Firstly, as it was supported by the Liberals, it dented that party's claim to be a bulwark against socialism and, especially in Scotland, the right turned against them and reduced them to an electoral rump. This meant that politics would be dominated by two parties that based their electoral appeal primarily on class interests. Secondly, it reinforced claims that Labour was not a doctrinaire party and that the electorate did not need to fear radical change. The emphasis was placed on responsible government and the Wheatley Housing Act demonstrated that social reform was possible via the parliamentary route.

THE INTER-WAR ERA

The Scottish Parliamentary Labour Party's performance in the twenties enhanced the idea that the organisation was first and foremost a party committed to working-class welfare, rather than a theoretical advocate of socialism. The party stalwarts, James Maxton, David Kirkwood, George Buchanan, Tom Johnston and James Barr, were proponents of what might be called a 'wives and weans' socialism. There was little in the way of a sustained intellectual output from the Scottish party with most endeavours focusing on working-class grievances. Suspension from the House of Commons on a regular basis for unruly behaviour enhanced their image as working-class heroes, as did their tendency to stick together in lowly digs away from mainstream parliamentarians. This promotion of working-class interests was heightened by the economic background of the twenties. Structural dislocation in the Scottish economy meant that there were regularly some 100,000 unemployed and employers were engaged in a campaign of pushing back workers' rights and curtailing the power of the trade unions. Cuts in government expenditure meant that housing improvements by local authorities were limited in scope. Only John Wheatley, a much neglected figure in the intellectual history of the Labour Party, gave serious consideration as to the practical implications of achieving a workable system of socialism (Howell 1984). For most in the party, however, socialism was associated with an ethical belief in social justice that would reward the working class and improve their material standard of living. Little thought or attention was paid to when socialism would arrive or, for that matter, how it would arrive. It was a matter of belief that it would come. In the meantime, the party would operate within the parameters of the capitalist system, while at the same time promoting and protecting working-class interests.

This approach began to unravel when Labour took office in 1929 for the second time as a minority administration, just as the Great Depression was beginning to gather momentum. Some of the contradictions in this approach were revealed at the party conference in 1929 when Ramsay MacDonald in talking about the rising unemployment following in the wake of the depression claimed that it was not the government which was at fault, but the capitalist system. For a government committed to orthodox fiscal policy until socialism arrived, contradictions soon became apparent. The worst of the depression fell disproportionately on Labour's working-class constituency and they looked to the party to do something about it. Labour's commitment to 'responsible' government and a belief in the main tenets of fiscal orthodoxy placed the party in a quandary. Within the capitalist system, the best way to deal with unemployment was protection through the benefit system, yet as the recession bit deeper and government funds became depleted, nothing in the form of an answer was forthcoming.

By 1931, an international bank loan was predicated on cuts in state expenditure and this split the party with Ramsay MacDonald and a handful of his Cabinet taking the decision to form a 'Government of National Emergency'. The 'débâcle' of 1931 had a number of important consequences for the Labour Party, both in Scotland and in the United Kingdom. First, it demonstrated that the party was intellectually ill-equipped to deal with a crisis of the magnitude of the Great Depression. Labour was wiped out in the 1931 general election; even though the party polled almost a third of the vote in Scotland the first-past-the-post system meant that only seven MPs were elected. Those who survived represented solid working-class constituencies and had proven credentials as defenders of working-class interests. Speaking out against public expenditure cuts and rising unemployment maintained support. Second, it focused minds towards pragmatism rather than ideology. The secession of the ILP under James Maxton in 1932 further reinforced this trend as it removed the committed left-wing ideologues. For the party to reassert itself in politics, it was necessary to concentrate on organisation, propaganda and the building up of the infrastructure that would recapture lost seats.

In essence this focused minds back on airing working-class grievances, promoting better welfare provision, improvements in housing and high-lighting poverty, all of which had been exacerbated by the recession. This emphasis in Scottish Labour policy was reinforced by the fact that those who survived the electoral cull of 1931, such as David Kirkwood and George Buchanan, were stalwart traditionalists with little interest in economic arguments or ideology. Passion and commitment was more admired than intellectual ability. Much time and effort went into getting people such as Tom Johnston back into Parliament to provide leadership. The 1935 general election showed that Labour had recovered much ground in terms of its share of the vote (41.8 per cent), but the first-past-the-post system meant that this was not translated into seats (24). In many ways, it is difficult not to conceive of Labour as primarily a party of protest in Scotland during the thirties. Labour did not have its problems to seek and in addition to the ILP, there was a challenge from communists and nationalists, each advocating their own particular solutions to the problems of the recession. The extent of the difficulties facing a party designed to protect and promote working-class interests can be illustrated by a few telling facts and figures. Overcrowding in Scotland was six times greater than south of the border, infant and maternal mortality figures remained higher, unemployment was about twice the UK average and those on poor relief continued to grow until 1937 (Finlay 1994). The difficulty for Labour was to attain some form of ideological apparatus that would address and provide solutions for these problems. Gradualist socialism could not square the circle, while the party was still committed to orthodox fiscal policy. In part, some of the difficulties faced by Labour in Scotland could be ascribed to a lack of ideological development and political imagination. In many respects, the party canted the same mantra emanating from London. For example, Labour was hostile to a programme of rearmament which, had it been more extensive, would have reflated (as did eventually happen) many of the traditional industries in Scotland which were languishing as a result of the depression. Ideologically, facing up to the threat from Fascism should have posed little difficulty. Furthermore, the party was slow to pick up on specific aspects of London economic policy which worked against Scotland. Rural subsidies, low interest rates and cheap money and tariff protection all worked to the advantage of the south but brought little benefits to the north. Indeed, Scottish Tory criticism was often more trenchant than Labour.

While many historians have traced the origins of post-war corporatism to the experience of economic dislocation in the thirties, it was a debate in which Labour seldom took part (Hutchison 2001; Saville 1985). As business increasingly looked to government intervention in order to shore up the economy, especially the shipbuilding industry, Labour politicians were slow to grasp the opportunities realised by the use of the state as an economic regulator. Rather, the main focus of their criticisms centred on business getting money which should have gone to social welfare. The tense atmosphere of class conflict at this time goes some way to explaining this state of affairs in that businesses were quite keen to dip into the public purse but were forever moaning about the prohibitive costs of welfare. It was in response to this situation and the programme of rearmament, which was consolidating the power of the traditional industrialists, that increasing reference was made to the project of Scottish home rule. Labour had vacillated on this issue throughout the inter-war period. The debate on home rule gives some insights into the ideological state of play within the Labour Party during this period.

In the early twenties, home rule belonged to the wish list of radical reforms that formed part and parcel of the Labour staple, but as the economic reality bit in, the party moved away from the idea as it was believed that it was no longer feasible because the resources needed for social reconstruction would have to be utilised at a British level. This situation was reinforced by the appearance of the National Party of Scotland in 1928 and its transformation into the Scottish National Party in 1934 which made a number of unhelpful by-election interventions and in 1932 cost Tom Johnston the possibility of a return to parliament. It was only in the mid-thirties that the party began to have a rethink on the whole issue of Scottish home rule. Firstly, the nationalists were no longer conceived of as a threat. Secondly, government reforms had considerably enhanced the powers of the Scottish Secretary of State which effectively consolidated the powers of the state north of the border. Thirdly, the roots of corporatism were growing deeper and this meant that Labour and the unions were effectively frozen out of the decision-making process. Home rule was conceived as a means to break the power of the Tory business alliance.

Perhaps the most adventurous intellectual argument in favour of a socialist vision of Scottish home rule came from Thomas Burns of the Scottish Self-Government Committee. In *The Real Rulers of Scotland* (1939), Burns argued that the Scottish economy was dominated by a relatively small number of major capitalist owners who between them and their shared interests were responsible for most control over the economy. Furthermore, this oligarchy was closely involved with the government. In order to liberate the economy from such control and divert resources to social and economic reconstruction, Burns argued, it would be necessary to break the hold of monopoly capitalism in Scotland. This could be done by using Scottish home rule as a way to check the political power of the industrial barons and use the democratic process for the redistribution of economic power. Central to Burns' thesis was the primacy of economic power as this could always be used to circumvent democracy. Just as ideology was re-emerging within Labour, this argument was soon overtaken by events as the war ushered in a revolution in the nature of British politics and state power. In order to fight a 'total' war, reliance on the free market came to an end and the era of the command economy arrived.

THE SECOND WORLD WAR

The appointment of Thomas Johnston as Secretary of State for Scotland in 1941 is often seen as a turning point in Scottish political history (Walker 1988). By using his considerable talents as a propagandist, administrator and negotiator, Johnston was able to screw out of the Cabinet concessions for Scotland. In short, he was able to revitalise the Union and demonstrate that it could work to Scotland's advantage. This was especially the case as the issue of reconstruction was looming large in the wartime public mind. The use of the command economy to prosecute the war was an ample demonstration that where there was political will there was a way, which was demonstrated by an ability to provide full employment and redistribute wealth on a more socially just basis. It was strongly believed that this revolution should continue after the war and emerged as part of a wider British political consensus that the 'bad old days' of unemployment and depression should not be repeated. This was a necessary part of the government's campaign to mobilise hearts and minds for the war effort, and was enshrined in the Beveridge Report of 1942, which argued for the creation of the welfare state. Public opinion ensured that it would be implemented after the war.

Furthermore, the reign of Johnston was able to set in place a number of developments that seemed to point forward to the welfare state and the corporate economy in Scotland. The health service was reorganised under government control as part of the wartime emergency, but as Scotland experienced comparatively light injuries from aerial bombing, Johnston used the services to provide free health care to workers as part of a campaign to increase industrial efficiency. Furthermore, the Secretary of State was active in promoting government production north of the border and argued for an increased proportion of the factory space that was allocated to Scotland. Most ambitiously of all, he set in motion the plans for the reconstruction of the western central belt economy which had suffered most during the depression. Under the chairmanship of Sir Patrick Abercrombie, the Clyde Valley Plan was wide-ranging in its scope. It also took into account social factors and proposed that government oversee an ambitious redevelopment of the economy. New light industries were to be promoted to encourage diversification and end reliance on the old staples. Population was to be dispersed away from Glasgow into new towns and settlements to relieve urban congestion and tackle the problem of poor housing conditions. It was an ample demonstration of what the British state could do and it propounded a solution to the endemic social and economic problems which had plagued inter-war Scottish society.

While much attention has focused on how the use of the command economy and the development of the welfare state were important in revitalising a sense of British political identity in Scotland, a number of features would have a significant impact on the subsequent political development of Scotland. Firstly, Johnson did not really do anything new in terms of government north of the border. The seeds of corporatism had been planted in the thirties and the developments during wartime simply extended the corporate consensus to include the Labour Party and the trade unions. Furthermore, Johnston was a big fan of the corporatist approach as is revealed by his use of his Committee of the Ex-Secretaries of State for Scotland to form an all-party political consensus on Scottish post-war reconstruction. In many ways, the big issues were ducked. One problem with corporatism was the assumption that it could satisfy the ambitions of politicians, business and the unions, and little attention was paid to the possibility of conflicting interests. Nationalisation offered significant compensation to the owners (with the exception of coal, most nationalised industry control was outside of Scotland) and capitalism still expected to do well out of the corporate economy. Whether the government or the free market filled the order books it did not matter, so long as profits were ensured. Unions expected better pay and conditions and full employment. Politicians expected to be rewarded for their ability to satisfy these demands. At the end of the day, post-war plans failed to become reality because of political expediency. The need for cash following the war meant that the British economy began an export drive to capitalise on European reconstruction which effectively meant that the south produced the consumer durable, while the north produced the staples. Diversification was not achieved and corporatism was used to shore up a failing economic structure.

A second issue relating to Johnston's regime was that it turned Scottish politics into an issue more of administration than government. The wartime obsession with 'management' was reflected back into Scottish political life with the key benchmarks of success and failure being measured by delivery of socio-economic benefits from Westminster. Ideas of wider public consultation and democracy were shunned in favour of the belief that the 'expert' knew best. This had significant implications for the development of Scottish politics as the era following the post-war retiral of many of Labour's characters such as Maxton, Kirkwood, Barr and others saw the arrival of 'grey' characters with little in the way of a public persona. It is also worth noting that Scottish Labour produced no figure of repute on the scale of Attlee, Dalton, Bevan, Bevin, Cripps or Citrine, who were absolutely essential to the revitalisation of Labour south of the border and in Britain generally. The tendency for administrative devolution which Johnston set in train meant there was little scope for public debate as Labour concentrated on policy implementation which usually had its intellectual origins in London, and was adapted to Scottish purposes by civil servants.

A third and final issue is that a distinctive Scottish politics died north of the border. Pragmatism and management became ingrained in Scottish Labour's post-war outlook. Political elevation was usually through the tried and trusty method of service in local government or through the trade unions. Intellectual horizons became fixed on the delivery of housing, local government and the local party organisation. Ideology and political imagination had never been Scottish Labour's strong points in the period before 1945, and would continue to languish until the sixties. Perhaps more importantly, faith in administration and experts meant that passion died and the party became distant from the people.

Notes

1. The history of Labour in Scotland has been well covered. See I. Donnachie, C. Harvie and I. S. Wood (eds), *Forward! Labour Politics in Scotland 1888–1988* (1989); R. Duncan and A. McIvor (eds), *Militant Workers: Labour and Class Conflict on the Clyde 1900–50* (1992); A. McKinlay and R. J. Morris (eds), *The ILP on Clydeside 1893–1932: From Foundation to Disintegration* (1991); W. Knox (ed.), *Scottish Labour Leaders 1918–39* (1984); J. Holford, *Reshaping Labour: Organisation, Work and Politics – Edinburgh in the Great War and After* (1988); W. H. Fraser, *Scottish Popular Politics: From Radicalism to Labour* (2000); D. Howell, *A Lost Left: Three Studies in Socialism and Nationalism* (1984); I. Maclean, *The Legend of Red Clydeside* (1983). For a general history of Scottish politics, see I. G. C. Hutchison, *Scottish Politics in the Twentieth Century* (2001).

2. This has engendered a wide-ranging debate. See Maclean, *The Legend of Red Clydeside*, and T. Brotherstone, 'Does Red Clydeside Really Matter Any More?', in Duncan and McIvor, *Labour and Class Conflict*, pp. 52–81.

References

Burns, T. (1939), *The Real Rulers of Scotland*, London Scots Self-Government Committee, Glasgow.

Finlay, R. J. (1994), 'National Identity in Crisis: Politicians, Intellectuals and the End of Scotland, 1928–39', *History*, 79.

Finlay, R. J. (1996), 'Continuity or Change? Scottish Politics 1900–45', in T. M. Devine and R. J. Finlay (eds), *Scotland in the Twentieth Century*, Edinburgh University Press, Edinburgh, pp. 64–84.

Howell, D. (1984), *A Lost Left: Three Studies in Socialism and Nationalism*, Manchester University Press, Manchester.

Hutchison, I. G. C. (1986), *A Political History of Scotland: Parties, Elections and Issues, 1832–1924*, John Donald, Edinburgh.

Hutchison, I. G. C. (1987), 'Glasgow Working Class Politics', in R. A. Cage (ed.), *The Working Class in Glasgow: 1750–1914*, Croom Helm, London.

Hutchison, I. G. C. (2001), *Scottish Politics in the Twentieth Century*, Palgrave, Basingstoke.

Knox, W. W. (1990), 'The Political and Workplace Culture of the Scottish Working Class', in W. H. Fraser and R. J. Morris (eds), *People and Society in Scotland: Volume II, 1983–1914*, John Donald, Edinburgh.

MacDonald, C. M. M. (2000), *The Radical Thread: Political Change in Scotland: Paisley Politics 1885–1924*, Tuckwell Press, East Linton.

Melling, J. (1983), *Rent Strikes: Peoples' Struggle for Housing in the West of Scotland 1890–1916*, Polygon, Edinburgh.

Saville, R. (1985), 'The Industrial Background to the Post-war Scottish Economy', in Saville, R. (ed.), *The Economic Development of Modern Scotland 1945–80*, John Donald, Edinburgh.

Walker, G. (1988), *Thomas Johnston*, Manchester University Press, Manchester.

Chapter 3

Labour in Scotland since 1945:
Myth and Reality

Bob McLean

The first post-war conference of the Scottish Council of the Labour Party took place in Musselburgh in October 1945. Far from Attlee lauding his Scottish troops as the van in the peaceful revolution, the Prime Minister scolded the Scottish party for achieving the lowest regional swing to Labour, from the last peacetime election in 1935, just 9.8 per cent compared with 17.5 per cent in London, 11.4 per cent in Wales and 12 per cent nationally. Labour in Scotland has distinctive roots, but one of its distinguishing features was its relative weakness when compared with the Party in other parts of the UK. It was that weakness that led to the collapse of an independent organisation after 1909, the subsequent creation of the Scottish Advisory Committee, of the NEC in 1915, and its incorporation in the 1918 constitution of the Party as a regional council with the same rights as the English regions (Midwinter et al. 1991: 26).

Another distinguishing, and debilitating, factor was the disaffiliation of the Independent Labour Party in 1932. The stated reason for the split concerned the whipping of ILP MPs at Westminster, although it also reflected growing left/right tensions between the ILP and Labour. In Scotland the ILP was particularly strong at the grass roots of the party. Those who sustained the local Labour Parties, attended Socialist Sunday School, wheeled around Scotland with the Clarion Cycling Clubs, sold *Forward* or sang in socialist choirs tended to be ILP. Their departure has been described as transforming the Labour Party in Scotland from 'a crusade into a machine' (Brown et al. 1998: 142). There were those eager to manage a more docile organisation, for example Sir Patrick Dollan, Lord Provost of Glasgow, Arthur Woodburn, Organiser and future Secretary of State for Scotland, and future Scottish Council Secretary Willie Marshall. As Chris Harvie has so colourfully described it: 'The time of the wee hardman had come' (Harvie 1981: 106).

So much for the vanguard, what about the revolution? Labour will forever be firmly associated with the creation of the welfare state but there is little doubt that if the Tories had won in 1945 they would have created something similar. The experiences of the late 1930s and the war years led the British state to sign up for corporatism, a superstructure co-ordinating capital, labour and government in the interests of social harmony and economic development. To the victor the spoils and Attlee's government inherited Beveridge's plan for universal insurance against sickness, unemployment and old age. It also took control of a framework of economic controls governing labour, raw materials, pricing and demand from Europe and the Empire for almost anything Britain could export.

The corporatist consensus was particularly strong in Scotland where Scottish Unionists were more pragmatic and paternalistic than their southern Conservative siblings.[1] Leading Unionist Walter Elliot argued in the 1920s for an interventionist Toryism that he implemented as Secretary of State for Scotland in the 1930s. There was general agreement that economic diversification and housing were Scottish priorities and the labour movement was included in the Scottish National Development Committee and the Scottish Economic Committee. Edinburgh increasingly resembled a seat of government and labour was within the pale.

At the heart of the Scottish consensus was ILP veteran Tom Johnston and his reign as Secretary of State for Scotland from 1941 to 1945. In accepting Churchill's offer of a place in his wartime coalition government, Johnston refused to accept a ministerial salary and insisted on the creation of a Scottish Council of State composed of previous Secretaries of State. If the Council unanimously agreed on any matter, Churchill agreed to effectively rubber-stamp it. In his years at St Andrew's House, Johnston created the Scottish Council Development and Industry which brought together the STUC, employers, local authorities, chambers of commerce and the banks. This 'industrial parliament' was welcomed by STUC General Secretary William Elgar, an enthusiast for the corporatist consensus. Johnston established the North of Scotland Hydro-Electric Board, brought the Forestry Commissioners under the de-facto control of the Scottish Office, pre-figured Labour's 1946 Heath Service proposals by extending the care provided by Civil Defence Hospitals, and instigated enquiries into various aspects of the Scottish economy to prepare for post-war reconstruction.

Evidence of the consensus is found in the actions of the incoming 1951 Tory government which only rolled back the recent nationalisation of the steel industry and aspects of road transport. Revolutionary? No. Effective? Yes. For the next twenty years politics in Scotland would be about delivering the consensus.

As Attlee inspected his Scottish troops in Musselburgh he may have harboured concerns about their abilities. With the departure of the 1922 generation, through death or disaffiliation, Scottish Labour MPs, with the obvious exception of Johnston, failed to stand out at Westminster and that is how it would remain until the 1960s. Johnston raised the question of supposed corruption in local government in 1941/42, threatening to appoint commissioners to run Glasgow. This involved the Secretary of State in a relatively public spat with Dollan who challenged Johnston to look beyond small-time licensing irregularities to the big money involved in council contacts: 'Wherever profit is to be made out of municipal trans-actions there is always a tendency for graft unless regulations are strict and enforced without fear or favour.' (*Glasgow Herald*, 19 February 1942)

Almost forty years after Dollan wrote those words, I heard George Galloway, then Secretary/Organiser of Dundee Labour Party, express similar sentiments regarding the scandals in that city in the 1970s. Isolated incidents across the decades, however, should not cause to be questioned the integrity of generations of Labour councillors who have given of themselves for the interests of their communities, nor that of the current generation, which, given the development of the local state, are increasingly professional.

NATIONALISATION = CENTRALISATION?

The achievements of the 1945–51 Labour governments demonstrated the ability of the British state to deliver for Scotland, and the old Scottish Labour commitment to home rule continued to decline in relevance.

It was a difficult act to follow, but Johnston's successor, Joseph West-wood, fell ill during 1945 and was absent from Cabinet deliberations from October 1945 until January 1946. His absence at that critical point may partly explain why Labour's nationalisations were organised on a highly centralist model with little or no Scottish dimension. The equation that nationalisation equals centralisation was raised at the Scottish Council of the Party's conference in October 1947 (*The Scotsman*, 27 October 1947).

Another source of discontent over centralisation was John MacCormick's Scottish Convention. Having split from the Scottish National Party in 1942, MacCormick was a gradualist advocating broad agreement around a scheme for home rule. Ever prepared to play the 'Scottish card', the Scottish Unionist Association published 'Scottish Control of Scottish Affairs' in 1949, in an attempt to distinguish between Unionism and 'amalgamation'. It promised Scottish authorities for transport, electricity, gas and coal, and a review of civil aviation (Scottish Unionist Association 1949).

During 1947, MacCormick was engaged in debate with Unionists with the intention of leading them along the decentralist path to home rule.

Earlier that year MacCormick had been selected as the Liberal parliamentary candidate for Paisley. In December 1947, Paisle MP, Oliver Baldwin, was elevated to the Lords, causing a by-elect much intrigue MacCormick emerged as a 'National' candidate, en the Unionists and their National Liberal allies and local Liberals. In a straight head to head, Labour's Douglas Johnston defeated MacCormick, whose actions provided Labour in Scotland and London with all the reason required to ignore the Scottish Convention and its National Covenant. Paisley raised Labour hackles, and although the details are long forgotten, the spectre that 'everyone else is against us' continues to haunt sections of Scottish Labour (*The Scotsman*, 20 February 1948).

If by-elections are an indicator of government popularity, the Attlee governments remained popular throughout their period in office. Labour also 'won' the October 1951 general election, out-polling the Tories across the United Kingdom by 1.6 per cent of the popular vote, but the vagaries of first past the post produced a Tory majority of seventeen. It was not solely a question of electoral systems, however. The continuing austerity of rationing and divisions in the government were also contributory factors (Haines 2000).

THE ONLY WAY IS DOWN

In the general election of May 1955, the Unionists in Scotland polled an all-time record 50.1 per cent, a mirror reflection of the Conservative performance in England. Four years later the Scottish Tories polled 3 per cent below that achieved by their English counterparts while Labour in Scotland out-polled the party south of the border. Why did the Unionists poll so effectively in 1955 and why did they go into a decline so steep that within forty-two years it would leave them without any parliamentary representation in Scotland?

The 1955 result was not only the high-water mark of Unionism, it was also the apogee of two-party politics in Scotland. Between 1955 and 1964, the Unionists polled an average of 46 per cent in Scotland to Labour's 47 per cent. As already demonstrated, the Unionists were ready to play the Scottish card, without yielding one inch on legislative devolution, and were prepared to outbid Labour on housing programmes and projects like the Forth Road Bridge. In the mid-1950s Scotland's heavy industries were still enjoying the Indian summer of the post-war boom but the failure to diversify would return to trouble both parties.

Tory decline from the mid-1950s reflected changes in Scottish society and institutions and the role of Labour within them. From the days of Keir

Hardie's Mid-Lanark campaign in 1888, Scotland's press had been consistently hostile to Labour. In 1956 the Kemsley Press sold its *Daily Record* title to the Mirror Group, which transformed it into a Scottish equivalent of the Labour-supporting *Daily Mirror*. From that time on the *Daily Record* has been a consistent Labour supporter. In October 1974, and as recently as the Scottish Parliament election of 2003, stunning *Record* front-page endorsements have been displayed by Labour supporters as posters (*Daily Record*, 10 October 1974 and 1 May 2003). There are limits, however, and at the Hillhead by-election of March 1982 the *Record* wobbled in its support for Labour (*Daily Record*, 24 March 1982).

Protestantism was once an important glue holding the Unionist alliance together and providing it with a working-class base, particularly in the West of Scotland. In an increasingly secular Scotland, however, working-class Catholics and Protestants found their shared economic and social aspirations to be increasingly in tune with Labour. While recent election surveys suggest that religion continues to decline as a determinate of political behaviour, there is still a residual relationship between politics and religion as demonstrated by the sectarian hostility encountered by Labour's Helen Liddell in the Monklands by-election in 1994. Empire was another important building block of the Unionist/Tory identity and its decline, so emphatically demonstrated by the Suez crisis, loosened another tie with Unionism.

The professions, particularly teaching, were once regarded as a recruiting ground for Unionism. The affiliation of the Educational Institute of Scotland to the STUC in the early 1970s was a symbolic shift of allegiance, as is the number of former teachers who have played a prominent role in Scottish Labour politics since the 1960s.

By 1959 the post-war boom was over and the decline of heavy industries hit Scotland particularly hard. Between 1954 and 1960, Scottish industrial production grew by 9 per cent, compared with 23 per cent across the UK as a whole. The Tories campaigned on the slogan 'Life is better with Conservatives. Don't let Labour ruin it'; the reality in Scotland was 100,000 unemployed.

At the 1956 Conference of the Scottish Council of the Labour Party, Attlee's successor, Hugh Gaitskell, pronounced that the notion of Scottish home rule within the United Kingdom was dead. Labour's achievements in government and the development of national planning had rendered the old policy obsolete. Rearguard actions, including the intervention of John P. Macintosh, delayed the inevitable for two years but a special conference, held in Glasgow in September 1958, formalised Labour opposition to Scottish home rule. It was to remain party policy for sixteen years (*The Scotsman*, 15 September 1958).

THE ECONOMY CENTRE STAGE

In 1963 the Scottish Conference of the Party approved 'Signposts for Scotland', a rolling manifesto for the general election expected the following year. At the centre of the paper was a commitment to national planning and targeting industrial development to areas where labour was available and work was required. Growth would be based on scientific research matched to commercial applications, as the document concluded: 'Every thinking Scot knows in his heart what Scotland needs now is the socialist policy of planned industrial expansion and the positive direction of that expansion to the places it is most needed.' (Labour Party National Executive et al. 1963)

It proved to be a signpost for victory. In 1964, the Unionists, fighting under that banner for the last time, slumped to twenty-four seats compared to Labour's forty-three. While Labour had a clear lead in Scotland, the pattern that had emerged in 1959 continued and Labour only narrowly pipped the Tories across the United Kingdom. Another election was expected soon. With Willie Ross, Harold Wilson's Secretary of State for Scotland, at the helm, Scotland benefited from an aura of good feelings. Doomed shipyards were rescued, the Highlands and Islands Development Board was established to counteract the rundown of the rural economy, and a National Plan granted development-area status to the whole of Scotland, with the exception of Edinburgh and Leith. Labour's regional strategy proved popular and Scotland rewarded Wilson and Ross with a then record forty-six seats in March 1966.

Socially and culturally, the Wilson governments chimed with the mood of the 'swinging sixties'. The Race Relations Act of 1965 was an opening salvo against racism, male homosexuality was decriminalised in England and Wales in 1967 (Scotland having to wait until 1980) and in that same year a private members' bill legalised the medical termination of pregnancy. Labour began to outlaw gender discrimination with the 1970 Equal Pay Act and Wilson claimed the Open University as his personal monument as learning was extended beyond the lecture theatre (Haines 2000). In Scotland, Labour sought to modernise institutions. Ross established a Scottish Law Commission and a Royal Commission on Local Government, which produced the two-tier regional and district councils that served Scotland from 1975 to 1995.

Within months of re-election, a sterling crisis led to the virtual abandonment of the National Plan. Despite the boost of Dounreay and the Invergordon smelter to the rural economy, a seaman's strike tarnished Labour's image in Scotland's island communities. The promise of the 'white heat of technology' was beginning to cool.

CHANGED UTTERLY: POST-HAMILTON SCOTLAND

The problems facing the government partly explain the Scottish National Party's by-election victory at Hamilton in November 1967. Until then SNP parliamentary representation had been confined to a matter of months in 1945 and had been due to the Nats flouting the war-time electoral truce. The SNP had polled credibly at by-elections in the 1960s, but Winnie Ewing's triumph was a political earthquake. Willie Ross's reaction was to tough it out against the SNP and to make no concessions. Ross used the threat of the SNP to win a larger slice of the UK cake with which he believed he could hold the line in Scotland. An insight into how Ross patrolled the Scottish beat at Westminster is revealed in Richard Crossman's diaries of the period (Crossman 1977: 48). Crossman was among those who urged Wilson to ignore Ross's advice, and in late 1968 the Prime Minister appointed a Royal Commission on the Constitution. It would not report until after the next general election, and Wilson hoped that it would see off further Nationalist advances. The plan worked in Scotland. Labour returned forty-four MPs while the SNP was restricted to just one seat, but Heath's Conservatives won an unexpected United Kingdom majority.

The Kilbrandon Commission, as it was popularly known, spent the spring and summer of 1970 taking evidence in Scotland. In its session with the representatives of the Scottish Council of the Labour Party, the Commissioners quizzed the Labour team on their response to the prospect of prolonged Tory tenure of the Scottish Office, based on an ever-declining Tory rump in the face of an increasing majority of Scottish Labour MPs. Scottish Council Chair John Pollock dismissed the scenario as 'hypothetical and almost impossibly extreme'. Pollock's colleague, Party Secretary Willie Marshall, denied that there was such thing as a 'separate political culture in Scotland' (Royal Commission on the Constitution 1971: 23).

Within weeks of the Commission reporting, in the autumn of 1973, Wilson was back in Downing Street but without a working majority. The SNP had won seven seats in February 1974 and Wilson needed a credible response to Kilbrandon to ensure there were no further SNP advances in a general election which had to take place in the autumn. Through the efforts of his ally Alex Kitson, the senior Scot on Labour's National Executive Committee and the powerful Transport and General Workers' Union fixer in Party affairs, a special conference of the Scottish Council of the Labour Party met in Glasgow in August and overturned its opposition to devolution in favour of 'An Assembly with legislative powers within the context of the political and economic unity of the United Kingdom.'

On 10 October 1974, the SNP increased its share of the poll from 22 per cent to 30 per cent and captured a further four seats, all of them from the Conservatives. Wilson had his overall majority.

The publication of Labour's detailed devolution proposals in November 1975 was the cue for the establishment of a breakaway Scottish Labour Party led by Jim Sillars, the MP for South Ayrshire. Disappointed with the economic powers proposed for the Assembly, and the absence of any reference to the European dimension, Sillars, and fellow MP John Robertson, believed they could further the debate more effectively from outwith the Labour Party. Fêted by the Scottish media, the formation of the Sillars Scottish Labour Party was its high point. Marginalised by a pro-devolution Labour Party and a pro-independence SNP, and debilitated by far-left entryism, the SLP was sidelined as a serious force by 1977 although Jim Sillars would continue to make an influential contribution to Scottish politics.

DIVIDED OVER DEVOLUTION

Legislating for Labour's Scottish Assembly was a marathon, dating from November 1975 to Royal Assent on 31 July 1978. Along the way it picked up a couple of unwanted boarders. In order to accommodate divisions within the Labour Party in Scotland, it was agreed to subject the legislation to a referendum, just as the party had done over EEC membership in 1975. In the case of the Assembly, however, success was set at 40 per cent of the registered electorate. On the basis of general election turnouts in the 1970s, the Assembly proposition required the support of more than 60 per cent of those voting in the referendum. It was a two-thirds rule, an obstacle that no British government has ever cleared.

Those in the party opposed to devolution organised themselves as Labour Vote No (LVN) in January of 1978, stealing a march on the official Labour Movement Yes Campaign (LMY), which brought together the party, STUC and Co-operative Party and was chaired by a young Gordon Brown. Working to prevent LMY from delivering Labour supporters for a Yes vote, Labour Vote No's greatest coup was to effectively pull the plug on a planned broadcast by Labour Prime Minister Jim Callaghan. Arguing that the Yes case had greater access to party political broadcasts during the referendum campaign, Labour Vote No succeeded in having an interdict issued to prevent the Prime Ministerial broadcast from going ahead.

What did the leaders of LVN achieve by their actions? The Callaghan government depended on a Yes vote, as the proposed Assembly was a building block of the Lib-Lab pact sustaining a government which had lost its majority. Not content with campaigning against government and party policy, they had gone to the courts to prevent a Labour Prime Minister from addressing the country on an issue on which the survival of the government depended (Bochel et al. 1981).

By any conventional democratic practice, Scotland voted for an Assembly on 1 March 1979 by a margin of 51.6 per cent to 48.4 per cent. The winning total translated into 32.9 per cent of the electorate and the Assembly fell on the 40 per cent rule. With the Liberals ending the pact, the only lifeline was a parliamentary vote to override the referendum, but that would rely on the support of every Labour anti-devolutionist. Jim Sillars recalls a House of Commons encounter at that time with future Labour leader Neil Kinnock, who had led the Labour No campaign against a Welsh Assembly. Sillars put it to Kinnock that his failure to support this parliamentary ploy would result in an immediate election and almost certain defeat for Labour. 'So be it then' was the future Labour leader's reply! (Sillars 1986: 72)

Among the ranks of Labour Vote No in Scotland were Brian Wilson MP, Tam Dalyell MP, Robin Cook, UK minister, Adam Ingram, Holyrood Health Minister, Malcolm Chisholm and other luminaries. On the basis of their subsequent careers in the party, it is difficult to disagree with the assessment of Arthur Midwinter et al.:

> It is an indication of the relative lack of importance of the issue to the Party that none of those [Ingram, Wilson, etc.] suffered a political penalty for their defiance of party policy or indeed the role that their actions on devolution played in the fall of the Labour Government. (Midwinter et al. 1991: 32)

REACTING TO THATCHER

While the failure to deliver the Scottish Assembly was one of the triggers for the downfall of the Callaghan government, different perspectives in the party had their own views as to the reasons behind the defeat.

In early 1970, the Tory Shadow Cabinet agreed that their next administration would be different from those of Macmillan and Home. They agreed to break with consensus in favour of a more free-market approach: a more discriminating stance on welfare; a determination to let so-called 'lame ducks' drown; and a readiness to confront trade union power with an Industrial Relations Act. Within months of being elected in June 1970, Heath was fighting on several fronts. The campaign of the shipyard workers of UCS to save their jobs became a Scottish-wide movement while conflict with the National Union of Mineworkers, in late 1973, forced Heath to go to the country. He posed the question 'who runs Britain?'. By a narrow majority the answer was 'not you'. Within eighteen months, Heath received a more emphatic rejection, from a party which chose Margaret Thatcher as a more resolute champion of the break with consensus and the new Toryism.

The left's reaction to Thatcher's 1979 election victory was to criticise the Wilson/Callaghan governments for refusing to embrace socialist policies in response to the international economic crisis which buffeted them. Better leaders were required to ensure that the next Labour government would not repeat the same mistakes. With Michael Foot as leader, the left-leaning National Executive Committee of the Party drove through constitutional changes which would see future leaders elected by an electoral college of MPs, trade unions and local Labour Party members. Labour MPs became subject to mandatory reselection in every parliamentary cycle. There were those on the left who argued that the correct policies and the right leaders were not enough. If Labour was to match a resolute Thatcher, it must become a mass party of 'permanent persuaders for socialism', linking activists from the trade unions and Labour parties with single-issue campaigners and those radicalised by the youth and student politics of the 1960s and 1970s (Hain 1980). The lead organisation articulating this analysis was the Labour Co-ordinating Committee founded in 1978 (Thomson and Lucas 1998). The LCC struck a note with a Scottish Labour left influenced by those who had quit the Communist Party of Great Britain in the 1950s and '60s, and by those who remained within it. The involvement of as many as fifteen of the post-2003 crop of MSPs with the LCC is partly explained by its emphasis on the women's movement and the forum it provided for progressive Scottish councillors who saw themselves on the front line against Thatcher in the early 1980s. The extent of Scottish involvement in the LCC is demonstrated by the number of Scots who served on the organisation's UK Executive (Thomson and Lucas 1998: 25–7).

The LCC was not the only left organisation active in the Scottish Labour Party of the 1970s and '80s. Founded by Ted Grant, a contender for the British franchise of world Trotskyism since the late 1940s, the Militant Tendency's simple and confidently expressed blend of entryism and utopianism won control of the Scottish Region of the Labour Party Young Socialists in 1973. Prior to mandatory reselection, at least two Scottish Labour MPs owed their position to Militant support while Militant Ronnie Stevenson came to within one vote of becoming the official Labour candidate at the 1980 Glasgow Central by-election. Armed with the rule changes, Militant targeted the Glasgow constituencies of Pollok and Provan prior to the general elections of 1983 and 1987. In Provan, in 1985, Militant supporter Jim Cameron came to within one vote of securing the candidature. These Militant near misses led to the first round of Scottish Militant expulsions in 1986 (Allison 1995).

Twenty years on, and following two splits with their London-based founding fathers over the Scottish question and the poll tax campaign, the majority of Militant supporters made the 'open' or 'Scottish' turn which saw them emerge as an open political party, Scottish Militant Labour, which captured a clutch of council seats in Glasgow in 1992. Following involvement with others in the Scottish Socialist Alliance, the Militant pilgrims reached the promised land of the Scottish Socialist Party in time to see their convenor, Tommy Sheridan, elected as an MSP in 1999. Following the 2003 Scottish election, Sheridan has been joined by five SSP colleagues, at least two of whom are former senior figures in Militant.[2]

The Militant threat was cited by the leaders of the Social Democratic Party who broke with Labour in 1981 over reselection, Foot's poor leadership, and Labour Party Conference support for unilateral nuclear disarmament and withdrawal from the EEC.

The new party, either on its own or in Alliance with the Liberals, achieved a run of stunning by-election successes in 1981 and 1982. The Social Democrats' Scottish high point came in March 1982 when Roy Jenkins won in the last remaining Tory outpost in Glasgow at a by-election in Hillhead. The pressures heaped on the Labour Party at that point are reflected in the stand taken by the *Daily Record*. For the first time since its relaunch by the Mirror Group in the early 1960s, the *Record* equivocated on support for Labour. In its eve-of-poll edition it attacked Foot's ineffective leadership and left-wing policies associated with Tony Benn. If registered in Hillhead, its editorial writer concluded:

> we would seriously consider voting for the SDP – and in view of the political shambles in Britain today not feel guilty about betraying old loyalties. We dismiss carpetbagger jibes against Jenkins. He is entitled to try his hand in Scotland. (*Daily Record*, 24 March 1982)

Addressing Labour Party workers following the close of poll, Scottish Organiser Jimmy Allison conceded defeat but stressed the positives for Labour. He claimed that the anticipated result would demonstrate that Jenkins would have failed to win any Labour-held seat in Scotland, that the Labour Party had 1,000 activists on streets on polling day and that many of those who had voted for Jenkins had done so because they fancied the notion of being represented by a statesman, a former Home Secretary and Chancellor. Within eight days of Jenkins' victory, Argentina invaded the

Falkland Islands. Domestic politics went on the back burner and the momentum of the Liberal–SDP Alliance stalled.

The only Scottish Labour MPs to defect to the SDP were Robert MacLennan (Caithness and Sutherland) and Dickson Mabon (Greenock and Port Glasgow). In the general election of June 1983 the SDP/Liberal Alliance polled 25 per cent in Scotland, an impressive increase on the Liberal's 9 per cent share in 1979, but returned only eight MPs. The Liberals added Gordon and Roxburgh and Berwickshire to take their total to five while the SDP lost Mabon, retained Jenkins and MacLennan, and added Charles Kennedy in Ross, Cromarty and Skye. By the general election of June 1987, the Alliance had lost five percentage points and George Galloway displaced Jenkins in Hillhead. In the UK as a whole the 'third force' had remained static and the Alliance collapsed in the acrimony of merger negotiations. In 1992 the Liberal Democrats retained the nine seats won in Scotland in 1987 but their vote dropped a further 6 per cent.

LABOUR: THE NATIONAL PARTY OF SCOTLAND?

The general election of 11 June 1987 was one of the most important in modern Scottish history. It was the doomsday scenario, the term coined to describe the prospect of an anti-Tory Scotland ruled by an increasingly unrepresentative Tory rump. In 1987 the Conservatives polled less than half of the poll won by their Unionist forebears in 1955, and returned only ten MPs compared with the thirty-six seats won thirty years earlier. The outcome presented challenges for all political parties, but for Scottish Labour, and its record fifty seats, in particular. In 1983 brief talk of a campaign around the Tories' lack of a mandate to run Scotland had come to nothing. How would Labour, led by Donald Dewar, respond to a new political landscape which looked particularly harsh in the light of the controversial poll tax?

In the spring of 1985, Scotland's councils carried out a rates revaluation. The exercise had been postponed from 1983 and the result was large increases that produced a cry of pain from the Tory suburbs. In search of a quick fix, the Tories turned to their ideologues who came up with the Community Charge, a standard charge in each local authority to be paid by every adult, regardless of housing tenure, income or any other indicator of ability to pay. Commonly known as the poll tax, it was against the grain of progressive and redistributive taxation. The news that it was to be introduced in Scotland in April 1988, one year ahead of the rest of the UK, increased resentment.

One of Labour's first initiatives following the 1987 general election was the Canvass for Scotland, a canvass of electors in the Glasgow constituencies of Cathcart and Garscadden to ask their views on Labour's devolution proposals. In August 1987, the LCC in Scotland staged a one-day conference on the post-election situation. It was an encouraging event but definite proposals, regarding Labour's relationship with the cross-party Campaign for a Scottish Assembly and its proposal for the convening of a Scottish Constitutional Convention, were not followed up.[3] In September, a Festival for Scottish Democracy on Glasgow Green was well attended. Unfortunately, it was marred by inter-party wrangling, but it was an early indication that the STUC's Campbell Christie intended to involve the trade union movement in the constitutional debate. A special conference of the Scottish Council of the Labour Party was held in Edinburgh in 1987 but produced very little in terms of policy or strategy. In January 1988, Dewar decided to present Labour's revised devolution proposals at Westminster. On the day in question, Tory Scottish ministers engineered a statement on the future of Paisley Grammar School and blew the Labour initiative off the front pages.

It was against that background that a new internal pressure group was established at the March 1988 Scottish Conference. The founding statement of Scottish Labour Action (SLA) contained the following action points:

1. Recognition of the right of the Scottish people to self-determination
2. To assert that the Tories had no mandate to run Scotland
3. Non-payment of the Poll Tax
4. Labour participation in a Constitutional Convention
5. Non-co-operation at Westminster on Scottish business
6. Greater autonomy for Labour's Scottish organisation

In September 1988, a special conference of the Scottish Council of the Labour Party rejected non-payment of the poll tax but on 20 December Donald Dewar led a Westminster walkout of opposition MPs in protest at the Tories' refusal to staff the Scottish Affairs Select Committee. The return of Jim Sillars in late 1988, as the SNP victor of a by-election in Glasgow Govan, demonstrated the political danger of doing nothing. In late 1988/early 1989, Donald Dewar led Labour into the Constitutional Convention. The SNP, on a high with opinion poll ratings of 32 per cent, decided against participation. Their poll ratings soon plummeted and their absence allowed Labour to position itself as a party prepared to put Scotland before narrow partisan advantage, the real national party of Scotland (Deacon 1990). In 1990 the Scottish Constitutional Convention produced its first report, 'Towards Scotland's Parliament', which formed the basis of Labour's manifesto commitment in the 1992 general election. Agreement was made possible by Scottish Labour's rejection of first past the post for elections to what was by then referred to as a Scottish Parliament. Defeat in 1992 allowed time for further fine-tuning of the Convention scheme with George Robertson having replaced Donald Dewar as Shadow Secretary of State for Scotland. In 1995 Robertson committed the Party to the Convention's revised scheme, 'Scotland's Parliament, Scotland's Right'. Assumptions that the detail of the home rule model was now settled proved to be premature.

THE SETTLED WILL:
DELIVERING SCOTLAND'S PARLIAMENT

When John Smith succeeded Neil Kinnock as Labour leader in the summer of 1992, he was beyond doubt the senior Labour figure with the greatest experience of working in government, having been part of the team that steered the 1970s devolution legislation through Westminster. A brilliant debater, Smith told the first meeting of the Constitutional Convention, in March 1989, that support for a Scottish Parliament was the 'settled will of the Scottish people'. Following his election as leader in 1992, he described a Scottish Parliament as 'unfinished business' for Labour. There would have been further oratorical flourishes from the great phrasemaker had he not died in the summer of 1994.

Labour's new leader, Tony Blair, demanded some changes to the Constitutional Convention scheme in the summer of 1995, but New Labour was not finished with revisions. With Smith gone there were few in frontline politics who could recall the time and effort required to legislate for constitutional change, and in the spring of 1996 the Shadow Cabinet expressed concern that back-benchers, and Lords, might balk when faced with the complexities. Why not short-circuit the process with a pre-legislative referendum in the early months of a Labour government? There were also concerns as to how the debate in Scotland over limited tax discretion for a Scottish Parliament, the so-called 'Tartan Tax', would play in England, mindful of how tax had been used against Labour in 1992. Why not insulate the rest of the country by subjecting the Scottish tax power to a second, specific, question in any referendum, and by making it clear that a Labour Scottish administration would not use the tax power in its first term in office? There were concerns at the way London had intervened and what it meant for the practical operation of devolution in the future and also a view that the second question was an open invitation to reject that particular component of the scheme.

Resignations abounded and guerrilla warfare continued in the party throughout the summer of 1996. By early September, the leadership had its way as both sides of the argument collapsed in exhaustion.

Eventually, Prime Minister John Major could run no further and, on 1 May 1997, one of the most anticipated general elections of recent times took place. All of Scotland's remaining Conservative MPs lost their seats as the process that began in 1959 came to its culmination. Tony Blair asked Donald Dewar to return as Secretary of State to complete John Smith's 'unfinished business'. Dewar returned with Murray Elder and Wendy Alexander, Labour staffers from the early days of the Convention, re-united to steer the project through to conclusion. Dewar published a White Paper on 24 July 1997. When selling the referendum to opinion in Scotland, Blair promised that Labour would play a leading role in a genuine cross-party campaign for a double Yes vote. In August 1997 'Scotland Forward' was launched with the active support of Labour, the SNP and the Liberal Democrats.

It was an odd campaign. The shell-shocked Tories put up little fight, and campaigning was put on hold for a number of days following the tragic death of Diana, Princess of Wales. Normal campaigning resumed on 7 September, just four days prior to judgement day. Despite the distractions, 74.3 per cent voted Yes to the substantive proposition of a Scottish Parliament while 63.5 per cent voted Yes to tax-varying powers. It really was the settled will of the Scottish people.

Epilogue: Unfinished Business Part Two

In the second term of a Scottish Parliament, what are the fault lines in Scottish Labour? In March 1994, the party dropped the little-used title of 'Scottish Council of the Labour Party' in favour of the 'Scottish Labour Party'. Given the obvious associations with Sillars' 1976 breakaway, the change of title appeared to be the actions of a party increasingly comfortable with its Scottish identity (*The Scotsman*, 14 March 1994). One outstanding action point from SLA's founding charter is Scottish control of party resources in Scotland. In 1992, Jack McConnell's trek to Preston, to be interviewed for the post of Scottish General Secretary, was greeted with derision (*The Scotsman*, 17 September 1992). In the intervening years an easier relationship has worked between constitutional structures and in-formal arrangements.

McConnell's party title, 'Leader of Labour in the Scottish Parliament', and not 'Leader of the Scottish Labour Party', is more than semantics when it comes to developing new relationships with the reduced group of Scottish

MPs at Westminster and the evolving post of Secretary of State for Scotland.

Following the first Scottish election in 1999, commentator Iain Mac-whirter speculated on the likelihood of a re-grouping of Scottish Executive ministers with SLA pedigrees, including McConnell, to carry the autonomy agenda to its conclusion (*Sunday Herald*, 12 September 1999). The manner in which the First Minister dispensed with his erstwhile comrades in late 2001 suggests otherwise.

Autonomous structures are not only a matter of political will; they have to be paid for. Since 1945, Scottish Labour has lagged behind the levels of membership, fundraising and organisation achieved by the party in the regions of England, London and Wales. Curing this Scottish weakness remains 'unfinished business' for the current generation of Scottish Labour leaders.

The search for Scottish solutions to Scottish problems is at the heart of the home rule project. Four years on from its establishment, is our Labour-led Parliament a robust and confident legislature, or a gathering content to 'thistle-stamp' ideas from elsewhere? Time will tell.

NOTES

1. From 1912 until 1965, Conservatives in Scotland operated under the title of 'Unionist'.
2. I am grateful to Alan McCombes, National Policy Co-ordinator of the Scottish Socialist Party, and former senior Militant organiser, for assisting in separating the wheat from the chaff.
3. For an early advocacy of the Constitutional Convention proposal, see Lawson (1988: 36–45).

REFERENCES

Allison, J. (1995), *Guilty By Suspicion: A Life and Labour*, Argyll, Glendaruel.

Bochel, J., Denver, D. and McCartney, A. (eds) (1981), *The Referendum Experience: Scotland 1979*, Aberdeen University Press, Aberdeen.

Brown, A., McCrone, D. and Paterson, L. (1998), *Politics and Society in Scotland*, 2nd edn, Macmillan, Basingstoke.

Crossman, R. (1977), *The Diaries of a Cabinet Minister, Volume Three: Secretary of State for Social Services 1968–1970*, Jonathan Cape, London.

Deacon, S. (1990), 'Adopting Conventional Wisdom – Labour's Response to the National Question', in A. Brown and R. Parry, *The Scottish Government Yearbook 1990*, Unit for the Study of Government in Scotland, Edinburgh, pp. 62–75.

Hain, P. (1980), *Refreshing the Parts Others Cannot Reach*, Institute for Workers' Control, Nottingham.

Haines, J. (2000), 'Labour 100 Years of Struggle', *Inside*, special souvenir issue, vol. 1, no. 4, Labour Party, London.

Harvie, C. (1981), *No Gods and Precious Few Heroes: Scotland Since 1914*, Edward Arnold, London.

Labour Party National Executive Committee, Scottish Council of the Labour Party, Scottish Parliamentary Labour Group (1963), *Signposts for Scotland: Policy Statement for Scotland*, London.

Lawson, A. (1988), 'Mair Nor A Rauch Wind Blawin' . . .', in D. McCrone and A. Brown (eds), *The Scottish Government Yearbook 1988*, Unit for the Study of Government in Scotland, Edinburgh, pp. 36–45.

Midwinter, A., Keating, M. and Mitchell, J. (1991), *Politics and Public Policy in Scotland*, Macmillan, Basingstoke.

Royal Commission on the Constitution (1973), Minutes of Evidence IV, Scotland (4/5 May 1970 and 20 July 1970), London.

Scottish Unionist Association (1949), *Scottish Control of Scottish Affairs*, Edinburgh.

Sillars, J. (1986), *Scotland: The Case for Optimism*, Polygon, Edinburgh.

Thomson, P. and Lucas, B. (1998), *The Forward March of Modernisation: A History of the Labour Co-ordinating Committee 1978–1998*, Labour Co-ordinating Committee, London.

CHAPTER 4

The Economic and Social Context of Scottish Labour

Christopher Harvie

The shout of the welder in the din of the great Clyde shipyards; the speak of the Mearns, with its soul in the land; the discourse of the enlightenment, when Edinburgh and Glasgow were a light held to the intellectual life of Europe; the wild cry of the Great Pipes; and back to the distant cries of the battles of Bruce and Wallace. The past is part of us. (Donald Dewar, 1999)

WORKSHOP OF THE WORLD

Donald Dewar's speech at the inauguration of the Scottish Parliament looked forward, sure, but its most powerful imagery was about a past, much of which he knew, but which would be strange to the Parliament's forty-something MSPs. For Dewar, born in 1937, the Scottish economy was 'only the other day', in 1900, among the world's most advanced, and was truly Scottish.

Local consumer-goods producers – of footwear, foodstuffs, furniture, pottery, and so on – fed a Scottish market, in the shadow of the huge capital goods industries, centred on the Clyde, whose business was the making of steel and the supply of ships, marine, factory or mine engines, locomotives and structural engineering to the world. This was a segment of an interconnected industrial littoral stretching from the china clay and tin mines of Cornwall through the steam-coal, anthracite, steel and tinplate of South Wales, to the shipping and cotton trade of the Mersey and the iron and shipbuilding of Cumbria, to the Belfast Lough–Clyde basin. Essential to this, although politically alienated and indeed excluded from British statistics, was Ireland, where only agriculturally based industry had thrived outside the Lagan Valley, but whose supply of food and manual labour (and an unproclaimed inventiveness which matched the Scots') was essential to the economics of the Atlantic arc.[1]

Scottish parliamentary and municipal politics were by contrast primitive, constrained by the 1884 Reform Act, which permitted barely half of adult males to vote, and an archaic bias towards rural constituencies which would endure until 1918. This vested organisation and patronage in a small professional elite – principally the solicitors who directed Liberal politics from their chambers in the burghs – which coexisted with the small Scottish Office (essentially covering land, law and education) of 1885 opened, as it had done for nearly two centuries, 'a road west-awa yonder' for the educated and ambitious. If Scotland was the only European industrial state with strong out-migration, how much of its success ethic was derived from the careers of radical and socialist politicians abroad: Lyon Mackenzie in Canada, Andrew Fisher in Australia, Peter Fraser in New Zealand? Or such ambiguous but influential 'returners' as Andrew Carnegie?

Liberal hegemony lost way after the mid-1880s, when numerous unionist Liberals quit over Irish home rule and effectively took over the Scottish Tories. The boost the 1884 Act had given to rural radicalism was countered by the loss of monied Whigs, making the remaining Gladstonians favour carpetbaggers. The Unionists – cleverly deploying a Chamberlainite social-imperial programme on a west-coast electorate, Catholic as well as Protestant (on which more research is needed!) – eventually got a narrow majority of Scots seats (39 out of 71) in the 'khaki election' of 1900. Is Keir Hardie's Scottish Labour Party (1888–94) best seen as an attempt at an urban counterpart to the Crofters' Party, rather than a Labour Party precursor? Despite charismatic leaders, its contribution to the socialist movement was slight, compared to a Liberal revival which was overwhelming. Only twelve Unionists survived the wipe-out of 1906, their leader Arthur Balfour moaning that this was Britain's version of the international unsettlement of 1905, with revolution in Russia and social-democrat progress in Germany and France (Hutchison 1986).

Liberal triumph was followed by a chastening (though, again, little-researched) slump, in which production fell as rapidly as it was to do after 1920, though it did not stay down. Manufacturers had to cope with increased foreign competition, and friction with skilled trades unionism increased, along with a more utopian radicalism in Scots labour politics, hitherto Gladstonian, and the growth of a progressive intelligentsia, reflected in the student movement, advanced tastes in art (the Glasgow Boys, C. R. Mackintosh and co.), theatre (Ibsen, Shaw, Barrie) and a literary reaction (George Douglas Brown, James MacDougall Hay) against the commercialised ruralism of the Kailyard. This could be seen in such institutions as Fabian and Ruskin societies, the weekly *Forward*, the left-Liberal, anti-imperial and nationalist Young Scots' Society, as well as steady growth in the Independent Labour Party and satellites such as the Scottish

Home Rule Association, the retail co-operatives and the Clarion Clubs. It was at this level that the politics of 'the enthusiasts' – often boosted by the involvement of businessmen and rentiers (such as the tanner Roland Muirhead, the shipowner Thomas Allan, the coal merchant Sir Daniel Macaulay Stevenson, and exemplified by Glasgow's municipal Progressives) – met those of the trade unions, most articulate in the Amalgamated Society of Engineers and the Miners' Federation, and in burgh trades councils which brought together local unions. Only in 1909 did the Miners' Federation of Great Britain (MFGB) affiliate to the Labour Party, skilfully managed since 1901 by its ILP general secretary Ramsay MacDonald, but Labour was still not much more than a pressure group, poorly represented in Scots MPs: three in 1910. Its union-directed agenda had shrewdly been pre-empted by the Liberals under a substantially Scotland-based leadership – Premier Asquith sitting for West Fife and Winston Churchill, like Lloyd George a progressive President of the Board of Trade, sharing Dundee with the (rather conservative) Labour man George Wilkie. Scots socialism was good at projecting ideas, but not at originating them, unless one went back to such Victorian sages as Robert Owen, Carlyle and Ruskin. Patrick Geddes, the most remarkable social thinker of the period, belongs more to the anarchist tradition and the 'personalism' of Walt Whitman. Despite the intellectual impact of later American radicalism (Jack London and Upton Sinclair figured prominently in *Forward*), the Socialist Labour Party and the Wobblies were picturesque but highly marginal (see Donnachie et al. 1989).

War and After

In a very short space of time, Liberal Scotland would collapse, and in 1922 the competing groups for Scottish leadership were the Conservatives and Labour. Was this because of the tensions and adaptations necessary in running a 'total war' economy or the more specific challenge of the expansion of the electorate in 1918? The debate between Arthur Marwick (1962) and Jay Winter (1974) on one side and Ross McKibbin (1974) on the other remains a fruitful one, but the Scots situation was complicated by two nationalist sub-themes and overshadowed by a major economic reversal. First, the Coalition Liberals squared the immigrant Irish with the Education (Scotland) Act early in 1918, which saved the Irish National tradition from Sinn Fein, to the later benefit of Labour. Second, the collapse of the Liberal Party and the impotence of the ILP in responding to an enduring depression was to provoke the articulate Scottish nationalist and Communist responses which enlivened the 'Scottish renaissance' (McLean 1983).

The wartime 'nationalisation' of investment and industry, with the stormy history of 'dilution' on the Red Clyde, 1915–16, meant a redirection to armaments for which there was no peacetime demand. In 1918 the Scots had the world's largest and consequently most useless aircraft industry and an overstocked capital goods market provoked in 1920 a recession so severe that recovery was only possible with external assistance. Far from devolving power, Lloyd George's 'war socialism' concentrated it, notably in the shipping-dominated heavy industries, at the expense of urban rentiers who were penalised by rent control. The great shipowners had taken over the shipyards, which were further amalgamated with steelworks and collieries. Like roped-together mountaineers, they dragged each other over the cliff. Shipping recovered, but stayed (like the railways and most of the banks) London-based. The Bank of England became, as the lender of last resort, the life-support of inert industrial mastodons, while even his union opponents, like David Kirkwood MP, campaigned to stop William Beardmore's vast and varied manufacturing empire going to the wall (Campbell 1980).

All of this could only be speculated on by a new intake of Scots Labour MPs (from seven to twenty-nine in 1922) largely representative of mining, but with a few teachers, small businessmen and skilled workers, whose remedy was a mix of Adam Smith orthodoxy, dogmatic nationalisation, and Victorian moral reform. The last *did* diminish (or at least change) Scotland's narcotic culture; licensing reform and female advance meant that spirits and chewing tobacco gave way to sweeties, Irn Bru and fags. Despite some home rule noises, the key policy presence in the MacDonald ministry of 1924 was the elderly convert from Liberalism, Viscount Haldane, a brilliant political fixer whose 'Machinery of Government' report of 1918 underlay the 'magic lever in Whitehall' ethos which dominated Labour until the 1970s. Something of this rubbed off on the two real intellectuals of the Scottish intake: John Wheatley, who had discovered the 'underconsumptionism' of the left Liberal J. A. Hobson and created the key instrument of Scottish Labour, council housing, and Tom Johnston, more schematically devolutionist, but also deeply attracted to imperial co-operation.

The pre-war threat of direct union action ended in the 'nine days in May' of 1926, and the long lonely agony of the miners. It was the prelude to the commitment to the parliamentary road, albeit with a long hiatus after the catastrophe of 1931 (when Labour MPs fell from thirty-six to seven) and the fairly rapid capture of urban Scotland, which would set the (unambitious) tone of Scottish social democracy. But along with the Red Clyde the General Strike also left what MacDiarmid called 'a dream of beauty, dernin' yet' which was – thanks to him and Grassic Gibbon – to provide a unique and continuing myth for the Scots 'autonomous left': Scotland's peaceable equivalent to the Easter Rising, with John Maclean as her Connolly.

The Tories in Church and State were more Unionist and Protestant than they had been for several generations. Now that Ireland had quit Westminster, they had no need to negotiate with it, so Sir John Gilmour, Secretary of State, 1924–9, could come out as an Orangeman, which would have been *infra dig* a generation earlier, and the Kirk, united after 1929, danced to the tune of the equally bigoted Rev. John White. Divide and rule through sectarianism, which was perhaps most evident within the Scottish establishment, lasted: James MacGuinness, who ran economic policy in the 1960s and 1970s, was the first Catholic at that level in the Scottish Office, although a report from another Catholic, Sir Anthony MacDonnell, late Under-Secretary for Ireland, had proposed its reform in 1913. One senses, under the lip-service paid to democracy by the Scots professional classes, a deep hostility to the 'Irish' Labour Party after its forward thrust in 1922, an understated but effective 'Liberal-Unionist' coalition against it, and hovering in the background and not much talked about, an easy tolerance of fascist regimes in Europe, fostered by long-running cartel arrangements with German chemicals and Italian cotton.

Conservative collectivism – meaning the public funding of infrastructure for industry – was weakened by the fact that the Scottish state sector was burgh-based and suffering from economic recession, while 'local' *Mittelstand* capitalism dwindled. Not only did the firms that serviced the heavy industries – making gauges and special castings, donkey engines and ventilators – go bust, but local consumer-goods firms were wiped out by mass-production. The labour force, dominated by its skilled men, was usually the first casualty, something that may well have helped industrialisation elsewhere in the world, especially in the 1920s when the USA was still booming, as there was a steady emigration. This, along with the desire of Americans to sail to Europe, kept the 'hotel ship' market going until 1929, when the Wall Street Crash and its consequences brought catastrophe.

The years between 1931 and 1935 saw the low point of recession, although the Special Areas Act (1934) did something to build up the power of the Scottish Office (made a Department of State under Gilmour in 1926) in the economic field. When recovery came, it was 'more of the same'. The National Government's rearmament plan of 1935 called for battleships, aircraft carriers, cruisers and escorts, and over half of these orders came to the Clyde, together with a big Rolls-Royce aero-engine plant. In 1935 Scots government was headed up by a professional scientist, the liberal Tory Walter Elliot, who along with Sir James Lithgow, *Herrscher* of the heavy industries, launched the Empire Exhibition of 1938 in Glasgow's

Bellahouston Park. A more left-wing 'progressive', John Grierson of the GPO Film Unit, produced *Night Mail* in the same year. His and other 'Old ILP' careers showed up the implosion of the party itself: the attractive and picturesque Jimmie Maxton presided after 1932 over an impotent shell, outflanked on the left by the Communists, and fighting its affiliated rival the Scottish Socialist Party to a mutual standstill in the courts. A warning not lost on Maxton's biographer Gordon Brown? More positively, a welter of small-'n' nationalist reconstruction agencies, set up by Elliot, Johnston and others, tried to bind technology to industrial diversification, electrification, and urban reconstruction. The main instrument of social progress was housebuilding, the attempt to reform a level of overcrowding five times greater than that in the south. Andrew O'Hagan's novel *Our Fathers* (1999) rightly makes this symbolic of the Scottish left, its strengths and its severe flaws (Smout 1986).

ADMINISTRATIVE DEVOLUTION

Conventional capital goods industry, having bounced back in 1935, ruled the roost until the late 1950s. A sense of security, latterly delusive, affected trade union responses (a mixture of craft conservatism and declaratory, usually Communist-influenced, trades council radicalism). This formed part of a fairly stable tripartite division between union-dominated party, the 'strong' Scots civil society of the traditional 'estates' (of Scots Law, Kirk, local government and education) and the rapid rise of the Scots administrative state, symbolised by the building of Tommy Tait's grand art-deco headquarters, St Andrew's House, in 1939, and Tom Johnston's rule from it during the period 1941–5. Johnston was 'the greatest Secretary of State', but did he take a wrong turning, preferring a production-driven consensus with the sclerotic elite of the heavy industries instead of (as with Nye Bevan's friendship with Marcus Sieff of Marks and Spencer) sussing out how his people might be living twenty years on? Pat Dollan toured La Guardia's New York, and came back with the multi-storey notions of the Bruce Plan. The more humane conservationist approach of Geddes and hands-on socialists like Frank Tindall was confined to the New Towns and Overspill. Institutions can take ten, fifteen years to bed themselves down. By doing too much too fast did 1940s Scotland end up with the worst of both worlds?

The bureaucratic co-ordination of the Attlee programme of service industry nationalisation, as well as the institutions of National Insurance, Public Assistance and the National Health Service, detracted from the municipal socialist tradition, leaving the all-important housing drive to be managed by the one-party town. Think of the doctor as social reformer – one frequently used by the arch-Labour-unionist Nye Bevan – and there's a best-seller parallel in the novels of A. J. Cronin, a Scots Catholic medic working in Durham and South Wales, in *The Stars Look Down* (1935) and *The Citadel* (1937). 'The moment of Britain' had deep roots, not just in the war and the Blitz.

'The getting of wisdom' was also ambiguous, as the technical skills conveyed by education, apprenticeship and political/union activity often meant emigration (after a war which took a deadly toll of the well-qualified). This applied in particular to the two props of Scottish radical activism in the 1950s, the teacher and the journalist. R. F. Mackenzie showed the frustration of the first at home, James Cameron the opportunity available in London and abroad. These may account for the ambiguity attending a remarkable Labour revival in the 1940s. This was the first mass-membership party, yet it ended in a messy confrontation with John MacCormick's Scottish Covenant Movement. Apostasy about the national question in the 'long 1950s', from 1951 to 1964, meant that no one took any interest in social democracies of comparable size, whether in the Commonwealth or in Europe. The picture given in Iain Hutchison's political history (Hutchison 2001) is one of parochialism and incompetence, indeed of an irrelevance to the foreign affairs themes of 'high politics' which dominated Labour at Westminster in the age of Gaitskell and Bevan. Scotland's politics were irredeemably and incompetently 'low'.[2]

The Communist challenge was considerable, grown in local 'Little Moscows' as well as in the real place (Macintyre 1980; Thompson 1992). Figures like Willie Gallacher, Abe Moffat or Hugh MacDiarmid had a massive integrity which, despite their Stalinism, was not often paralleled in democratic Labour. The secessionists of 1955–6 would strengthen – but also stiffen – the Labour Party for a generation. But the essential conservatism of the 1950s – the women who formed an increasing part of the labour force had scarcely a handful of MPs: Jean Mann and Peggy Herbison were lonely – left lasting damage. Labour was ill fitted to fight when in the late 1950s the capital goods industries fell apart, while Scotland's efficient and internationalised financial superstructure assured continuing prosperity for its investing clients. Leaders like George Middleton of the STUC bargained and conceded, in bodies like the Scottish Council: Development and Industry, yet a double game was being played: the old commercial establishment co-operated in reforming the Scots economy with one hand, but with the other built up key interests elsewhere. Sir William Lithgow's involvement with green-field shipyards for super-tankers, developed by Hyundai in South Korea, is a classic case. The planning bonanza that followed the Toothill Report of 1961 (drafted by the academic and Labour sympathiser Tom Burns) was by the mid-1960s giving great opportunities to an expanding intellectual left in the universities, with results apparent in Westminster and some of the new region/district councils by the mid-1970s, but there was no guarantee that its schemes would bear fruit (see Scott and Hughes 1980; Harvie 1998: ch. 5).

In fact, a particular sort of Scots politics went into eclipse about this time. Much has been written about Gordon Brown's Rectorship of Edinburgh University, but he was the first Scots student politician to emerge *away* from the debating-floor. John Smith, Donald Dewar, Neil MacCormick, David Steel, Malcolm Rifkind and Robin Cook had been raised in the atmosphere of Union parliamentary debates, where the risk of being shot down in flames concentrated the mind wonderfully. Aficionados will treasure Cookie blowing away John Moore, one of Thatcher's handsome dauphins, on the floor of the Commons in 1988. By Brown's time at Edinburgh, this had evaporated in favour of the more gruelling politics of what he once despairingly called 'the five-nights-a-week activist'. The dedication to intrigue remained, but the political content would change, remarkably.

What happened in Scotland in the later 1960s was that grand plans came on line just as funding for them evaporated, leaving individual projects – from Ravenscraig down – isolated. The discredited Conservatives could not profit, so the SNP did, particularly at by- and local elections. It was on the wane by the 1970 general election, but not before it had forced Wilson into the expedient of the Crowther (later Kilbrandon) Commission on the Constitution. Even he could not have calculated that Kilbrandon's report would land in the middle of the altogether more serious SNP revival of 1973, prompted by the discovery of oil in the North Sea and its price escalation.

The oil was, and deserved to be, an SNP coup. Both the Heath and Wilson governments were neurotic about coal and miners, ran a huge staff devoted to atomic power and had next to no one dealing with petroleum, so for about a year the SNP was actually ahead of the game.[3] Gordon Brown's famous *The Red Paper* of 1975 might be thought to fit in here, but only three essays out of twenty-eight (of which under a third were actually by Labour Party members) dealt with it, in a rather marginal way. American opinion was certainly preoccupied with left-wing designs on the oil, but this boiled down to intense and Texan suspicion of Tony Benn as Energy Minister, less because he was half-Scots than because of his 'East Coast liberal' wife Caroline (Harvie 1994).

In fact the SNP soon put the brakes on its 'Scotland's Oil' campaign, realising that the Scots electors were actually feeling quite generous about the stuff, and had some fear that a high petropound Scots would not do the long-term development of the country much good – what came to pass in 1979–81 when Mrs Thatcher, in her monetarist spasm, jacked up interest rates just as the price per barrel hit a forty-dollar high in response to the Iran–Iraq war. There were promises all round of an oil fund, promptly forgotten about, but something of them survived in the Scottish Development Agency (1975) and in the Barnett Formula (1978) on public expenditure, which was generous to Scotland.

The 1970s are today viewed as the Jurassic Park of Old Labour, roamed by the dinosaurs of the unions and rank-and-file Bennism. Yet they were marked by three policies Downing Street forced on them: formal entry to Europe and devolution, as well as the unplanned-for beginning of monetarist policy, in Denis Healey's response to the IMF diktat of 1976. EEC membership was not popular with the Scottish left, the SNP included, yet it was carried by referendum in 1975; in 1978 the Scotland and Wales Bills wolfed down parliamentary time, resembling MacDonald's India Bill in 1934 at the pit of the depression, and equally unloved. Scotland and for that matter Britain in the 1970s was not the hell-hole Thatcherites and following them New Labourites have claimed, usually generalising from the pits of the 'winter of discontent' in 1978–9. There was still a substantial manufacturing sector at 34 per cent of GNP in 1976 (which got the oil out of the North Sea, for God's sake!) – it is now 19 per cent; social equality was at its greatest-ever level; women were at last getting some degree of equality. The British cultural scene was vibrant, from radical theatre to a television scene so brilliant (from *Play for Today* to *Monty Python*) that large parts of it have hovered around in a video afterlife and in endless re-runs, extenuating its influence over the next two decades.

All of these achievements – and indeed the liberties and licences of the 'permissive society' – stemmed from the welfare ethic of Attlee Labour and its union alliance. That old Anglo-British radical A. J. P. Taylor could still write in 1973 that the miners were getting their revenge for 1926. What had collapsed, shortly after its creator's sudden death in 1977, was Tony Crosland's notion of a British 'welfare citizenship' achieved by equality of entitlement. (The realisation that Crosland was Taylor's brother-in-law brings home the intimacy of the London–Oxbridge elite, when a Scots minister in a Labour Cabinet was a rarity.) The shift to a participative citizenship, ultimately taken on board by the left in Charter 88 a decade later – its Scottish modulation being the Constitutional Convention – took a long and painful time to root itself (Weight 2002).

New Labour, New Scotland?

In 1981, Bill Miller, politics professor at Glasgow, and formerly a stalwart of the Labour right, published *The End of British Politics* (Miller 1981). The timing seemed bad, given the result of the referendum of 1 March 1979, the election of Mrs Thatcher, and the eclipse of the SNP, yet Miller's contention was that the structure of politics had been so adapted to contain the national question that any return to the 'British homogeneity' beloved of Butler, Stokes, Blondel et al. was out of the question. He probably seemed at the time more percipient than other Scotland-based political scientists such as Henry Drucker and Gordon Brown, who saw devolution as loosening up Labour's ideological and organisational problems, through an effective federalisation of the party between unions, members and regional interests (Drucker and Brown 1980; Crick 1991).

Nothing like this happened. Instead there was a split in the metropolitan Labour elite (perhaps prompted by oil interests and pro-Europe pressure groups) producing the SDP and in several by-elections humiliating English Labour, while the far left, in such offerings as the Bennite *Manifesto* contributed to by Robin Cook and Jimmy Reid (Cripps et al. 1981) shut up about the territorial dimension. Intriguingly, the SDP made only limited progress in Scotland – although the right-wing Catholic element ought to have been receptive – and damaged the Tories more than Labour. Solidarity on the broad left was maintained to face down the devastating impact of sado-monetarism on Scots manufacturing, which claimed the ailing motor industry at Linwood and Bathgate, pulp at Corpach and aluminium at Invergordon. The establishment manoeuvring of the deftly non-confrontational George Younger saved the Weir Group, Ferranti and the Royal Bank of Scotland, an important factor for the later boom in financial services and privatisation, which RBS made a *specialité de la maison*, and probably did the Labour leadership a good turn by squashing the municipal far left before it could do major damage to the party.[4] Friends of Neil Kinnock, such as Brown and Cook, could help him carry the war to Militant after 1983 without having to look over their shoulders all the time. Meanwhile the likes of Dr Michael Kelly made over Glasgow after 1984 in a cuddly, tourist-friendly image, with quite bountiful help from 'she who must be obeyed', and returned her no thanks whatsoever (Harvie and Jones 2001).

Even so, Scotland went against the prevailing rightward grain. The Falklands war was not a patriotic runner, and the Conservatives stuck at twenty-one MPs in 1983. The miners' strike of 1984–5 increased the breach, and Mrs Thatcher muttered audibly about Thatcherism being 'rebuffed' up north. After the Westland crisis in 1986, and the translation of Younger to defence, she tried to remedy matters. Malcolm Rifkind, who was hard-working and a good debater, found himself forced into a Colonial Governor strait-jacket, with an intensely ambitious Michael Forsyth snapping at his heels, ostentatiously supported by Downing Street. Up against this lot, programmed for self-destruction, Labour did not really have to do very much.

In the 1987 election the Tory vote fell by 4.4 percentage points, and the number of MPs by half. The Scots, and particularly the professional middle class, had discovered the charms of tactical voting for 'A Tory-Free Scotland', and employed them to deadly effect. Behind this was the menace of the poll tax, and behind that the *Angst* of Scottish small businesses, more heavily rated than their English counterparts, which the poll tax (originally Younger's, with strong input from the Adam Smith Institute) was intended to help. It was a ham-fisted approach to a real problem, and the response did not show the Scottish radical bourgeoisie in an altogether positive light. State- or local-government-sponsored development bodies were good – because they created lots of jobs for the university-trained middle class. The culture of *Mittelstand* entrepreneurialism remained something alien, with new start-ups low and getting lower, although continental social democracy normally coped competently enough with it. The Constitutional Convention of 1989–95 was, however, positive: Labour's acceptance of perestroika in the shape of proportional representation ended that semi-East European 'leading role of the Party' which had throttled Scots pluralism. But the 1992 election proved a false dawn, because Shadow Chancellor John Smith's redistributive and pro-industry budget did not play in the English south-east, although we now know that John Major would have conceded a referendum on devolution, had the Tories suffered another Scottish wipe-out (see Major 1999: 415–30; Seldon 1997: 261–3). That they did not was due to 3 per cent of the voters falling off the roll because of the poll tax. They did not make the same mistake five years later (McSmith 1994).

There were success stories in the 1990s but they were ambiguous. Silicon Glen thrived as a provider of computer hardware but could have been anywhere; by the mid-1990s only about 5 per cent of its components were sourced from Scotland, and some of the most ambitious ventures, Chungwa at Newmains and Hyundai at Dunfermline, died in infancy or were stillborn. Edinburgh financial services seemed to boom exponentially, peaking in 1999; but what were financial services but means of avoiding or deferring tax, exporting capital, and protecting the rather indefensible policies of banks and insurance companies? House property, in a country where it was kept in short supply, could not but boom, and along with it retailing,

61

particularly from out-of-town centres; as a result private motoring grew relentlessly.

The less said about the ethics and social implications of bus and rail privatisations – producing very strange conglomerates like First Group and Stagecoach – the better. It was difficult for the left to get a bead on these (unions were at best only tolerated) yet the Labour establishment managed to remain on pretty good terms with most, if the sponsors of public sector conferences are anything to go on. The most explicitly New Labour element of the Parliament after 1999, around Wendy Alexander, stressed the need for 'A Smart, Successful Scotland' and imaginative high-tech policies which drew on Scotland's international connections (Scottish Executive 2001). Fair enough, but the country had managed, since 1945, a number of such makeovers – incorporating consumer-goods manufacture, the oil, Silicon Glen, financial services – but at each stage its weaknesses, as a small player in a global finance scene (which, ironically, it had partly created) found it out (Houston and Knox 2001).

Nats would brandish the counter-case of Ireland, where clever use of EU membership, and concentration on pharmaceuticals and software, took the republic from 56 per cent of UK GNP in 1976 to near parity twenty years later. Yet the survival in Ireland until the mid-1980s of Catholic marital piety had produced a population two-thirds of whom were under thirty with, as Professor Joe Lee put it, 'another thirty-odd years until they get ill and claim pensions'. No such luck for Scotland (Lee 1990).

Perhaps the nature of intellectual capital was itself skewed. Something must be said about the sociology of the left. The 'polyocracy' was said to have taken Labour over in the early 1980s – an aperçu maybe due to a sharp TV dramatisation of Malcolm Bradbury's *The History Man* in which Anthony Sher and various good-looking women had grave difficulty keeping their clothes on. The reality was that in a cold climate sociology (always, anyhow, a conservative ology; see Durkheim, Pareto, Weber, and so on) bifurcated into Lazarus (the poor) in academia and the public sector and Dives (the rich) in market research, media and adland. This division was geographical, and the fashioning of New Labour, commenced under Kinnock, left fallow under John Smith, and resumed under Tony Blair, offered countless positions within 'The Project'. Devolution at least held out the prospect that some cognate media milieu might accrue around a Scottish legislature, so Scotland followed at a distance. The irony was that the 'general staff' of the devolution movement, who persisted through countless heartbreaking setbacks for eighteen years, were not just Old Labour, but from a literally older, more moralistic and more pluralistic Scotland: civil servants like Jim Ross; diplomats like Paul Scott; architects like Jimmy Boyack. Most ironic of all, the Mr Standfast of the Constitutional Convention was, in a by now far from Godly Commonwealth, a clergyman, Kenyon Wright (Harvie and Jones 2001).

Few of the workaholic oldies made it into the first Parliament, and none onto the Labour benches. Trade unionists fared little better. Hence, perhaps, its social imbalance: the over-representation of activists from South Edinburgh or Glasgow Kelvinside, the non-appearance of MSPs from Motherwell or Airdrie, Kilmarnock or Paisley. In part this served male-dominated one-party politics right, but these former industrial towns were the literal factories of grievance.

But, even if rectified, the Parliament would be faced with an agenda familiar to Very Old Labour: the need for technical training, for economic redistribution within Scotland, as well as within the regions and nations of Britain, for (archaic though it may seem) a war on booze, drugs and cultural witlessness. Doing an actuarial job on contemporary Scotland would disclose huge (and under-researched) diseconomies – in primitive public transport, high-risk, low-quality nutrition, poor health, non-existent recycling, two-tier education, and a crime-dominated black economy which might clock up a £3 billion turnover – clearing up which could yield a significant civic dividend.[5]

Guessing and Fearing

Was New Labour a solution, or part of the problem? Its impact in Scotland was initially veiled by the persistence, until the death of Donald Dewar in October 2000, of 'John Smith Labour' as an ethos if not a programme. But Labour's second term disclosed whole tranches of British policy where Blairite 'spin' – an interminable rhetoric of action: projects; initiatives; targets; tsars – concealed inertia and decline and Blairite allies who seemed little different from Thatcher's courtiers. Blair's other predilection, for foreign intervention, managed twice to coincide with Scottish parliamentary elections – Kosovo in 1999, Iraq in 2003 – shifting the debate from 'low' to 'high' or 'Westminster' politics, where Labour traditionally enjoyed an advantage of ten or so percentage points. Even so, this was not much help to Jack McConnell in May 2003, who despite a robust populist fightback had to cope with a loss of six seats, a coalition with the increasingly mutinous Lib Dems, and an effective majority down from seventeen to five.

The Scottish Parliament was nailed to the walls of its expensive (and still future) Edinburgh home, the only issue about it capable of engaging the monosyllables of Europe's worst mass-circulation press. Down south was another, to quote Walter Scott, 'damned dangerous North British neighbourhood', the Downing Street bunker, housing Alastair Campbell, Ian Macartney, Douglas Alexander, Charlie Falconer and Blair himself, whose connections to the Red Clyde, through his Communist-turned-Tory father Leo, were actually rather closer than Gordon Brown's, and whose links to George Bush ran through Charlotte Square and the Gammells of Ivory and Sime (Harvie 1994: 108–9; *The Times*, 29 September 2003). As for the semi-detached figure at No. 11, Brown's surrender of banking control to the City in 1997, his close connection to the worrying Geoffrey Robinson MP, self-proclaimed originator of the PFI strategy (which turned out to be a scheme of outdoor relief for what remained of British capital goods and construction industries), his inability to set up either effective stakeholder pensions or, in the stuttering Financial Services Authority, an effective policeman for the City, his lack of interest in manufacturing industry: all induced suspicion about whether his replacement of Blair would in fact be a positive move (Bower 2001).

In 1994 Labour under John Smith seemed to be moving towards a 'stakeholder society' which roughly approximated to the 'social marketism' I was familiar with in Baden-Württemberg. Something touted by Will Hutton's *The State We're In* (Hutton 1995), this had a key role for decentralisation, not least of investment. This vanished from New Labour's programme when in power, as did any effective 'co-operative federalist' integration of the devolved bodies, something that reached its nadir in June 2003 with the spatchcocked amalgamation of the Scots Secretaryship with the overloaded and poorly performing Transport Ministry. In fact, such was the atrophy of Cabinet government under Blair that Scotland – as much as any other department – was willy-nilly granted a sort of post-modern autonomy. Blair's strongest card in 2003 was the impotence of the Conservative opposition, but it could rapidly recover. One remembers Michael Howard's Cook-like demolition of Straw and Blair over prison policy in 1996 and Peel's remark anent Cobden, 'Reply to him, sir, because I cannot', still has clout. Should Blair meet his nemesis – and the Commons *is* that sort of place – and should the Scottish coalition break up – which in no way can be ruled out – we could face very interesting times indeed.

Notes

1. This will be the subject of the present writer's forthcoming book from Oxford University Press, *North Britain, West Britain, 1860–1920*.
2. For this distinction I am much indebted to the late great Brummie Tory Jim Bulpitt (1995).
3. There are three long biographies of Harold Wilson, by Philip Ziegler, Austen Morgan and Ben Pimlott. None of them mentions oil.
4. Younger's uncle Kenneth was a well-thought-of moderate Labour MP who died young.

5. Crime, Jeremy Rifkin's 'Fourth Sector', is a very big Scottish business indeed if you explore the linkages between drugs, smuggled fags, illegal workers, loan sharks, prostitution, tanning studios, bookies and casinos, clubs, minicabs, protection rackets (Rifkin 2000). Add to this globalised companies behaving badly – Wall Street and the City going the way of the uncouth lot in their Buenos Aires branch. Could it get worse? Yes, if reports are true of the Russian mafia buying its way in, leaving local hoods looking squeaky-clean. With lots of loot to push around, our 'rest and recreation culture' seems a sitting duck (Harvie 2004).

References

Bower, T. (2001), *The Paymaster: Geoffrey Robinson, Maxwell and New Labour*, Simon and Schuster, London.

Brown, G. (ed.) (1975), *The Red Paper on Scotland*, Edinburgh University Student Publications Board, Edinburgh.

Bulpitt, J. (1995), *Territorial Politics in the United Kingdom*, Manchester University Press, Manchester.

Campbell, R. H. (1980), *The Rise and Fall of Scottish Industry*, John Donald, Edinburgh.

Crick, B. (ed.) (1991), *National Identities*, Blackwell, Oxford.

Cripps, F., Griffith, J., Morrell, F., Reid, J., Townsend, P. and Weir, S. (eds) (1981), *Manifesto: Radical Strategies for Britain's Future*, Pan, London.

Dewar, D. (1999), *First Minister's Reply to the Queen*, Formal Opening of the Scottish Parliament, Edinburgh, 1 July 1999.

Donnachie, I., Harvie, C. and Wood, I. S. (eds) (1989), *Forward!: Labour Politics in Scotland 1888–1988*, Polygon, Edinburgh.

Drucker, H. M. and Brown, G. (1980), *The Politics of Nationalism and Devolution*, Longman, London.

Harvie, C. (1994), *Fool's Gold: The Story of North Sea Oil*, Hamish Hamilton, London.

Harvie, C. (1998), *Scotland and Nationalism: Scottish Society and Politics 1707 to the Present*, 3rd edn, Routledge, London.

Harvie, C. (2002), *Scotland: a Short History*, Oxford University Press, Oxford.

Harvie, C. (2004), 'The Case of the Postmodernist's Sore Thumb, or the Moral Sentiments of John Rebus', in E. Bell and G. Wilson (eds), *Scotland in Theory*, forthcoming, Rodopi, Amsterdam.

Harvie, C. and Jones, P. (2001), *The Road to Home Rule*, Polygon, Edinburgh.

Houston, R. A. B., and Knox, W. (eds) (2001), *The New Penguin History of Scotland*, Penguin, Harmondsworth.

Hutchison, I. G. C. (1986), *A Political History of Scotland 1832–1926*, John Donald, Edinburgh.

Hutchison, I. G. C. (2001), *Scottish Politics in the Twentieth Century*, Palgrave, Basingstoke.

Hutton, W. (1995), *The State We're In*, Jonathan Cape, London.

Lee, J. J. (1990), *Ireland 1912–1985*, Cambridge University Press, Cambridge.

Macintyre, S. (1980), *Little Moscows: Communism and Working Class Militancy in Inter-war Britain*, Croom Helm, London.

McKibbin, R. (1974), *The Evolution of the Labour Party 1910–24*, Clarendon Press, Oxford.

McLean, I. (1983), *The Legend of Red Clydeside*, John Donald, Edinburgh.

McSmith, A. (1994), *John Smith: A Life 1938–1994*, 2nd edn, Mandarin, London.

Major, J. (1999), *John Major: The Autobiography*, Harper Collins, London.

Marwick, A. (1962), 'The Independent Labour Party in the Nineteen Twenties', in *Bulletin of Historical Research*, vol. XXXV, pp. 62–74.

Miller, W. L. (1981), *The End of British Politics? Scots and English Political Behaviour in the Seventies*, Oxford University Press, Oxford.

O'Hagan, A. (1999), *Our Fathers*, Faber and Faber, London.

Rifkin, J. (2000), *The Age of Access*, Penguin, London.

Scottish Executive (2001), *A Smart, Successful Scotland: Ambitions for the Enterprise Network*, The Stationery Office, Edinburgh.

Scott, J. and Hughes, R. (1980), *The Anatomy of Scottish Capital*, Croom Helm, London.

Seldon, A. (1997), *Major: A Political Life*, Weidenfeld and Nicolson, London.

Smout, T. C. (1986), *A Century of the Scottish People*, Collins, London.

Thompson, W. (1992), *The Good Old Cause: British Communism 1920–1991*, Pluto Press, London.

Weight, R. (2002), *Patriots: National Identity in Britain 1940–2000*, Macmillan, London.

Winter, J. (1974), *Socialism and the Challenge of War: Ideas and Politics in Britain 1912–18*, Routledge and Kegan Paul, London.

II

Scotland's Leading Party

CHAPTER 5

The Scottish Electorate and Labour

Paula Surridge

Since 1964, Labour has occupied the position of majority party in Scotland both in terms of share of the vote and the number of Scottish seats won at Westminster elections and more recently at elections to the Scottish Parliament in 1999 and 2003. Until the Westminster election of 1997, it was widely believed that Labour would need their Scottish seats in order to form a majority government in Westminster. However, the rapidly changing political landscape since 1997 has left many unanswered questions. It has been suggested that the rise of 'New Labour' south of the border may alienate its more traditional supporters (see, for example, Heath et al. 2001: ch. 8). Furthermore, the establishment of the Scottish Parliament has led to distinctive policy agendas and indeed to policy differences between 'Scottish Labour' in Edinburgh and 'New Labour' in London. This chapter is not concerned with the internal mechanics of these differences, discussed elsewhere in this volume, rather it is concerned with how these changes have been received and interpreted by the Scottish electorate. The chapter firstly considers the changing image of the Labour Party in Scotland over the period 1992–2001. How do the Scottish electorate view the party? Is it perceived as a party of the working class, one that keeps its promises, or one that is divided? Secondly, the chapter considers changing patterns of support for Labour in Scotland, particularly the extent to which the social basis of Labour support has changed and the extent to which they face particular competition for their traditional basis of support.

THE DATA

This chapter draws on nationally representative data sets of the Scottish electorate which allow changing images of the Labour Party in Scotland to be charted over the last decade. Data for 1992 and 1997 are drawn from the

Scottish Election Surveys; for these surveys fieldwork was conducted by the National Centre for Social Research (formerly Social and Community Planning Research) as part of the British Election Studies, with the sample in each year being boosted to allow data to be analysed separately for Scotland. Full analysis of the 1992 data set can be found in Bennie et al. (1997) and for the 1997 data in Brown et al. (1999). Data for 1999 is taken from the Scottish Parliamentary Election Survey, also conducted by the National Centre for Social Research. Full details and analysis of this data are available in Paterson et al. (2001). Data for 2001 is available from two sources: the 2001 British Election Survey and the 2001 Scottish Social Attitudes Survey. Where available data is comparable over time, the 2001 British Election Survey (Clarke et al. 2003) is used, as each of the earlier surveys was conducted immediately after an election and this gives greatest comparability. However, some measures were not available in this data and in these instances data from the 2001 Scottish Social Attitudes Survey is used. The 2001 British Election Survey was conducted by a team of investigators at the University of Essex (Clarke et al. 2003) with fieldwork conducted by the NOP Research Group.[1] In each case the election surveys were funded by the Economic and Social Research Council. The Scottish Social Attitudes Survey of 2001 was funded from a number of different sources including three grants from the ESRC, a module funded by the Scottish Executive and one by Scottish Homes. Full details of the survey and its findings are available in Bromley et al. (2003).[2]

LABOUR PARTY SUPPORT IN SCOTLAND

In any consideration of the perceptions of the electorate about political parties it is necessary to control for political partisanship. Whilst the data in the chapter are drawn from surveys taken immediately after national elections, for the purposes of analysis party identification rather than vote is used as a measure of partisanship. This is for two key reasons. Firstly, as well-documented elsewhere (Heath and Taylor 1999), turnout in recent elections has been problematic. Thus, using vote as a measure of partisanship may cause inconsistencies over time as it is not clear that those predisposed to Labour will always abstain from voting in the same numbers. Secondly, the electoral system itself may influence members of the electorate to vote for a second-choice party in some circumstances (Evans et al. 1998); again it is not straightforwardly predictable how this may affect those predisposed towards Labour. Hence, when controlling for partisanship in the analyses that follow, party identification is used rather than vote at the relevant election. Political partisanship, or party identification, is a measure of people's attachment to

70

political parties. It was first developed in the American context (Campbell et al. 1960) and later imported to the British context in the first British Election Studies (Butler and Stokes 1974). It is designed to measure the voter's long-term attachment to a party, as Butler and Stokes put it:

> The values which the individual sees in supporting a party usually extend to more than one general election . . . As a result, most electors think of themselves as supporters of a given party in a lasting sense, developing what may be called a 'partisan self-image'. (Butler and Stokes 1974: 39)

It is this measure, rather than vote, which is used in this chapter to look at Labour support within the Scottish electorate.

Table 5.1 Party identity in Scotland, 1992–2001

	1992	1997	1999	2001
None	6	7	8	14
Labour	37	47	42	44
Conservative	28	16	17	14
Liberal Democrat	8	12	13	9
SNP	21	18	21	18
Unweighted N (=100%)	934	860	1427	692

Table 5.1 shows the pattern of party identification between 1992 and 2001. The table clearly shows the growth in the proportion of the Scottish electorate identifying with Labour between 1992 and 1997, from 37 per cent to 47 per cent; this proportion remained above two in five of the Scottish electorate until the end of the period. This rise in the proportion identifying with the Labour Party is accompanied by a fall in the proportion identifying with the Conservative Party, whilst support for the Scottish National Party (SNP) remains constant at around one in five. These figures clearly demonstrate that the position of the Labour Party electorally is reflected in party identification; the party is clearly the majority party within the political hearts of the Scottish electorate. The findings are also in line with the theoretical idea of a stable party identity which voters develop and retain across multiple elections (Butler and Stokes 1974) as it shows remarkable stability over a ten-year period. At first glance these figures seem to suggest Labour's position in Scotland is solid, with a large majority of the Scottish electorate declaring support for the party. However, as we shall see below, the picture is not entirely clear and there may be some cause for concern for the party in terms of their image and the competition they face for their key heartlands of support.

Changing Images of the Labour Party in Scotland

The change in the political fortunes of the Labour Party in Britain has been attributed in part to a successful rebranding of the party as 'New Labour'. Heath et al. find that 'New Labour was no longer distinctively associated with any particular group. It had successfully become a catch-all party' (2001: 141).

However, this finding stems from analysis of the electorate immediately following the 1997 general election; subsequent experience of New Labour in office may be expected to impact heavily on the images of the party held by the electorate. In this section the changing images of Labour in Scotland are explored. In some models of voting behaviour it is assumed that people will vote (and support) the parties associated with looking after their interests. This is, however, premised on the belief that people have clear ideas about which groups the parties look after. Respondents to the 1997 and 2001(e) surveys were asked to what extent the different parties looked after the interests of different groups. Table 5.2 summarises these responses for social class groups.

Table 5.2 Looks after the interests of working class and middle class

	1997	2001
Looks after working class		
Very closely	35	8
Fairly closely	58	53
Not very closely	6	30
Not at all closely	1	8
Unweighted N (=100%)	731	426
Looks after middle class		
Very closely	12	16
Fairly closely	76	64
Not very closely	11	16
Not at all closely	1	4
Unweighted N (=100%)	715	404

Table 5.2 suggests a very clear change in the image of New Labour in terms of whom it looks after. In 1997, 93 per cent of respondents felt that New Labour looked after the interests of the working class very or fairly closely, but by 2001 this figure had dropped to 61 per cent. By comparison, whilst the proportion who believed New Labour looked after the interests of

the middle class very or fairly closely also dropped from 88 per cent to 80 per cent, this represents something of a reversal as in 1997 a greater proportion thought Labour looked after the interests of the working class but by 2001 a greater proportion believe Labour look after the interests of the middle class.[3]

Table 5.3 Looks after the interests of trade unions and big business

	1997	2001
Looks after trade unions		
Very closely	26	10
Fairly closely	63	57
Not very closely	10	26
Not at all closely	1	7
Unweighted N (=100%)	712	369
Looks after big business		
Very closely	19	33
Fairly closely	56	52
Not very closely	23	11
Not at all closely	2	4
Unweighted N (=100%)	713	370

Table 5.3 considers the same question for big business and trade unions. A similar pattern is revealed when we consider whether new Labour looks after the interests of these groups. In 1997, 75 per cent believed New Labour looked after the interests of big business; this had risen to 85 per cent by 2001. Whilst 89 per cent believed that New Labour looked after the interests of trade unions in 1997, by 2001 this had fallen to 67 per cent.

This evidence confirms, to some degree, Heath et al.'s assessment (2001) that Labour have succeeded in becoming a 'catch-all' party as for each of these groups the perception is that Labour looks after their interests very or fairly closely. However, there is also a clear perception within the electorate that Labour have moved away from their traditional roots but perhaps now look after the interests of the working class and trade unions less than before. Thus, while it remains the case that a large majority of the Scottish electorate perceives Labour as continuing to look after the interests of the working class and trade unions, there has been a marked decline in this since 1997, not as yet a serious cause for concern for the party but nonetheless a trend which shows that the Scottish electorate are sensitive to changes in policy within the party.

Evidence in Scotland has shown that the Scottish electorate have tended to move away from parties they do not perceive as looking after the interests of Scotland (Brown et al. 1999); the Conservative Party has long suffered electorally from being perceived as an 'English' party. Respondents in 1999 and 2001(s) were asked whether 'New Labour' and 'Scottish Labour' looked after the interests of 'Scots in general'. The distribution of these questions is shown in table 5.4.

Table 5.4   Looks after the interests of Scots in general

	1999	2001(s)
New Labour		
Very closely	2	3
Fairly closely	40	37
Not very closely	46	52
Not at all closely	12	8
Unweighted N (=100%)	1100	1355
Scottish Labour		
Very closely	7	8
Fairly closely	56	60
Not very closely	29	28
Not at all closely	7	3
Unweighted N (=100%)	1093	1335

Table 5.4 highlights two important features of the image of Labour as a party looking after Scotland. Firstly, it shows remarkable stability between 1999 and 2001 (although this is a shorter time period than 1997 to 2001 so we would expect changes to be on the whole smaller). However, and more striking, there is a clear difference between perceptions of 'New Labour' and perceptions of 'Scottish Labour'. Around 40 per cent in each year believe New Labour look after the interests of Scots in general very or fairly closely, compared with a little under 70 per cent for Scottish Labour. It is worthy of note that this is the only social group, that we have looked at, where a clear majority did not perceive New Labour as looking after the interests of the group very or fairly closely. Furthermore, and a possible source of concern for Labour in Scotland, when asked if the SNP looked after the interests of Scots in general (in 2001), 72 per cent believed the SNP did so very or fairly closely, a small difference compared to Scottish Labour but almost twice the proportion who believed that New Labour did so. This signals something of huge importance for the nature of party competition in Scotland and for Scottish Labour. Przeworski and Sprague suggest that when a formerly

socialist party moves to the centre of the political spectrum, the 'workers' who would previously have voted for them have three possibilities open to them: 'They can vote for bourgeois parties, they can abstain from voting altogether, and in some countries, they can vote for other parties that appeal to them as workers.' (1986: 61)

In the Scottish context Labour have two potential pitfalls here. First, the potential loss of 'the workers', the working-class voters who perceive New Labour as moving away from their interests. Second, the nationalist vote. We could, in the quote above, replace 'workers' with 'Scots' and see some of the potential danger in New Labour's position in Scotland: 'They can vote for English parties, they can abstain from voting altogether, or they can vote for other parties that appeal to them as Scots.'

This potential weakness in Labour's support in Scotland can be examined further by looking at how these images vary according to social group. Is it members of the working class, or those who feel strongly nationalist, who believe Labour does not look after their interests? If this is the case then the danger of losing support to a party these voters feel looks after them better is a real possibility. However, it is also possible that a party may succeed in convincing each group that it looks after their interests and not those of others. Table 5.5 explores this possibility by considering images of Labour as looking after the working class, by occupational class.[4]

Table 5.5 Looks after the interests of working class, by occupational class

	Salariat	Routine non-manual	Petty bourgeoisie	Manual foremen and technicians	Working class
1997					
Very closely	32	29	27	44	39
Fairly closely	61	64	57	50	55
Not very closely	6	7	14	5	4
Not at all closely	1	1	3	2	2
Unweighted					
N (=100%)	194	160	37	62	237
2001					
Very closely	7	9	4	6	13
Fairly closely	58	59	54	61	39
Not very closely	28	25	14	29	39
Not at all closely	7	7	27	3	9
Unweighted					
N (=100%)	139	84	25	33	129

Table 5.5 suggests that there is some evidence that Labour's image among the working class has declined more than amongst other class groups. In 1997, 93 per cent of the salariat thought of Labour as looking after the interests of the working class very or fairly closely; by 2001 this had fallen to 64 per cent. Similarly, in 1997, 94 per cent of the working class thought Labour looked after working-class interests very or fairly closely; this had fallen to 52 per cent by 2001. Thus, in 2001, only half of the working class in Scotland perceived Labour as looking after their interests. Unfortunately an equivalent question was not asked of the SNP in 2001, so it is not possible to assess the extent to which they are now perceived as looking after working-class interests more closely than Labour.

Table 5.6 considers whether there is any evidence of nationalists losing faith in Labour to look after the interests of Scots; it shows the extent to which the party is perceived as looking after the interests of Scots in general according to national identity.[5] As described above, the question was asked both of 'New Labour' and 'Scottish Labour'.

Table 5.6 Looks after Scots in general, by national identity, 2001(s)

	Scottish not British	Scottish more than British	Equally Scottish and British	British more than Scottish	British not Scottish
New Labour					
Very closely	2	3	3	5	4
Fairly closely	27	38	47	65	33
Not very closely	59	52	46	23	57
Not at all closely	12	7	4	7	6
Unweighted					
N (=100%)	482	413	322	39	51
Scottish Labour					
Very closely	6	10	9	16	4
Fairly closely	57	63	62	58	50
Not very closely	33	26	26	21	38
Not at all closely	4	2	3	5	8
Unweighted					
N (=100%)	472	407	318	39	51

Table 5.6 clearly demonstrates a relationship between perceptions of the party as looking after the interests of Scots and national identity, with those expressing an exclusive Scottish identity (that is, say they feel Scottish and not British) being the least likely to think New Labour looks after the

interests of Scots in general. Among this group, just 29 per cent believed New Labour looked after the interests of Scots very or fairly closely in 2001; this figure increases gradually as we move along the national identity scale from the 'Scottish' to the 'British' ends of the scale, with 41 per cent of those who felt Scottish more than British and 50 per cent who felt equally Scottish and British taking this position.[6] A similar trend is discernible when considering perceptions of Scottish Labour, with those who expressed an exclusive Scottish identity being least likely to think that Scottish Labour looks after the interests of Scots very or fairly closely. However, in all identity groups a majority believe this is the case (63 per cent of those who are 'Scottish and not British', rising to 73 per cent among those who feel 'equally Scottish and British').

There is then some cause for concern for Labour in these figures: there is a clear change in the perception of the party as looking after the working class, and this is especially marked among the working class themselves. It is unlikely that these changes are specific to Scotland. However, the nature of party competition in Scotland means that these social groups have alternatives; in England these changes may result in low turnout but in Scotland the electorate have the option of moving to another left-of-centre party with a strong Scottish agenda, the SNP. Moreover, the party at Westminster is not perceived as a party that looks after the interests of Scotland. This was a key element in the demise of the Conservatives in Scotland (Brown et al. 1999) and as with the changing perception of their social class interests, those who feel that Labour do not look after Scots' interests closely clearly have other choices in the four-party Scottish system. As has been shown elsewhere (Brown et al. 1999), the relationships between class, national identity and party in Scotland are complex, and in particular the way in which these social locations and identities interact in competition between Labour and the SNP. These issues will be considered in detail below.

However, first there is a further dimension of party image to be considered. Until now we have considered the image of the party in terms of how well it looks after particular groups, but there are other facets of party image – such as whether parties are perceived as extreme, united or capable of strong government – which contribute to the way parties are received within the electorate. Changes in Labour Party image are presented in table 5.7. For some of these key measures of party image, data are available from 1992 which enable trends before and after the transition to New Labour to be examined.

Table 5.7 Party image, 1992–2001

	1992	1997	2001
United/divided			
United	28	–	40
Divided	69	–	50
Neither/both	3	–	10
Unweighted N (=100%)	915	–	708
Extreme/moderate			
Extreme	31	16	19
Moderate	64	79	76
Neither/both	4	5	5
Unweighted N (=100%)	907	819	659
Capable of strong government			
Capable	46	91	79
Not capable	52	6	14
Neither/both	2	2	6
Unweighted N (=100%)	904	805	737
Keep promises			
Keep	–	66	39
Break	–	20	45
Neither/both	–	14	16
Unweighted N (=100%)	–	685	737
In/out of touch			
In touch	–	–	40
Out of touch	–	–	50
Neither/both	–	–	10
Unweighted N (=100%)	–	–	708

In 1992, Labour were clearly a party with something of an image problem: 69 per cent of the Scottish electorate viewed the party as divided while 52 per cent viewed the party as not capable of strong government, this in an area of Britain usually seen as one of the party's heartlands. The measures that are available suggest that the party's image improved dramatically between 1992 and 1997, but has suffered small but significant set-backs since 1997. For example, in 1992 only 46 per cent believed Labour was capable of strong government; by 1997 this had risen to an astonishing 91 per cent, but fell back again to 79 per cent in 2001. Similarly, in 1997, 66 per cent believed that Labour kept its promises; this had fallen to 39 per cent in 2001. The Scottish electorate have not, over the last decade, perceived Labour as an 'extreme' party. In 1992 around one third of the Scottish electorate chose the label 'extreme' for the party; this fell to just 16 per cent in 1997, and 19 per cent in 2001. There seem, then, to be few weak spots in the party's overall image. The only measure where the party do not have a majority choosing the 'positive' image on these measures in 2001 is whether Labour 'keeps its promises', and it is arguable that is more likely to be a problem for a party in government than for a party that is not having its promises tested on a regular basis.

Overall, the Labour Party's image in Scotland remains extremely positive. On all but one of the measures of looking after particular groups, more than 50 per cent of the Scottish electorate believe that the party looks after the interests of the group very or fairly closely, whilst on the more general measures of image, in all but one case the majority of the Scottish electorate perceive the party positively. The picture then seems to be of a secure position for the Labour Party in Scotland. However, whilst the images of the party held by the Scottish electorate remain extremely positive, there have been changes in these images over the last decade and in particular there has been a fall in the proportion of the Scottish electorate who perceive the party in positive terms on general issues such as whether they keep or break promises and a fall in the image of the party as looking after the interests of the working class. These changes are not currently serious enough to represent a threat to Labour's position in Scotland. However, if they were to continue in this direction there is an alternative party waiting in the wings to capture Labour votes. The extent to which this is a real threat depends on how close the supporters of Labour and the SNP are in terms of both their social locations and their ideological profiles. This is examined below in order to better understand the relationship between class, nation and party in Scotland and to assess the extent to which the SNP poses a threat to Labour by competing for the same section of the voting public.

PARTY COMPETITION IN SCOTLAND

Due to restrictions of space and the wide availability of the data elsewhere, this section will not review systematically the way in which different measures of social location are related to party identity in Scotland. For full reviews of these issues, see Brown et al. (1999), Paterson et al. (2001), Curtice et al. (2002) and Bromley et al. (2003). Rather, this section attempts to find those characteristics which discriminate between Labour and SNP supporters in Scotland. In order to assess this, a binary logistic regression model was fitted to the data for each year. Only those respondents who identified with either Labour or the SNP are included in the model, therefore significant coefficients represent those factors which discriminate between the two groups of party supporters.[7] The results of this model are presented in table 5.8.[8]

Table 5.8 Models of party support, Labour vs SNP, 1992–2001(s)

	1992	1997	1999	2001(s)
Age (in years)	0.010	–0.022	0.010	–0.002
Gender				
Female	–0.110	1.383	0.351	–0.067
Education (Degree)				
Post-compulsory qualifications	–0.971	1.172	0.052	–0.145
Compulsory-level qualifications	–1.133	1.588*	0.168	0.080
No qualifications	–0.931	1.393	0.125	–0.163
Housing tenure				
Owner	0.291	0.573	0.322	–0.024
Trade union membership				
Member	0.030	0.856	0.232	0.001
Religion (No religion)				
Roman Catholic	0.719*	1.900**	1.042**	1.254**
Protestant	0.138	8.854	–0.089	–0.134
National identity				
(Equally Scottish and British)				
Scottish not British	–1.037*	–0.941	–0.222	–1.018**
Scottish more than British	–0.618	–0.972	–0.043	–0.791*
Class identity (Middle class)				
Working class	–1.212*	–2.245	0.064	0.363
No class	–1.964**	–1.205	–0.292	0.010
More in common with				
(Neither/both)				
Same class English	0.971**	0.649	0.348	–0.032
Opposite class Scottish	0.444	–0.316	0.139	0.295
Constitutional preference				
(Devolved Parliament)				
Independence	–1.368**	–1.911**	–1.892**	–1.580**
No Parliament	2.247**	7.383	5.860	0.442
Left–right scale	–0.124**	0.019	–0.004	0.008

Notes
Full details of variables included in the models are given in the Appendix to this chapter.
* Indicates significance at the 5 per cent level.
** Indicates significance at the 1 per cent level.

The results in table 5.8 demonstrate which characteristics, both social and ideological, discriminate between Labour and SNP supporters. The table shows that there has been substantial change in this over the last decade, with far more differences between the parties in 1992 than in 2001. This is true of both differences according to social characteristics and those arising from ideological differences. Factors that have not played a significant role in distinguishing between Labour and SNP supporters at any point in the last decade include gender, educational qualifications, housing tenure, age, and trade union membership. In other words, since 1992, it has never been possible to predict whether a person would support Labour or the SNP on the basis of these social characteristics. Social identities, however, appear to have a greater significance. Those who belong to the Roman Catholic church have been more likely to support Labour throughout the period, whilst those who prioritise their Scottish identity over any British identity have been more likely to support the SNP. These identities remain significant in 2001.

Of particular interest are differences in ideology between the different supporters. In 1992, the respondents' position on a left–right attitudinal scale distinguished between SNP and Labour supporters with those further to the left of the scale being more likely to support Labour. By 1997 these differences in attitudinal position had disappeared and have not reappeared in subsequent surveys. Thus, in 2001 it was not possible to predict whether a person was a Labour or SNP supporter on the basis of their position on a left–right attitudinal scale; Labour and SNP supporters in Scotland were equally 'left-wing'. Finally, constitutional preference continues to predict whether or not a person will support Labour or the SNP, with those who favour independence over a devolved parliament being more likely to support the SNP.

The results from the logistic regression models indicate that at the 2001 general election, Labour and the SNP were largely competing for the support of the same social groups. However, the SNP appear to be ahead in the 'Scottishness' stakes, with those who feel more Scottish than British or Scottish and not British being more likely to support the SNP than those who feel equally Scottish and British. As this is the dimension which most strongly differentiates between SNP and Labour supporters, the image of New Labour as not looking after the interests of Scots in general (seen above) could pose a real danger to the Labour Party in Scotland. However, for the time being this effect is to some extent ameliorated by the more positive image of Scottish Labour.

Table 5.9 Perceived differences between Labour and the SNP, 1999–2001

	1999	2001(s)	2003[a]
Great deal of difference	43	35	37
Some difference	43	44	37
Not much difference	15	20	23
Unweighted N (=100%)	1411	1508	1100

Note
(a) Data for 2003 are taken from an ICM poll conducted by telephone immediately after the Scottish Parliament elections of 2003. Full details can be found in Boon and Curtice (2003).

A further way of assessing the seriousness of this threat is to consider how far apart Labour and the SNP are perceived to be by the Scottish electorate. Table 5.9 shows the perception of the differences between Labour and the SNP. This table may offer some comfort to the Labour Party in Scotland but equally suggests that there is little room for complacency. Whilst a large majority of the Scottish electorate perceive Labour and the SNP as having at least 'some' difference between them, less than 50 per cent perceive this to amount to a 'great deal of difference', and a growing proportion indicate they see 'not much difference' between the parties.

CONCLUSION

It is clear that Labour in Scotland remain the majority party and have continued to dominate electorally at both Westminster and Holyrood. The images of the party held by the Scottish people are very positive, and suggest that, in Scotland, Labour is perceived as a catch-all party, looking after the interests of both middle and working classes, big business and trade unions. It is also clear that images of the party have changed, as the party has changed over the last decade. The party's image clearly improved in 1997 but whilst remaining positive, has fallen a little over their period of office. However, Labour cannot afford to be complacent in Scotland, as they may have been elsewhere in traditional Labour areas. In the Scottish context, disillusioned Labour supporters can find a comfortable home among supporters of the SNP with whom they largely share the same social location, identities and ideology.

APPENDIX

The models presented in table 5.8 are logistic regression models of Labour vs SNP identification for each year. In each model the same set of independent variables is used. These are described in detail below. In each appropriate case the reference category is shown in brackets.

Age (Measured in years)
Gender (Male)
Education (Degree-level education)
  Qualifications achieved in post-compulsory education, below degree level
  Qualifications achieved in compulsory education.
  No qualifications
Housing (Non-owner occupier)
Trade union membership (Non-member)
Religion (No religion)
  Roman Catholic
  Protestant
  (Those belonging to other religions were omitted from analysis due to very small numbers)
National identity (Equally Scottish and British)
  Scottish not British
  Scottish more than British
  (Those belonging to British more than Scottish and British not Scottish were omitted due to very small numbers)
Class identity (Middle class)
  Working class
  No class identity
Respondent feels they have most in common with (Neither or both)
  Same class English
  Opposite class Scottish
Constitutional preference (Devolved Parliament)
  Independence
  No Parliament
Left–right scale
The scale is constructed from the following items; it may take values between 0 and 30:
- Ordinary people get their fair share of the nation's wealth
- There is one law for the rich and one for the poor
- There is no need for strong trade unions to protect employees
- Private enterprise is the best way to solve Britain's economic problems
- Major public services ought to be in state ownership
- It is the government's responsibility to provide a job for everyone who wants one

NOTES

1. The original data creators, depositors, funders and the UK Data Archive bear no responsibility for the analysis or interpretation contained herein.
2. For ease of reference, the surveys are referred to as 1992, 1997, 1999, 2001(e) for the 2001 British Election Survey and 2001(s) for the 2001 Scottish Social Attitudes Survey.
3. As the questions are asked separately it is perfectly acceptable for a respondent to believe that Labour looks after the interests of both the middle and working class very closely.
4. The measure of occupational class used is that devised by Goldthorpe (1987), which has been used extensively in the analysis of social attitudes and electoral behaviour. See, for example, Heath et al. (1985).
5. The measure of national identity used is that devised by Moreno (1988).
6. Due to small numbers of respondents, figures for the 'British' end of the scale, 'British more than Scottish' and 'British not Scottish' are subject to larger standard errors and are therefore less reliable.
7. The dependent variable is code 1 for Labour and 0 for SNP identifiers, therefore significant positive coefficients increase the odds that a person with that characteristic will support Labour whilst a significant negative coefficient increases the odds that a person with that characteristic will support the SNP.
8. There are some inconsistencies in question-wording which make it impossible to construct identical models over time. The 2001 Scottish Social Attitudes Survey does not include a directly comparable measure of social class, while the 2001 British Election Survey does not include questions on constitutional options and socialist–*laissez-faire* attitudes. As models for each year suggest that occupational class does not distinguish between Labour and SNP voters, the models presented use data from the Scottish Social Attitudes Survey 2001 and omit occupational class. For full details of the measures used in the models, see the Appendix to this chapter.

REFERENCES

Bennie, L., Brand, J. and Mitchell, J. (1997), *How Scotland Votes*, Manchester University Press, Manchester.

Boon, M. and Curtice, J. (2003), *Scottish Election Research*, The Electoral Commission, Edinburgh.

Bromley, C., Curtice, J., Hinds, K. and Park, A. (eds) (2003), *Devolution – Scottish Answers to Scottish Questions?*, Edinburgh University Press, Edinburgh.

Brown, A., McCrone, D., Paterson, L., and Surridge, P. (1999), *The Scottish Electorate: The 1997 General Election and Beyond*, Macmillan, Basingstoke.

Butler, D. and Stokes, D. (1974), *Political Change in Britain*, 2nd edn, Macmillan, London.

Campbell, A., Converse, P., Miller, W. and Stokes, D. (1960), *The American Voter*, Wiley, New York.

Clarke, H. et al. (2001), *British General Election Study, 2001*, computer file, UK Data Archive, 18 March 2003, SN 4619.

Curtice, J., McCrone, D., Park, A. and Paterson, L. (2002), *New Scotland, New Society?* Polygon at Edinburgh, Edinburgh.

Evans, G., Curtice, J. and Norris, P. (1998), 'New Labour, New Tactical Voting?', in D. Denver, J. Fisher, P. Cowley and C. Pattie (eds), *British Elections and Parties Review*, vol. 8, Frank Cass, London.

Goldthorpe, J. (1987), *Social Mobility and Class Structure in Modern Britain*, Clarendon Press, Oxford.

Heath, A., Jowell, R. and Curtice, J. (1985), *How Britain Votes*, Pergamon Press, Colchester.

Heath, A., Jowell, R. and Curtice, J. (2001), *The Rise of New Labour: Party Policies and Voter Choices*, Oxford University Press, Oxford.

Heath, A. and Taylor, B. (1999), 'Turnout: New Sources of Abstention?', in G. Evans and P. Norris (eds), *Critical Elections: Voters and Parties in Long-Term Perspective*, Sage, London.

Moreno, L. (1988), 'Scotland and Catalonia: The Path to Home Rule', in D. McCrone and A. Brown (eds), *The Scottish Government Yearbook*, Unit for the Study of Government in Scotland, Edinburgh.

Paterson, L., Brown, A., Curtice, J., Hinds, K., McCrone, D., Park, A., Sproston, K. and Surridge, P. (2001), *New Scotland, New Politics?*, Polygon at Edinburgh, Edinburgh.

Przeworski, A. and Sprague, J. (1986), *Paper Stones: A History of Electoral Socialism*, University of Chicago Press, Chicago. Cited in Heath et al. (2001).

CHAPTER 6

The Politics of Scottish Labour's Heartlands

Jane Saren and James McCormick

This chapter explores the politics of Scottish Labour's heartlands in the context of what might be called 'the new politics': the changing patterns of political loyalties and engagement which are common across the western world, in which ideology is a less dominant force and social democratic parties, in particular, seek to construct broad coalitions of support based on redefined approaches to the welfare state, full employment and market regulation.

We begin by presenting a contemporary view on what constitutes Scottish Labour's heartlands, based on an analysis of election results in the period from the 1987 UK election to the second Scottish Parliament election in 2003. This is followed by some observations on the Scottish picture relative to the rest of Britain. Consideration is then given to the possible impact of specific Scottish Labour commitments on proportional representation (PR) for local government and modernisation of public services. Finally, some suggestions are made about the features that might define the kind of party which could thrive in the changing context of 'new politics'.

SHIFTING HEARTLANDS

In our analysis of Scottish Labour's heartlands, we propose a threefold typology of parliamentary constituencies based on the party's fortunes across the six UK and Scottish parliamentary elections between 1987 and 2003:

- **Consistently Labour** – where a Labour MP/MSP has been elected on each occasion in this period
- **Swing seats** – where a Labour MP/MSP has been elected on some/most occasions (ranging from two to five elections)
- **Peripheral seats** – where Labour has never won in the period 1987–2003

CONSISTENTLY LABOUR

In total, forty-two of the seventy-three parliamentary constituencies are in this first category – a clear sign of Scottish Labour's effectiveness in translating its support into seats, even when the party's share of votes across Scotland falls as low as 35 per cent as in 2003, a lower vote than the party achieved in its *annus horribilis* of 1983.[1] At the 2003 Scottish Parliament election, Labour remained clearly ahead in this cluster of seats, polling on average 20 per cent more support than the second-placed party (in most cases the SNP).

Table 6.1 shows that Labour's average share of the vote was almost 10 per cent higher than across Scotland as a whole (44.5 per cent). This figure masks a significant variation in performance, ranging from just under 60 per cent in Glasgow Springburn and more than 50 per cent support in seven other seats, to less than one-third of votes in the three city seats of Edinburgh Central, Aberdeen Central and Dundee West. Although the most marginal Labour seat is found elsewhere (Cumbernauld and Kilsyth, reflecting a large swing to the SNP's Andrew Wilson), the party must be concerned by the poor showing in these east-coast city heartland seats and by the recent advance of the Liberal Democrats in Edinburgh. On this evidence, the pulse of Scottish Labour was beating too weakly for these seats to be considered part of the party's heartlands in 2003.

Table 6.1 Selected measures of Scottish Labour's electoral performance, 1987–2003

Constituency type	Average Labour share of vote	Average Labour majority	Average turnout	Average 'density' of Labour vote
Consistently Labour (Labour at each election, 1987–2003)	44.5% (2003) −3.2% change since 1999	20.2% ahead of second-placed party (2003)	47.3% (2003) −9.5% change since 1999	21.0% of electors
42 seats	Range: 59% to 32%		Range: 58% to 35%	
Swing seats (Labour at some or most elections in this period)	32.5% (2003) −3.9% change since 1999	Average 4.4% behind winning party (2003)	52.8% (2003) −8.7% change since 1999	17.2% of electors
14 seats	Range: 40% to 17%	4 of 14 seats returned Labour MSPs in 2003	Range: 58% to 43%	

| Labour's periphery (Never returned a Labour MP/ MSP in this period) 17 seats | 14.4% (2003) −4.3% change since 1999 Range: 27% to 6% | Not applicable | 51.4% (2003) −9.3 % change since 1999 Range: 57% to 46% | 7.4% of electors |

It is worth noting that the fall in Labour's support in this category (on average just over 3 per cent) was lower than across Scotland as a whole and lower than in the two other constituency groups. A more efficient distribution of its support could have helped Labour in 2003 – the party could have afforded to lose more votes in most of these heartland seats without losing MSPs, whereas the slightly higher loss of support among the 'swing seats' resulted in the loss of seven seats. Indeed, Labour's share of the vote actually rose in eight of these seats, concentrated in Glasgow and Lanarkshire including the First Minister's Motherwell and Wishaw seat, where the party scored an impressive increase in support of more than 8 per cent.

Turnout was down in every constituency across Scotland. The average level of turnout in this group was lowest of the three, at just over 47 per cent, and fell furthest compared with 1999 (down by 9.5 per cent). Turnout ranged from 52 per cent or higher in five seats (reaching 58 per cent in the Western Isles) to less than 40 per cent in another five, all in Glasgow, falling to just 35 per cent in Shettleston. The change in turnout varied from a 12 per cent drop in five seats stretching from Midlothian to Kilmarnock, to a drop of less than 4 per cent in three seats including Dundee West, where a drop in turnout closer to the average would almost certainly have led to Labour losing.

To explore further the underlying pattern of Labour's support, we have used an indicator of 'density' of electoral performance based on share of the vote relative to turnout. Thus, winning half of the votes on a turnout of 50 per cent of the electorate (Falkirk East) gives a density score of 25 per cent – Labour won the support of one in four electors. This counts as a better result than a 50 per cent share of the vote on a turnout of just 37 per cent (Glasgow Maryhill), giving a density of around 18 per cent. On average, Labour persuaded only one in five electors in these seats to actually vote for the party – a sobering figure for Scotland's dominant electoral force. The even poorer performance of its opponents will be of little comfort.

Labour's best performance by this measure was in the Western Isles, where just over 27.4 per cent of electors voted for the party. Table 6.2 shows the eleven seats with a density score of at least 23 per cent – which we might consider as Scottish Labour's 'true heartlands' in 2003. Labour's heartlands are by no means confined to the cities and central belt: some smaller towns and semi-rural seats have proved to be more fertile territory latterly than some consistently Labour seats that now appear to be fading from the heartland.

Table 6.2 Highest 'density of support' scores in consistently Labour seats 2003

Density (%)	Constituency
27.4	Western Isles
26.5	Motherwell and Wishaw
26.0	Coatbridge and Chryston
25.3	Carrick, Cumnock and Doon Valley
25.3	Falkirk East
25.1	Airdrie and Shotts
24.6	Hamilton North
23.6	Paisley North
23.2	Clydesdale
23.1	East Lothian
23.0	Midlothian

The variation in density scores is revealing. In five seats, Labour secured the votes of fewer than one in six electors, as shown in table 6.3.

Table 6.3 Lowest 'density of support' scores in consistently Labour seats 2003

Density (%)	Constituency
13.8	Aberdeen Central
14.1	Glasgow Kelvin
14.9	Edinburgh Central
16.0	Dunfermline West
16.0	Dundee West

SWING SEATS

This is the smallest of the three categories. In total, fourteen seats have returned Labour representatives on at least two of the six occasions considered in this chapter, and in five of them on all but one occasion. Glasgow Govan is included here as a special case, the Westminster seat having been held for four years by the SNP's Jim Sillars following a by-election in 1988. At the 2003 election, Labour lost seven of these seats won in 1999 (remarkably, the margin of defeat being less then 1 per cent in four cases) and held just four. Stirling and Eastwood were the safest among them with Labour majorities of just under 10 per cent.

Labour's average level of support fell further in these seats than in the 'consistent' category (to 32.5 per cent) despite the premium on each vote being highest. The party's share of the vote was higher than the average across Scotland in half of these seats, peaking at 40 per cent in Dumfries and falling to just 19 per cent in Aberdeen South and 17 per cent in Falkirk West. While the latter result can be explained by the unique circumstances surrounding Dennis Canavan's position as Independent MSP, the former is more significant for Labour. Despite having returned a Labour MP with an increased majority in the 2001 UK election, the Holyrood seat must be considered currently as safe for the Liberal Democrats. Transport Minister Nicol Stephen recorded a sizeable swing in his party's favour in 2003. In fact, Labour fared better in two of its most peripheral seats than it did in this, one of its key target seats.

Reflecting the marginal nature of most seats in this category, average turnout was highest at close to 53 per cent, although this was substantially down on 1999. Turnout was below 50 per cent only in the three city seats of Aberdeen North, Dundee East and Glasgow Govan – the first two having been considered safe Labour seats for most of the period in question – and peaked at 58 per cent in Eastwood and Strathkelvin and Bearsden.

The density of Labour support varied widely in this category. In ten of these swing seats, including six lost by Labour, the party fared better on this indicator than the average consistently Labour seat. The party's best performance among this group came in Edinburgh Pentlands, where 21 per cent of electors voted Labour and the party's vote share actually *increased* by 1 per cent despite Enterprise Minister Iain Gray losing to Conservative leader David McLetchie. Similar density scores in Dumfries and Eastwood were higher than in a host of seats long considered part of Scottish Labour's heartland including Paisley South, Kirkcaldy and Hamilton South. On the other hand, the party attracted support from only one in ten electors in Aberdeen South. To put this in perspective, a higher density score was recorded in Argyll and Bute, which has never returned a Labour representative.

PERIPHERAL SEATS

A total of seventeen seats can be described as Scottish Labour's periphery, never electing a Labour MP/MSP in this period and having seldom elected a Labour representative before. Labour's support fell faster in the periphery than in the other categories, on average down by more than 4 per cent to around 14 per cent of votes. While the party managed to win more than 20 per cent support in two seats,[2] Labour support was weakest of all in five seats held by the Liberal Democrats (at between 6 per cent and 10 per cent), and in the two seats represented by the current SNP leader and his predecessor (11 per cent). It is hard to see any target seats emerging from this category on recent trends. Average turnout was just above 50 per cent in Labour's periphery. It varied from 57 per cent in the tightly contested seats of Argyll and Bute and Galloway and Upper Nithsdale to 46 per cent in Moray.

The density of Labour's support was exceptionally low in most of these seats. On average, 7 per cent of electors actually voted for the party, varying from a high of 14 per cent to less than 5 per cent in three seats. The lowest density score in Scotland was recorded in Orkney, at 3 per cent.

LESSONS FROM THE HEARTLANDS

Scottish Labour is not a homogeneous entity. While its image has been defined in stereotypes of Clydeside and the wider central belt, manufacturing industry, council housing and the trade union movement, these account for only a minority of the party's support base and have done since the 1960s. Even within the four largest cities, Labour has pursued different priorities over time. For example, key constituency and local authority activists from Edinburgh/Lothian appeared to be more closely involved in debates about constitutional reforms than those from Glasgow during the 1980s. Recent elections have seen Labour's support base diversify further: it represents a coalition of interests including Eastwood as well as Pollok, the Western Isles as well as the New Towns. Distinctive political cultures within these different areas are reflected, to some extent, in the type of Labour politics found in each. While it is not clear how well these differences are understood or how significant they have proved to date, we believe the long-term renewal of the party calls for a more conscious recognition of the diversity as well as common ground existing across these areas.

Our findings demonstrate that Scottish Labour's heartlands are shifting. While Labour's position looks unassailable in a sizeable group of consistently loyal seats, other seats have become highly vulnerable to the second-placed party, having been considered as secure in recent years. We describe these as 'fading' from Labour's heartlands – this is not intended as a prediction of the trend in 2007 or beyond, but as a description of where the party is losing ground against its own expectations. These are not necessarily the seats with the smallest Labour majorities, since other seats are more marginal but have a tradition of being tightly contested in the past (for example, Cumbernauld

91

and Kilsyth, Kilmarnock and Loudoun). In contrast, a small number of seats can be thought of as 'emerging' or 'new' heartland seats. These have been gained from the Conservatives in recent years, and have returned a higher share of the vote for Labour than in some traditional heartland seats. Table 6.4 identifies some key seats in each category.

Table 6.4 Examples of shifting heartland seats, 2003

Fading	Emerging
Aberdeen Central	Dumfries
Dundee West	Eastwood
Edinburgh Central	Stirling

Looking ahead, what might this imply for Scottish Labour's strategy for targeting resources before and during election campaigns, and its 'reading' of the changing electoral map? The heartlands have become more diverse, containing traditionally Labour seats in the urban central belt, consistently Labour seats in rural and semi-rural areas, and largely middle-class seats which swung to the party at the time of Tony Blair's first election victory in 1987. This diversity is a strength, but it is not self-evident that the party's decision-making machinery has adapted to this new reality. When resources are limited, targeting tends to be too narrowly focused on those seats that appear to be most winnable from Labour's opponents, or on traditionally Labour wards within more marginal constituencies.

These findings suggest to us that Scottish Labour needs to be more sophisticated in its approach to the 2007 election. It needs to develop a political strategy that is more broadly based, in order to:

- reverse its declining support in the 'fading' heartland seats (for example, Aberdeen Central and Edinburgh Central);
- win back seats that have been consistently Labour but were lost in 2003 (for example, Dundee East and Edinburgh South); and
- make gains elsewhere, including seats where Conservative support has strengthened recently (for example, Edinburgh Pentlands and Ayr).

Moreover, such a strategy has to respond to the strong challenge from three different parties in these seats. Given the pattern identified earlier of lower turnout in consistently Labour seats, efforts to 'get the vote out' in traditionally Labour areas – including Labour wards in swing seats – will not be enough for the party to make progress. Within most swing seats, there are wards with lower levels of support for Labour as a share of votes, but significantly higher levels of turnout. In these neighbourhoods, the density of Labour support – and thus the number of votes contributed to the overall constituency total – may therefore be higher than expected.

From discussions with key party figures, we conclude that the attachment between Scottish Labour and a substantial number of voters is at risk of being neglected. The incentives for swing voters to continue supporting Labour or perhaps to vote at all may be further weakened without an active strategy to nurture the diversity of its support base. This is, certainly, a question of the party's capacity to invest resources, but only in part. We believe it also reflects how Scottish Labour understands the concept of heartlands. For example, how effective is the party in putting down roots in the large number of new private housing developments across Scotland and what assumptions are made about the loyalties of electors in such areas?

Renewing Heartlands

It appears from the available evidence that the views of Labour Party members in Scotland on key questions of economic and social policy do not diverge significantly from those of their colleagues in England. There are parallels to be observed also in the challenges facing the party leaderships. Consider the following comment by Gerry Stoker:

> A . . . substantial area of difficulty for New Labour is that some leading figures in the Government, some parts of the parliamentary party and considerable elements of the active party membership in local government and in the constituencies do not sign up to all of New Labour's programme. Electoral success is wanted, but there is resentment at the so-called neglect of the traditional 'heartlands' because of the efforts made to attract new voters and interests . . . The bottom line is many just want to raise taxes and spend more . . . Modernisation is adopted at the level of rhetoric but not at the level of substance, with only a few exceptions. (Stoker 2000: 13)

Scottish Labour or British Labour? In fact, Stoker is describing the challenges facing the Blair leadership, but it seems likely that Jack McConnell would recognise the outlook.

Loss and Renewal

There are, however, some important differences in perspective on re-engagement and reform between Scottish and English Labour. The political psychology is different. To a large extent, Scotland stood at a distance whilst the Labour Party under Kinnock's leadership began the long and painful process of analysing the reasons for dramatic electoral defeat in 1983 and the loss of so much of the skilled working-class base to the Conservatives.

Labour in Scotland simply did not experience the same degree of lost voter support and indeed a disproportionate number of the party's gains across Britain at the 1987 general election were secured in Scotland, as it consolidated its position as the most viable alternative to the Conservatives.[3]

It was in this period that the foundations for New Labour were laid, by separating out policy from fundamental values, and seeking contemporary expressions of both in ways related more closely to how ordinary people lived their lives. As Wendy Alexander MSP acknowledged, speaking to a 'Progress' conference in Edinburgh in June 2003, there was a live discussion in the Labour Party south of the border in the 1980s about the appropriate place of markets, choice, diversity and the limitations of command and control approaches to both economic policy and public services. Scotland missed out on that. This was compounded, in the main, by an assumption that it was not necessary in Scotland:

> At a time when political activists in the Labour party south of the border were grappling with the need to revisit shibboleths such as Clause Four, interventionist economic policy and the internal democracy of trade unions, Scotland was more exercised with devolution as the route to modernisation, a new politics and maintaining a connection with the party's traditional base. (Saren 2002: 34)

Thus Scottish Labour has never had to face the stark electoral rejection that prompts fundamental reappraisal and questioning. Must Scottish Labour lose before it adapts more fully to the changes taking place in people's lives? In England, the experience of losing four general elections from 1979 to 1992, and being in majority government for only eleven years of the twentieth century, was key to the development of a core element of New Labour – the ambition for social democracy to dominate the politics of the twenty-first century, just as Conservatives had dominated the previous century.

Due to PR in the voting system for Holyrood, and for the first time in fifty years, Scottish Labour has been denied a majority of parliamentary seats. The response has been mixed to say the least. It may be that a small working majority in coalition with another party will prove more likely to prompt a serious examination of the Labour Party's relationships with members, voters, communities and interest groups than will a large majority at Westminster. But this is not inevitable. Realpolitik may dictate that the relationship with its coalition partner claims more attention. The scope for fundamental thinking on the changing role of the party may be restricted if a single-party majority in Scotland were to be replaced with a semi-permanent coalition between Labour and the Liberal Democrats. One paradox to emerge from the 2003 Scottish Parliament election may be that the two parties could be unable to secure a working majority in 2007, following the loss of a small number of seats, but an alternative coalition government may be even harder to envisage unless the fortunes of the SNP improve markedly. In future, Scottish Labour may be faced with the choice of forming a minority administration or seeking a second coalition partner in order to govern. The implications for party renewal are far from clear.

Scottish Labour has always been pragmatic and focused on winning power. Its acceptance of some form of proportional representation for a Scottish Parliament at its 1990 Conference in Dunoon was a close-run thing, won only by some traditional trade union vote fixing and a recognition that the Constitutional Convention could go no further without a deal on voting reform. However grudgingly the additional member system (AMS) is regarded, one can see that Scottish Labour is adapting to it and beginning to learn how best to benefit from it. It is perhaps useful to bear in mind this transition as Scottish Labour approaches another period of robust internal dispute over voting reform.

PRESSURES AND CHALLENGES FOR SCOTTISH LABOUR'S MODERNISING PROJECT

THE POSSIBILITIES OF PROPORTIONAL REPRESENTATION

The pledge to introduce the single transferable vote system of PR (STV-PR) for local government elections will deny Labour the automatic majorities the party has become used to enjoying in several authorities on a minority of votes. In other areas, such as Glasgow, North Lanarkshire and Midlothian, Labour would have to poll badly by the standard of recent elections to lose control, but a larger and more diverse set of opposition politicians is guaranteed.

The introduction of PR for local government will be strongly resisted by many members of heartland constituencies and local authorities, although survey evidence in recent years has shown that a clear majority of supporters of each major party including Labour favour voting reform. It will be interesting to test the views of Labour Party members across a variety of constituencies – old and new heartlands as well as authorities where first past the post currently leads to the under-representation of Labour supporters.

PR could create a powerful impetus for parties to revisit their assumptions about heartlands, core voters and marginal seats. In addition, by exemplifying the notion of 'no no-go areas', it has implications for party capacity to contest elections. The costs of over-concentrating resources, or of misjudging the critical areas on which to focus in order to maximise seats, will be brought into sharper focus.

We consider the introduction of PR as a necessary condition for Labour – and other parties – to approach local government in Scotland differently. Behaving as if one party has won a clear mandate, when a majority of electors in every authority has either voted for another party or not voted at all, deserves to be challenged. But it is far from being a sufficient condition for reform.

On the one hand, Labour critics of PR will talk in terms of 'betrayal' and being forced to give up 'control' to political opponents, ignoring the likely arithmetic in the Scottish Parliament that would result in Labour being forced to legislate for voting reform. It will be argued that a single ward councillor should represent 'natural communities', when the force of that claim varies from inner city to remote rural areas and voting systems can be adapted to reflect such differences. Urban neighbourhoods familiar with low levels of investment and political neglect would be better served by four local representatives (in almost every case from more than one party) competing to serve them than by one time-served councillor elected irrespective of commitment. Too often in discussion of electoral reform the emphasis is on numbers when the fundamental need is for an improvement in the *quality* of representation.

On the other hand, some supporters of PR tend to be starry-eyed about its consequences. Electing the Scottish Parliament by the additional member system has demonstrated that PR brings with it a new set of pros and cons. It has resulted in a more diverse pattern of representation, better aligned to changing preferences and allowing an increase in voter choice (which may have helped prevent turnout in 2003 falling even further). It has helped to produce a significantly higher share of women in parliament. But there are simmering tensions between single constituency and regional list MSPs, and a small working majority for the coalition could result in Labour MSPs being acutely risk-averse.

We believe that PR in Scottish local government *could* serve as a catalyst for Labour to select a group of candidates who are much more representative of the electorate as well as Labour supporters, across a broader spread of wards. The party will win rather fewer than the 500 councillors elected in 2003, but the face of Scottish Labour could become more diverse in terms of sex, age, ethnicity and economic status. The geography of Labour's local representation is likely to change, perhaps broadening the pool of talent from which leading politicians in future will be chosen.

The increase in competitiveness in all authorities *might* work in the interests of the public. Under the first-past-the-post system in previous years, Labour and its closest opponents – such as the Conservatives in Stirling and Edinburgh – have been unable to take winning for granted, resulting in the parties working hard to develop distinctive policies. There are other examples where tight contests have tended to bring out the worst in the Labour/SNP relationship, to the detriment of the authority as a whole (notably Renfrewshire).

These contrasting examples should caution us against making early judgements about the likely effects of PR. Local political cultures can be influenced as much by personalities as electoral arithmetic. Whether PR contributes towards a renewal of local democracy will turn largely on the decisions made by political parties. There is no guarantee that the resulting degree of change will be more than superficial. However, Scottish Labour has an opportunity to use voting reform to achieve higher standards of representation and decision-making, marked by a desire to look outwards and to the future on behalf of citizens. Tougher even than introducing STV-PR, the party must soon articulate a vision for local government and take steps towards realising it.

APATHY AND DISCONNECTION IN LABOUR'S HEARTLANDS

Besides voting reform, we can point to other factors pressing Scottish Labour to examine the concept of its heartlands and to consider afresh the relevance of the modernising project. At the most basic level, historically low levels of turnout in traditional heartlands are not a healthy indicator. Furthermore, they imply a worrying level of disconnection between the party and those it claims to represent.

A narrative of 'betrayal' may also be offered to explain low turnouts, based on incumbent Labour governments (at Westminster or Holyrood) being viewed as having turned their backs on poor and working-class households in order to cultivate the voters of middle England – and indeed middle Scotland. We believe this tends to ignore the longer-term effect of redis-tributive measures taken by UK Government, especially through the Treasury, which specifically target lower-income families and, in respect of Scotland, the influence of the Liberal Democrats in pushing 'universalist' provision in higher education and long-term care of the elderly which in practice is likely to benefit most the middle classes.

Furthermore, the call to appeal specifically to heartland voters makes important assumptions about the differences in priority concerns of people living in traditionally Labour areas, and overlooks the fact that the new middle class has grown at least in part as a result of successful measures taken by previous Labour governments. The challenge for progressive governance is to build a coalition in society that is capable of winning power and committed to changing society for the benefit of the majority. As Paul Thompson has put it: 'Successful politics in the more fluid structures of modern societies is constructed from universal themes and ideas that are robust and sensitive enough for different groups to find a home within.' (Thompson 2000: 6)

The feature of declining turnout at elections is not peculiar to Labour heartlands. Indeed the most striking characteristic in 2003 was the consistency of this pattern across different types of constituency. Nor is it unique to Scotland or Britain. It is part of a broader phenomenon across the OECD, affecting most countries, though each from a different baseline. Nevertheless, it is striking how recent this trend is in Britain and how firmly it has taken hold. Turnout in the UK general election of 1997 was above 70 per cent. A few months later, the devolution referendum in Scotland attracted only 60 per cent of electors to vote. By European standards, and on a vote of such constitutional significance, this was a relatively low level of participation. During the six-year period to 2003, Scottish turnout dropped by almost a quarter.

It is not that people are uninterested in politics – the number involved in campaigns and in pressure groups is testament to their interest. Rather, as Douglas Alexander MP has observed, it is parties, not politics, that are struggling. Addressing the same 'Progress' conference in June 2003, he commented: 'No democrat can be anything but disappointed with a turnout of 49 per cent [as happened in the 2003 Scottish Parliament election] – and no one can claim it does not speak to the difficulties all political parties have in communicating their politics.'

A Future for Social Democratic Politics

At least in part, the greater individualism of modern western societies helps to explain the reluctance to exercise the vote. This phenomenon also challenges the ability of parties to attract and hold members. The rise of individualism is sometimes decried as an expression of selfishness or the corruption of human interaction by consumerism, promoted by the market economy. Anthony Giddens acknowledges that these traits exist, but argues that it is highly misleading to equate them with individualism as such:

> Individualism is a structural phenomenon in societies breaking free from the hold of tradition and custom, a transition that is again taking place on a widespread basis. We live our lives in a more open, reflective way than was the case in the past. (Giddens 2001: 107)

98

This seems to us to be a more hopeful basis for analysing the future of political parties. It implies that party membership is not a remnant from an earlier age that will survive only through appealing to selflessness. Instead, it suggests that the challenge is for political parties to adapt the membership model to changed conditions. Labour's quest to become a 'mass party', which might have seemed viable in the mid-1990s, may prove to have been part of a brief moment in history. Nonetheless, it is difficult to imagine a healthy democratic political process in which decision-making powers are not mediated through parties – thus the continuing role of members, and a need to address the familiar tensions around party discipline, unity and effectiveness.

Is there a model for the modern social democratic party? In its submission to the 21st Century Party consultation, the Labour Renewal Network (Scotland) suggests that attention needs to be paid to the balance of the 'psychological contract' between members and the party, in order to sustain involvement, commitment and effort. They identify the needs of the party for campaigning and linking to communities, candidate development, co-ordination, and contributions. The needs of members are categorised as identity, ideas and influence.

The question of how Labour Party members exercise influence over policy is a vexed one. In their 1999 survey of a representative sample of Labour Party members across Britain, Paul Whiteley and Patrick Seyd found that participants in national, regional and local policy forums found the experience interesting, even enjoyable, efficiently run and easy to understand. They reported that there were misgivings about how influential the policy forums were and commented just before the 2001 general election that 'we will know better whether their misgivings are valid or not when we see the extent to which their views have been incorporated into the party's election manifesto' (Whiteley and Seyd 2001).

There is a widespread perception that the policy forum process has diminished the influence of ordinary members over party policy and that things were better in the days of conference resolutions. This version of how things have changed seems to overlook how baffling and alienating the resolution process was to all but a small group of hardened activists. Compositing meetings and conference decision-making were largely determined by the trade unions. At both Scottish and British party levels, those involved in the manifesto process are able to point to concrete examples of the influence of policy forums. For example, the Scottish Executive's commitment to legislate on anti-social behaviour is highlighted as a recent development from sustained concerns expressed in policy forums involving party members in the traditional heartlands.

In the past Scottish Labour has appeared uncertain on how to take action against anti-social behaviour. The prominence of this issue has risen since the Scottish Executive was formed. Critics within Scottish Labour, as distinct from political opponents, respond that the party can share the commitment to address this kind of problem without necessarily agreeing that the proposed solutions are appropriate or effective. Others argue that the policy forums are drawn upon only selectively, and risk being used to justify populist initiatives rather than to help make hard choices for the long-term. Nevertheless, we believe they offer one important means of ensuring Scottish Labour policy takes into account the diverse views of its membership. The assertion that we have moved away from a golden era of membership influence over policy towards one of increasingly tight control from the centre deserves to be challenged.

There is a serious issue about the level of resourcing by party staff demanded by the policy forum process. To say the least, Scottish Labour has a remarkably lean party infrastructure despite being one of the most successful election-winning parties in Europe. Yet its ability to engage proactively in setting the political agenda between elections, to develop its own policy-making capacity and indeed to run election campaigns is significantly less than would be expected in other European countries. The downside of Scottish Labour's success, and the relative lack of competition, is to be found in its status as the establishment party: the incentives to innovate may be only weakly felt, and its ability to attract members with reforming energy is sporadic, especially when in government. It represents a distinctive blend of voter loyalty (even if among a relatively small share of the electorate), pragmatism, incumbency and limited organisational capacity – one which might be characterised as leading to social conservatism.

Whilst the party has struggled to develop a politics of diversity and innovation, it is not alone. Moreover, these attributes might confer a comparative advantage in adapting to devolution, compared to the three other mainstream parties. The current level of entrenchment of Scottish Labour interests in both Westminster and Holyrood may render it better placed to articulate a robust sense of national identity whilst operating within a multi-tier system of governance, without getting too bogged down in the complexity of asymmetric devolution or absolute sovereignty. In this, it is perhaps most closely in tune with most Scottish voters.

It remains to be seen whether Scottish Labour is adequately equipped for perhaps its most critical modernising challenge, the future of public services. The Scottish Labour manifesto for the 2003 election talks in bold terms about the goal of 'first class, responsive and efficient public services', acknowledging that investment must be matched by reform if this is to be achieved. The Scottish public is not immune from growing consumer expectations arising from private service experiences being transferred to the public services. It is widely acknowledged that the investment of money, skills and political capital in mainstream public services since 1999 has not yet resulted in significantly better outcomes. It is no secret that ministers in the Scottish Executive are frustrated at the pace of progress. At the same time, we are likely to see highly public discussion of fragmented budgeting, the weight of central initiatives, target-setting and audit, local leadership and the appropriate role of trade unions in achieving reform.

The renewal and reform of public services are of critical importance to Scottish Labour's traditional heartlands. An unknown dimension arising from devolution, however, is whether a Labour–Liberal Democrat coalition with a small majority is as likely to address these challenges as a majority Labour government at Westminster, or whether any other party is likely to advance a more convincing strategy for public service reform.

Party Renewal In and Beyond the Heartlands

What would a modern social democratic party look like? We propose it would understand instinctively its purpose as representing the majority of society, seeking to build a progressive coalition based on clear values and not simply a rigorous evidence base, encompassing economic opportunity, security and responsibility, and democratic renewal. It would be European and internationalist in outlook. Its campaigning and organisational behaviour would recognise the fundamental importance of economic prosperity and sustainability. It would replenish its desire for improvement through periods of incumbency. It would tolerate diversity and promote discussion of ideals, within a framework of professionalism and appropriate types of discipline. It would embrace new forms of technology, reflecting how we share information in other areas of our lives. And it would recognise the responsibility to build links in many communities and restore lost trust in its relationship with voters.

Much of this ground was covered in the 1998 Labour Party document 'Building a Healthy Party'. It received some circulation in Scotland but, given the timing, probably not much attention. In any event it deserves revisiting, both north and south of the border, in the current context. Five years on, what can be added? Firstly, in the context of devolution, there is a need to create avenues for party activists in different parts of Britain (and ideally with sister parties in Europe) to engage in discussion and sharing of views and experiences. Currently such contacts tend to be confined to an elite of politicians, special advisers and party staff. It cannot be healthy, for example, for the number of Scottish constituencies sending delegates to UK Labour conferences to continue to decline. However the broader point is how to use a wide range of communication methods and forms of engagement to promote such interaction between members and indeed between the party and the electorate. The assumption that the primary or only relationship has to be locally based deserves to be challenged. It has been suggested that the first political grouping to create the 'networked party' will sweep the board.

Is it fanciful to imagine that it could be Scottish Labour? Perhaps. But consider this. In 1992, Andrew Marr wrote that 'Scotland has one of the worst records in Europe for electing women MPs; its political culture, like those smoke-hazed drinkeries that used to line every main street with curt "No women" signs sellotaped to the door, remains deeply male.' (Marr 1992: 206)

Eleven years later, in July 2003, Scottish Communities Minister Margaret Curran could say, 'In the Labour Party we have now got more than 50 per cent representation. It's an astonishing achievement. If we can achieve gender equality in the Labour group in Scotland, we can achieve anything.' (Curran 2003)

Mixed in with the caution likely to meet this view ought to be a dash of optimism laced through with vision. The nature of Scottish Labour's heartlands is changing. The way the party understands economic and social change across Scotland, and thus its own role, will also have to change. The pressures to do so are not as strong as we would hope, but the consequences of ignoring these trends are likely to be counted in growing party irrelevance and disconnection from the democratic process.

NOTES

1. Our analysis is concerned with first-preference votes in the 2003 and 1999 Scottish Parliament elections to ease comparison with first-past-the-post constituency contests in Westminster elections.
2. Caithness, Sutherland and Easter Ross where support actually increased since 1999, and Tweeddale, Ettrick and Lauderdale.
3. Among these, Glasgow Kelvin, Cunninghame North, Edinburgh Central, Renfrewshire West and Western Isles appear in the 'consistently Labour' group throughout the period to 2003 (despite boundary changes).

REFERENCES

Alexander, D. (2003), 'The New Scottish Politics', speech by Douglas Alexander MP to 'Progress' Scottish Conference, Edinburgh City Chambers, 21 June 2003.

Curran, M. (2003), quoted in A. Crawford, 'Executive to put feminist ideals at core', *Sunday Herald*, 20 July 2003.

Giddens, A. (2001), 'The Global Third Way Debate', *Policy Network*, issue 1, summer 2001, pp. 102–21.

Marr, A. (1992), *The Battle for Scotland*, Penguin, London.

Saren, J. (2002), 'The Implications of Devolution for Scotland: "Shaken, not stirred" ', in S. Henig (ed.), *Modernising Britain*, The Federal Trust, London, pp. 29–46.

Stoker, G. (2000), 'The Three Projects of New Labour', *Renewal*, vol. 8, no. 3, summer 2000, pp. 7–15.

Thompson, P. (2000), 'It really *is* the message', *Renewal*, vol. 8, no. 3, summer 2000, pp. 1–6.

Whiteley, P. and Seyd, P. (2001), 'Party People', *The Guardian*, 27 March 2001.

CHAPTER 7

Women and the Labour Party in Scotland

Fiona Mackay

The results of the 2003 elections confirmed the female face of the Labour Party in twenty-first-century Scotland. Women comprise more than half of the Labour MSPs in the Scottish Parliament. They also hold influential positions as ministers and parliamentary committee conveners. In respect of women's political representation, the Labour Party is head and shoulders above its main electoral rivals in Holyrood and Westminster. This is the most visible sign of a remarkable process of transformation: the twin trends of modernisation and feminisation of the party in the UK and Scotland over the past two decades.

This chapter provides a brief account and analysis of the changing role and status of women in the Scottish Labour Party. It asks how the Labour Party, once characterised as stereotypically masculine, got to this point, and what the prospects are for the future. It draws upon the small literature that exists on women and the Scottish Labour Party, a selection of party documents and also upon interviews with women party activists and party officials conducted as part of related comparative research into gender and constitutional change in the UK.[1] After giving some historical context, the chapter summarises some of the key developments since 1979. This is a complex and relatively under-researched area and this chapter does not claim to provide a comprehensive account; there is a clear need for further work on the historic and contemporary roles of women in the Labour Party and also the other Scottish political parties.

The chapter is organised around the theme of women's representation, broadly defined. We distinguish between two main ways of thinking about representation. First, representation as a *place at the table* by which we mean women as internal elected party office-holders and as candidates and politicians at different levels of government. Second, representation as a *voice in the party* by which we mean the structures and opportunities that exist for women *as women* to organise within the party, to share experiences and build capacity, to campaign and lobby for women to take their place in the mainstream, and to articulate gendered policy concerns.

Women and the Labour Party: The Historical Context

From the earliest days women have played an active role in socialist politics and the Labour movement in Scotland although their numbers were small and much of their contribution has since been neglected and forgotten. Women participated in both 'mainstream' groupings and through separate women's organisations such as the Women's Labour Party, which existed in Glasgow in the 1890s and was allied to the Labour Party; The Women's Labour League, which was established in 1906, with its first Glasgow branch in 1908; and the Scottish Women's Co-operative Guild (Smyth 1992; McCrae 1991).

Smyth's work on women and the Clydeside rent strikes of 1915 demonstrates the vibrancy of women's organising and also the strong lines of continuity over time and across different issues. Key players in the rent strikes also played active roles in socialist and Labour movement groupings, peace activism and suffrage campaigns, and the co-operative movement. This can be illustrated in the person of Helen Crawfurd. A leading Clydeside rent-striker, Crawfurd was also an activist in the ILP (subsequently joining the Communist Party), the Glasgow Women's Housing Association and the Scottish Co-operative Women's Guild. She had also been a militant suffragette[2] and was a prominent peace and anti-conscription campaigner during the War, playing a leading part in the Women's International League and the more radical Women's Peace Crusade. Other leading rent-strikers such as Agnes Dollan and Mary Barbour had similar patterns of activism and networking (Smyth 1992). Smyth notes that women's self-organisation and self-activity were important, providing organisational experience and networking and helping to break down some of the structural and institutional barriers that existed to women's greater participation in the Labour movement (Smyth 1992: 184).

Certain trends can be discerned from this early period about the relationship between women and the Labour Party, some of which continue to have a contemporary resonance. Gordon (1991) provides the most comprehensive history of the late nineteenth and early twentieth century and notes the ambivalence of the Labour Party to women activists and the balancing act that women themselves performed in pursuing gender equality within existing stereotypes about gender roles. The nature of the ambivalence related on the one hand to the formal ideology of gender equality in the labour movement, championed by male leaders such as Keir Hardie, and on the other, the suspicion and 'deeply rooted antipathies towards women' amongst Labour men (Smyth 1992: 189; see also Gordon 1991; McCrae 1991).

Opportunities for women to press their claims for a place and a voice in the party have been contingent upon the shifting fortunes of the party and the congruence between women's agendas and party leadership concerns and priorities (Smyth 1992; Burness 1992). So opportunities for women opened up in the period immediately before and after gaining partial enfranchisement in 1918 when the Labour Party (in common with other political parties) amended party rules and structures and made conscious efforts to accommodate women as party members and as voters. In particular women activists were able to press home arguments that Labour needed to organise and involve women in order that their votes were not 'captured' by the parties of 'reaction' (Burness 1992: 156). This was done through the development and support of women's structures to encourage women to join the party and to assist in their political education.

However, as economic conditions worsened in the inter-war period and working-class politics was increasingly put on the defensive, then the space for women and 'women's issues' shrank and Labour 'ambivalence reasserted itself' (Smyth 1992: 19; see also Hughes 1999). Women's participation in the public sphere of politics was regarded with suspicion by many male activists and the self-organisation of women and articulation of gendered concerns was seen as diversionary to class struggles at best and divisive at worst.

The political identity of women as a group was recognised early in the Labour Party. The 1918 rule changes provided women with a constitutional position alongside trade unions, constituency parties, and socialist societies like the Fabians and the ILP. However, 'the key role of male-dominated trade unions in this structure combined with a low female membership, left women less visible in the Labour Party than in either the Liberal or Unionist Parties' (Burness 1992: 157). In 1918 the Women's Labour League was formally integrated into the Labour Party (McCrae 1991). In that year the Scottish Conference also elected one seat on the Scottish Executive Committee to a representative of women's organisations. Clarice McNab Shaw (Leith) took the first women's seat and in 1919 went on to chair the 5th Annual Conference of the Labour Party Scottish Council, the first woman to do so.[3] She used her address to condemn the resistance and indifference of men in the party to women's sections and the need for women to participate in the movement and the party (McCrae 1991; Burness 1992).

In 1919, Agnes Hardie (later to become MP for Springburn) was appointed as the first paid Scottish women's organiser and set about increasing women members through women's sections and kitchen meetings. The number of women's seats on the Scottish Executive increased from one to four (Burness 1992) and the first Scottish Labour Women's Conference was held in Glasgow, which was to become an annual event for eighty years until it was abolished in the late 1990s as part of the reorganisation of women's structures. Despite the initial growth in women's sections,[4] periodic dissatisfaction with the indifference or resistance of Labour leadership at various levels to locally involving and organising women continued to be expressed by women into the 1930s and beyond. The verdict from elsewhere in the party was that Scotland was backward in this respect with lower-than-average female membership and relatively weak women's organisations (Burness 1992).

Nevertheless, women's sections did grow in the 1920s before declining in the 1930s and 1940s and female activists pioneered new forms of political communication and political education to reach and engage women in working-class communities (Gordon 1991; Smyth 1992). As with their sisters south of the border, women's sections pursued a range of issues including equal pay, birth control (and subsequently abortion rights), family allowances, maternity services, housing and health. They worked with organisations such as the Scottish Co-operative Women's Guild, women in trade unions, and community groups (Hughes 1999). McCrae lists some of the agenda items discussed by delegates at the 1919 Scottish Women's Conference: Russia; Conscription; Food Prices; Old Age Pensions; Housing; Municipal Trading; Mothers' Pensions; Political Organisation of Women; Unemployed Women; and Protests. Commenting on the striking similarities of the women's conference agenda in 1919 with concerns in the 1990s, and the slow progress towards equality, McCrae remarked, 'Patience indeed has been our weakness' (McCrae 1991: 48).

'Women's reforms' were seldom seen as 'bread and butter' issues and were sidelined to mainstream concerns such as mass male unemployment. The issue of birth control provides a good case in point. Despite strong support amongst rank-and-file women's sections for access to birth control, their concern 'received scant support from the official labour movement either in Parliament or in the city chambers' (Smyth 1992: 192). There was bitter disappointment amongst Labour women when John Wheatley, as Health Minister, in 1924 refused to revoke regulations that banned doctors and health visitors from giving advice on contraception (Smyth 1992; Hughes 1999).

The role of women's self-organising in the Labour Party was noted earlier but where were the women in the mainstream in the early decades of the twentieth century? From the relatively little we know, women seldom played leadership roles within the Labour Party and ILP or were selected as candidates and were more often active as 'propagandists' developing the tools of 'kitchen politics' and 'practical socialism' to mobilise women (Hughes 1999).

Between 1918 and 1945, just five Labour women were returned to Scottish seats at Westminster and eleven women were selected as Labour or ILP candidates. The first Labour woman MP in Scotland was the 24-year-old Jennie Lee (for the ILP) in the North Lanark by-election in 1929. She gained victory despite claims that the Catholic Church had advised parishioners to vote against her because of her supportive stance on birth control. She was to lose her seat in 1931, after the ILP and the Labour Party split, but would later serve as an MP for an English constituency. Agnes Hardie followed in 1937–46 for Glasgow Springburn. In 1945 three Labour women were returned: Clarice McNab Shaw (Kilmarnock); Jean 'haud the wean' Mann (Coatbridge); and Margaret (Peggy) Herbison (North Lanark) (Burness 1992: 166).[5]

At GB level the party returned more women to Parliament than the other parties in the period 1918–45. However, Labour in Scotland actually performed more poorly than the Scottish Liberals and the Unionist parties in promoting women candidates and giving a visible role for women within mainstream party structures. Considering 'the long slow march' of Scottish women MPs, Burness notes that, in contrast to the attention the issue was to attract in the future, 'the lack of women at Westminster does not seem to have been a burning issue over the period.' (1992: 169)

The role of women in the Labour Party in Scotland in the post-war years is little documented until the 1970s (see the following discussion). So women had a place and a voice in Labour party structures and politics but it was uncertain and marginal. Despite the vote and a history of activism and organisation, the party was ambivalent about the inclusion of women and there remained in place significant structural, cultural and institutional barriers to women's equal participation.

For most of the post-suffrage period, the percentage of women MPs at Westminster fluctuated at between 2 and 5 per cent, one of the poorest records of female representation in advanced liberal democracies (along with France and the US). As table 7.1 demonstrates, it was not until 1987 that the proportion of female MPs broke through the 5 per cent barrier (6.3 per cent). This figure increased to 9.2 per cent in the 1992 general election and doubled to 18.2 per cent in 1997 (before falling back to 17.9 per cent in 2001). These increases were primarily as a result of improvements in one party, the Labour Party, and the use of controversial gender quotas in the 1997 general election.

Table 7.1 Women in Westminster Parliament, 1979–97

Year	Labour	Conservative	Lib Dem[a]	Other	Total	%
1979	11	8	–	–	19	2.9
1983	10	13	–	–	23	3.5
1987	21	17	1	2	41	6.2
1992	37	20	2	1	60	9.2
1997	101	13	3	3	120	18.2

Note
(a) Including Liberal/SDP/SLD in appropriate years.
Source: Eagle and Lovenduski (1998: 1).

CONTEMPORARY ISSUES

THE CAMPAIGN FOR AN EQUAL PLACE AND A VOICE IN LABOUR POLITICS

If we fast-forward to 2003 we encounter a radically different Labour Party in Scotland where women are highly visible and play a role that would have been unthinkable in previous periods. Women are 42 per cent of party members, a record high (Scottish Labour Party 2003). Under current party rules, out of the seven key posts in each Constituency Labour Party (CLP) – chair, secretary, treasurer, two vice-chairs, women's officer, and youth officer – at least three must be women. Out of seventy-two CLPs, currently twenty-five CLP secretaries are women. The Labour Party has a standard 50:50 quota on party bodies, such as Scottish Policy Forum, the National Policy Forum and the Scottish Executive Committee. The majority of members of the Scottish Executive Committee, elected in March 2003, are women (eighteen out of thirty-one seats) and the Party Chairperson for 2003–4 is female. Some 80 per cent of Scottish Labour Party staff are women. The career trajectory of Lesley Quinn, who rose from office junior to become current Scottish General Secretary, provides a striking personal illustration of this process of feminisation.

In terms of women's political representation, the achievement of gender balance in the Scottish Parliamentary Labour Group has received inter-national plaudits. In 1999 women were 50 per cent of Labour MSPs and in 2003 they comprised 56 per cent. The Labour Party's performance on this issue is key to the Scottish Parliament's overall performance of 37.2 per cent in 1999 and 39.5 per cent in 2003. The proportion of Scottish Labour women at Westminster is less impressive at 18 per cent, but still represents considerable progress on past records of representation. It has proved harder to make headway at local government level: women are around 22 per cent of Labour councillors, a figure that has been virtually unchanged for three successive elections. Labour currently has three MEPs representing Scotland, of whom one is a woman. Labour will field equal numbers of male and female candidates in the next European elections.[6]

How did this come about? As has been argued elsewhere, the unprecedented voice and place of women in the Scottish Parliament did not happen by evolution, incremental progress or chance but was the result of a concerted lobbying by women activists inside the political parties, particularly the Labour Party, women trade unionists and women's organisations (Brown 2001a, b, c; Breitenbach and Mackay 2001; McDonald et al. 2001; Brown et al. 2002; Mackay et al. 2002). Likewise, women's agency and activism over a sustained period of time has also been significant in the internal transformation of the Labour Party.

There are a number of stories to tell, all closely interconnected: Labour in Scotland has only limited autonomy from the centre and therefore Scottish developments cannot be unpicked from related trends in the party at GB level; it is also the case that the developments around women's representation in Scotland cannot be considered without discussing the context of devolution.

As noted above, Labour in common with the other political parties has sought to mobilise women as activists in order to win women's votes. However, those women activists were seldom given the opportunity to take up leadership positions within the party or to serve as elected politicians. It was not until the 1980s that the issue of women's political representation began to gain prominence, the result of a confluence of pressures. Changing social attitudes resulted in increased public support for parties to take special measures to increase the number of women in politics. Meanwhile, global political actors such as the United Nations began to advocate gender balance in decision-making as a key means for delivering gender equality. Feminists who had first moved into mainstream politics in the Labour Party after 1979 worked in alliance with long-standing women's advocates in the Labour movement to organise around the issue, and to build and maintain internal pressure (Lovenduski 1999). They were part of a wider international movement conducting similar campaigns in other socialist parties, co-ordinated by Socialist International Women (Eagle and Lovenduski 1998).

In the late 1980s and through the 1990s, a sea change occurred in the Labour party in response to concerted demands from women party activists and office-holders. As noted earlier, historically women's reforms have been contingent upon their relevance to party fortunes and to the leadership's wider concerns and priorities. In the wake of successive Labour defeats at the polls and the gender gap in support (apparent at GB rather than Scottish level), senior party men became increasingly 'willing to concede greater women's representation as part of a strategy to win the next election' (Eagle and Lovenduski 1998: 4). Campaigners linked arguments for greater gender parity of representation to the Labour Party's wider programme of modernisation, the need to appeal to women voters, constitutional reform and social inclusion (Perrigo 1996; Brown 2001b). In Scotland the issue of women's under-representation became a high-profile element of broader civil society campaigns and processes of constitutional reform.

The comparative literature suggests that the relative success of women's representation within political parties rests in part on the strength of internal women's organisation. From the late 1970s onwards, women from different parts of the Labour party had mobilised to campaign for a *place at the table* in terms of increased representation in party office and as elected politicians, and for an improved *voice in the party* through the enhanced influence of women's structures (see later discussion). Women worked within formal structures such as women's sections, women's committees and women's conference and also created a range of informal lobby groups at GB and Scottish level. Although there were female party members active on the issue within the other main UK parties, their campaigns were less organised and effective, which reflected, at least in part, relatively weaker influence and organisational capacity within their respective parties.

Steps to a More 'Women-Friendly' Party

Concerted strategic action by well-organised women activists inside the Labour Party at GB and Scottish level created the momentum to change party rules. The principle of special measures such as internal party quotas was agreed by Conference in 1989, starting with the introduction of three reserved seats for women on the Shadow Cabinet. From 1991–5, quotas were introduced to increase the proportion of women as office-holders at different levels of the Labour Party including the National Executive Committee and the Scottish Executive Committee, delegates to national and regional conferences and offices at constituency level (Eagle and Lovenduski 1998; Lovenduski 1999). There was a mixed reaction to internal party quotas, with entrenched resistance in some quarters and instances where quotas were ignored. However, the impact of policy was to alter dramatically the gender balance of power throughout the party.

It had proved harder to get agreement on quotas for parliamentary candidates. Throughout the 1980s, Women's Conference at GB level had proposed that all-women shortlists be imposed on all seats becoming

111

vacant as well as the party's target seats in order to improve the poor gender balance at Westminster but these proposals had been rejected annually by the party conference (Eagle and Lovenduski 1998). However, as women gained more influential positions in the party structures, they provided a further springboard for candidate quotas to be championed and accepted. Female activists used a range of discursive and political opportunities to press home their case. In particular they were successful in linking calls for more women MPs with programmes of party modernisation and electoral competition for female voters. Proposals for all-women shortlists for half of all vacant and target seats in the run-up to the 1997 general election were approved by Party Conference in 1993 with the backing of the then leader John Smith as part of a package of reform measures including one member one vote (OMOV) (Eagle and Lovenduski 1998).

The process by which constituencies were selected for all-women short-lists was managed by consensus conferences at regional level between constituency officers, many of whom, by this stage, were women. Although there was undoubted resistance to the policy in some areas, agreement was reached in most cases and 'compulsion was more sparingly used than press coverage suggested' (Eagle and Lovenduski 1998: 9). Between 1993 when the all-women shortlist policy was introduced and 1996, when the policy was halted following a legal challenge (Russell 2001), thirty-five women were selected using this mechanism including four Scottish women. The radical measures contributed to the doubling of women's representation at Westminster from 9 per cent to 18 per cent and women comprised a quarter of the Parliamentary Labour Group. However, a regional analysis reveals very different performances with Scotland and Wales trailing behind English regions in respect of women's representation. So, for example, women comprised 16 per cent of Scottish MPs and 12 per cent of Welsh MPs in 1997 compared with 48 per cent of South-West England MPs and 27 per cent of MPs from the West Midlands.[7]

Labour, Women and Devolution in Scotland

Women in Scotland shared the opportunities opened up by party moder-nisation and through the 1990s gained significant positional influence inside the Labour Party in Scotland as a result of GB-wide internal party quotas (see above). They were also active in GB-wide campaigns for candidate quotas. In addition, women inside the Labour Party – together with trade union women and women's groups – campaigned in the context of devolution to ensure that equal political representation would be a key priority in any new Scottish Parliament and that Labour, as a party, would deliver on this issue. In addition to modernisation and women's votes, arguments that had been well-rehearsed at GB level, activists argued that gender balance would provide a powerful and visible symbol of 'new politics' and a modern, relevant and democratic Scotland.

The twin processes of party transformation – feminisation and modernisation – were slower and more contested in Scotland. This was because the party was more complacent: it had delivered Scottish MPs to Westminster and had held on to local power; many in the party did not see the need to do things differently. The party in Scotland was also traditionally less hospitable to women as candidates and office-holders and had returned proportionately fewer female MPs than its counterparts in England. So, whilst devolution brought with it opportunities, women inside Labour had reason to believe they would need to fight hard to ensure that equal political representation would be a key priority in any new Scottish Parliament.

The detailed story of women's mobilisation in the 50:50 campaign – 'one of the most strategic campaigns for equality for women in Scotland' (McDonald et al. 2001: 233) – has been told elsewhere (Brown 2001a, b, c; Breitenbach and Mackay 2001). Labour women activists were key members of the campaign alongside trade unionists, grass-roots women's organisations, feminist academics and gender experts, and women activists from other political parties. The campaign for gender balance took place under the rallying banner of '50:50' which took its name from a proposal originally made by the Scottish Trades Union Congress (STUC) women's committee in 1989 to the Scottish Constitutional Convention. It was argued that with the creation of a new legislature there would be no problem of incumbents. Equal representation could be achieved simply by electing one man and one woman to represent each parliamentary constituency. By 1991, the proposal had become the official policy of both the STUC and the Labour Party in Scotland. Although the proposal was not enacted in this form because of subsequent decisions about electoral systems, the 50:50 demand quickly became the official title of a broad-based campaign.

In the run-up to the first elections to the Scottish Parliament in 1999, internal and external pressure was brought to bear on the political parties, particularly the Labour Party. All the parties stated their concern to see more women in politics and their intention to encourage women to come forward for selection. In addition, all of the parties improved their recruitment and selection procedures, for example through the introduction of equal opportunities considerations in the process. However, in the final event, the Scottish Labour Party was the only party to operate a mechanism to guarantee gender balance in representation.

Under the additional member system (AMS), 73 of the 129 MSPs are elected from constituencies. The remaining fifty-six members are selected from eight regional party lists (based upon the former European Parliament constituencies). Different strategies were therefore needed for promoting gender balance in constituency contests and in the regional lists. In the case of Labour, the party likely to gain most of its seats through the first-past-the-post constituency contests, a policy of 'twinning' was devised. The mechanism, which involved the pairing of comparable constituencies where a male candidate is selected for one of the seats and a female candidate is selected for the other, produced a more or less equal number of men and women in the Scottish Parliamentary Labour Group in the first Parliament. Twinning was designed by Labour women activists and academics in place of all-women shortlists, which had been ruled illegal (see above).[8] It was intended for use in the first election only as a one-off means of ensuring a fairer gender composition in the new political institution.

As table 7.2 demonstrates, a significant proportion of women was elected to the Scottish Parliament in 1999. This was largely due to the use of formal positive action by Labour, and informal measures in the case of Labour's main contender, the Scottish National Party (see Brown 2001c; Russell et al. 2002).

Table 7.2   Gender composition of the Scottish Parliament, 1999

Party	Constituency seats		List seats		Total	%
	Men	Women	Men	Women	seats	women
Labour	27	26	1	2	56	**50.0**
SNP	5	2	15	13	35	**42.9**
Conservative	0	0	15	3	18	**16.7**
Lib Democrat	10	2	5	0	17	**11.8**
Green	0	0	1	0	1	**0.0**
Scottish Socialist	0	0	1	0	1	**0.0**
Independent	1	0	0	0	1	**0.0**
Total	43	30	38	18	129	**37.2**

The story of the struggle within the Labour Party over this issue has yet to be fully documented and analysed. Early internal pressure groups included the Labour Women's Action Committee (LWAC), first formed in 1980 as part of the Campaign for Labour Party Democracy, which operated at both GB and (from 1986) Scottish level, and the women's network of the Scottish Left pressure group Labour Co-ordinating Committee (LCC), also formed in the 1980s. Later in the 1980s and the 1990s, other groupings emerged which brought together women from the left and the right of the party, together with non-aligned women, to campaign on the issue.[9] Prominent Labour women – sympathetic to gender balance – worked with others through broader structures such as the Scottish Constitutional Convention and its Women's Issues Group and, later, the Women's Co-ordination Group to engender debates about the shape and form of constitutional change over a period of ten years or so. It came to be expected that the so-called 'new politics' that was to be achieved through devolution would mean little if it did not address the gender question (Mitchell 2000). Labour women worked with the Women's Co-ordination Group to broker an Electoral Contract in 1995 signed by the leaders of Labour and the Liberal Democrats, committing each party to field equal numbers of male and female candidates in winnable seats in the first elections and agreeing upon the AMS electoral system and a Parliament of 129 members (see Brown 2001a, b).[10]

Inside the party, women – sometimes with significant political differences – worked together to influence internal party debates, to sell positive action and to devise a suitable mechanism in the form of 'twinning'. It is difficult from an initial scrutiny of party documents and papers to discern which groups or individuals were particularly influential at any particular point. Party factionalism, alternative agendas and personalities, as well as gender politics, played a part in the internal struggles. So for example, the arguments over gender quotas were also influenced by other agendas, including those of party modernisation and centralisation of candidate selection procedures (Bradbury et al. 2000; Russell et al. 2002) and other kinds of horse-trading. The issue received support from key men in the party. These included Jack McConnell who as Scottish General Secretary played a part in promoting positive action in the Scottish Party and was instrumental in securing the endorsement for 'twinning' – the Scottish solution – from the party nationally in 1997. He saw women's representation as inextricably linked with modernising the party and creating 'New Labour', a vision radically at odds with some of the high-profile feminist reformers allied to LCC and the Scottish Women's Caucus.

Nevertheless it is evident that the debate, activism and lobbying of both 'troublesome women'[11] and women regarded by party leaders as 'safer' worked in combination to provide the impetus for significant gains in women's representation. Brown (2001b) argues that there were various points at which the issue – and women – might have been sidelined and that it was the persistence of women that kept the issue on the agenda.

115

Women Organising

Equality Achieved . . .
But on Second Thoughts . . . But Then Again

This chapter turns now to issues of women's collective voice within the party. As noted earlier, there has been a long history of women's structures within the Labour movement although their fortunes have waxed and waned and their existence has sometimes been viewed with suspicion. In the wake of equal pay and sex discrimination legislation, the Scottish Conference – in line with the party centrally – decided to abolish women's seats on the Scottish Executive in 1978 with the support of many prominent women. This was done on the grounds that equality had been achieved and that special measures were no longer needed. By 1981 just fifteen women's sections had survived and the Scottish Women's Committee had fallen into decline, despite the manful efforts of the then Women's Officer Gerry O'Brien to encourage participation (McCrae 1991).

The decision spurred women activists at GB level and in Scotland – including those who had been influenced by second-wave feminism – to rebuild and increase the influence and accountability of the women' structures, in tandem with promoting women into mainstream positions and pressing for more women candidates (see earlier discussion). Groups such as the LWAC and LCC Women's Network were instrumental in these campaigns. In 1983 the Scottish Women's Committee was elected by women for the first time (rather than by the party as a whole). By 1985 five reserved women's seats on the Scottish Executive had been reinstated, two of which were directly elected by the Scottish Women's Conference (activists in the party at GB level never managed to achieve directly elected seats). At the same time, women organised to get greater numbers of females elected to seats in the union and constituency sections of the Scottish Executive Committee. Over the 1980s and 1990s, women's structures were further strengthened. The Scottish Women's Committee was directly elected by the Scottish Women's Conference and the Women's Conference also succeeded in its demands to nominate a certain number of its motions be debated by the Scottish Conference.[12]

Campaigners of the period therefore had multiple strategies. First, to reinvigorate women's structures, spaces where women could organise separately, build capacity to enter the mainstream, and articulate a gendered analysis of policy issues. Second, to enhance the recognition of women as a group and the voice of women as a group in the structures of the Labour Party through the reintroduction of reserved women's seats and through a proportion of those seats being directly elected by women themselves through the Women's Conference. The idea was that accountability and responsiveness would be increased if positions were held by women with direct links with women in the party, rather than women chosen by men on the basis of factional loyalty.

During the 1980s and 1990s, women campaigned through women's structures on the issue of women's representation and also developed a raft of policies relating to women. They provided a platform to defend women's reproductive rights from attack in the 1980s and developed policies and lobbied the party at GB and Scottish level on a whole range of issues such as pay, benefits, poverty, health, violence against women and transport. The women's manifestos produced over this period fed into party policy in a number of areas. Labour women's sections were also important in supporting local government women's committees in Scotland and radical local initiatives such as the Zero Tolerance campaign against men's violence against women.

Coming Full Circle . . . Again

However, the relative strength of women's structures was to be short-lived and they were extensively reorganised in 1998 at GB and Scottish levels. Following on from a consultation paper entitled *Building a Healthy Women's Organisation*, women's sections were abolished and replaced with women's forums, which were to be less formal and more accessible than their predecessors. The women's seats on the NEC and SEC were abolished on the grounds that internal party quotas made them redundant. The national (GB) Women's Conference has been amalgamated with the Youth and Local Government conferences and now comprises of some workshop sessions as part of the party's spring conference. There is no longer a Scottish Women's Conference[13] or a Scottish Women's Committee. The changes were ostensibly intended to rejuvenate the structures and make them more open and attractive, as part of the general restructuring of Labour structures and the introduction of policy forums, which is explored elsewhere in this book. However, there is general agreement, from both supporters and critics of the changes, that in practice the women's structures have been down-graded. Indeed, so low profile are the new women's forums that many of our interviewees were under the impression that women's structures had been abolished altogether. Many activists within Scotland see this move as the price paid for winning the argument for twinning in the Scottish Parliament and the extensive programme of party quotas.

Prior to the 1998 reorganisation there were twenty-four women's sections and women's councils in Scotland, one fewer than existed in 1919 (Burness 1992: 156). The current position is that constituency parties must elect a

Women's Officer who may, in turn, establish a women's forum. However the Labour Party in Scotland does not have figures for how many women's forums have been set up nor is there available information in order to evaluate how active or successful women's forums have been at encouraging women's participation, providing training and support for potential women candidates and working with other women's forums to feed the views of women into the policy process. Those women who had been most active in the 1980s and 1990s have been most disappointed with the reorganisation. Some have boycotted the new structures, whilst others have tried to work within them but their initial assessments are largely negative.

The significance of the downgrading of women's structures is subject to differing interpretations. On the one hand, there are fears this has resulted in a shrinking of spaces where women can share experiences and develop a political analysis of gender inequality. Concerns are expressed that there is no longer the organisational base upon which to promote a 'women's agenda'. Finally there is some anxiety that there may be a longer-term impact on the supply of women candidates.

On the other hand, the argument is made that with the successful implementation of internal quotas, women are now visibly integrated into the mainstream, and the role of women's structures is less important. As a Scottish party official noted: 'Regarding the structures, I think you will see the involvement of women at the highest levels of the Scottish Labour Party has shown that the change has not adversely affected women's involvement.'

These debates are ongoing and, in part, relate to whether individuals perceive that such a collective voice and consciousness exists beyond a common concern for equal opportunity of access. Drawing upon our interviews with party activists, generation and political position also appear to be significant factors. In this respect, women who saw themselves as New Labour and younger women tended to be more sanguine about the weakened women's structures – 'women are mainstreamed in the party now', 'the arguments have been won' – than did older women and those who placed themselves on the Left. However, this was not always the case, as illustrated in the concerns of one young, woman activist: 'It will be much, much harder to raise issues and argue a way forward without a women's section; there's just not the right vehicle anymore.'

Conclusions

The last two decades have seen the twin processes of feminisation and modernisation transform the Labour Party. In Scotland these processes have been inextricably linked with the opportunities raised by the campaign for devolution and the engendering of mainstream debates about democracy and participation. The female face of the party provides a visible symbol of this transformation. Through the implementation of internal quotas and special measures for candidates, women have taken their place at the table. They hold key positions in the party hierarchy, in local organisations and in elected bodies. The achievements of the Labour Party are considerable with respect to women and political representation in the Scottish Parliament and they have consistently outperformed their main political rivals. As noted earlier, Labour was the only party to achieve 50:50 in 1999 and it further improved its performance in 2003 when women comprised 56 per cent of Labour MSPs. Despite recent enabling legislation passed by the UK government, only the Labour Party and the Scottish Socialist Party used specific measures in 2003 (both on the lists) (Mackay 2003). To put the party's achievements into perspective, as table 7.3 shows, Labour has over three times as many women MSPs as the next largest party, the SNP.

Table 7.3 Gender composition of the Scottish Parliament, 2003

| Party | Constituency seats | | List seats | | Total | % |
	Men	Women	Men	Women	seats	women
Labour	20	26	2	2	50	**56.0**
SNP	6	3	12	6	27	**33.3**
Conservative	3	0	11	4	18	**22.2**
Lib Democrat	11	2	4	0	17	**11.8**
Green	0	0	5	2	7	**28.6**
Scottish Socialist	0	0	2	4	6	**66.7**
Independent	1	1	1	1	4	50.0
Total	41	32	37	19	129	**39.5**

To be sure, the progress of women is uneven, and there is work to be done. There are still barriers to women's participation, including entrenched sexism in certain sections of the party. There are also issues as to which women get a place at the table: many prominent feminist campaigners, from the Left of the party, failed to be selected to stand as candidates in the 1999 Scottish Parliament elections. Meanwhile, progress on implementing all-women shortlists at Westminster appears to have stalled in Scotland, in the context of boundary changes and the overall reduction of Scottish constituencies.[14] Scottish councils remain male bastions, although positive-action measures may form part of the proposed reform of local government (Fraser 2003).[15] Nevertheless, the party and the party leadership have demonstrated firm commitment to women's political representation. As one female party official put it, 'The political argument on positive action has been won – on the basis of the need for women's talents and the need to be more representative; it is part of the vision.'

Women as individuals have made huge strides forward in terms of gaining a place. However, this has been accompanied by a dilution of women's collective voice in the party. To some observers, the issue of women's representation is no longer viewed as an assertion of collective female identity and allied with a feminist agenda for social change – as was the original vision in the 1980s – but has instead become part of a New Labour modernisation package. In an English context, McRobbie (2000) has called this strategy one of including 'women without feminism'. The Scottish position is more complex. Many Labour women MSPs and female office-holders share feminist sensibilities and are committed to the representation of women in a substantive as well as a descriptive sense. Labour women MSPs are more likely than their counterparts to have connections with women's groups. The responsiveness of women MSPs across the party to the concerns of women can be discerned across a range of policy areas, most notably domestic violence (Brown et al. 2001; Mackay et al. 2003). However, an important channel of communication and line of account-ability has been diminished. History has shown the strategic importance of women's self-organising in developing policies for women, building alli-ances and in developing political careers. Critics of the recent changes doubt whether the next generation of party women, office-holders and elected politicians will be able in the future to build the sort of alliances necessary to sustain campaigns such as 50:50.

NOTES

1. The project *Gender and Constitutional Change* (L21925202333) was funded as part of the Economic and Social Research Council's *Devolution and Constitutional Change* research programme. We draw here on a sub-set of twelve interviews undertaken with Scottish Labour activists, office-holders and officials carried out between 2001 and 2003. Further information about the project can be found at http://www.pol.ed.ac.uk/gcc. Thanks also to Alice Brown and Ann Henderson who provided documents and papers relating to the 1980s and 1990s.
2. There were close links between socialist groups, particularly the ILP and suffrage groups in Glasgow (Smyth 1992; Burness 1992). However, Smyth warns that 'tempting' though it may be to claim a direct connection between pre-war *militant* suffrage activism and the war-time rent strikes, this is not borne out with the exception of Crawfurd (1992: 187).
3. It was to take her another twenty-six years to be selected to fight a winnable seat at Westminster for the Labour Party, taking Kilmarnock in 1945.
4. By 1923 there were 42 women's sections in Scotland and Burness estimates this would

have given the Labour Party in Scotland a female membership of between 1,266 and 8,400 (Burness 1992: 157).

5. Jean Mann was unusual even by contemporary standards as a female politician with a young family of five. She was apparently known as 'haud the wean' Jean and was teased by James Maxton that all over Scotland 'the comrades had to decide who would take the chair, who would lift the collection, and who would "hold her bairn" ' (Mann cited by Burness 1992: 168).

6. All figures supplied by Scottish Labour Party, July 2003, unless otherwise stated.

7. Although the performance of English Labour strongholds such as North and Yorkshire were only marginally better.

8. The twinning mechanism was used to select Labour candidates for all constituencies with the exception of four Highlands and Islands constituencies. See Russell et al. (2002) for more detail.

9. For example, McCrae discusses an informal women's network operating in the late 1980s and early 1980s to support female candidates in the run-up to the 1992 general election (1991: 54–5). A GB-wide support group, Labour Women's Network, was launched in 1988, with Scottish activists involved such as Rhona Brankin. In 1993, the Scottish Labour Women's Caucus was created to promote 'feminist analysis in our policy processes and greater representation for Labour Women at all levels of the Party' (Scottish Labour Women's Caucus, 'Who Are We?', Scottish Conference '94 Conference Briefing). Founding members were Rosina McCrae and Johann Lamont, and Caucus members mentioned in the pamphlet include Jackie Baillie, Marilyn Glen, Esther Quinn, Margaret Curran and Moira Findlay.

10. The Liberal Democrats did not implement special measures, despite this commitment, stating the party feared such action might be illegal. 'They had the poorest gender performance of the main political parties in both 1999 and 2003' (Mackay 2003).

11. This reference to 'troublesome women' comes from press coverage of the time, reported in Scottish Labour Women's Caucas pamphlet (see note above).

12. For example, in 1998, Scottish Conference supported a motion originating from the Scottish Women's Conference, which condemned the then new Labour government's decision to cut lone-parent benefit. This proved to be one of the last opportunities for the collective voice of Scottish Labour women to be raised and heard.

13. The last one appears to have been held in 1998 or 1999, replaced by a Scottish Women's Forum. However, to date, only one has been held (in Stirling in December 2001). A second event has been scheduled for autumn 2003.

14. According to the Scottish Labour Party, it has been exempted, by the NEC, from the UK policy of all-women shortlists in the selections for the next Westminister elections. 'However as we are constantly attempting to increase women's representation, we may look at some of the seats on this basis.' Communication, July 2003.

15. The party's SEC has recently taken a decision to use positive action for the next local government elections through all-women shortlists. This follows a similar decision taken by the NEC regarding the English regions. According to a party official, support for positive discrimination in terms of women in local government also came through strongly in the consultation exercise 'Our Vision for Local Government', which took place between March and August 2002, in a series of very well attended cluster events all around Scotland. Communication, July 2003.

REFERENCES

Bradbury, J., Denver, D., Mitchell, J. and Bennie, L. (2000), 'Devolution and Party Change: Candidate Selection for the 1999 Scottish Parliament and Welsh Assembly', *Journal of Legislative Studies*, 6 (3), pp. 51–72.

Breitenbach, E. and Gordon, E. (eds) (1992), *Out of Bounds: Women in Scottish Society 1800–1945*, Edinburgh University Press, Edinburgh.

Breitenbach, E. and Mackay, F. (eds) (2001), *Women and Contemporary Scottish Politics: An Anthology*, Polygon at Edinburgh, Edinburgh.

Brown, A. (2001a), 'Women and Politics in Scotland', in E. Breitenbach and F. Mackay (eds), *Women and Contemporary Scottish Politics: An Anthology*, Polygon at Edinburgh, Edinburgh, pp. 197–212. (Originally published in *Parliamentary Affairs*, vol. 49, no. 1, 1996.)

Brown, A. (2001b), 'Deepening Democracy: Women and the Scottish Parliament', in E. Breitenbach and F. Mackay (eds), *Women and Contemporary Scottish Politics: An Anthology*, Polygon at Edinburgh, Edinburgh, pp. 213–29. (Originally published in *Regional and Federal Studies*, 8 (1), 1998.)

Brown, A. (2001c), 'Taking their Place in the New House: Women and the Scottish Parliament', in E. Breitenbach and F. Mackay (eds), *Women and Contemporary Scottish Politics: An Anthology*, Polygon at Edinburgh, Edinburgh, pp. 241–47. (Originally published in *Scottish Affairs*, 28, summer.)

Brown, A., Mackay, F. and Myers, F. (2001) 'Making a Difference? Women and the Scottish Parliament', ESRC End of Award Report, posted at http://www.pol.ed.ac.uk/gcc.

Burness, C. (1992), 'The Long Slow March: Scottish Women MPs, 1918–45', in E. Breitenbach and E. Gordon (eds), *Out of Bounds: Women in Scottish Society 1800–1945*, Edinburgh University Press, Edinburgh, pp. 151–73.

Burness, C. (2001), 'A Woman's Place? The Future Scottish Parliament', in E. Breitenbach and F. Mackay (eds) (2001), *Women and Contemporary Scottish Politics: An Anthology*, Polygon at Edinburgh, Edinburgh, pp. 179–94. (Originally published in L. Paterson and D. McCrone (eds) (1992), *The Scottish Government Yearbook 1992*, Unit for the Study of Government in Scotland, University of Edinburgh, Edinburgh.)

Eagle, M. and Lovenduski, J. (1998), *High Time or High Tide for Labour Women?*, Fabian Society, London.

Fraser, D. (2003), 'McConnell now turns on council male bastions', *Sunday Herald*, 1 June 2003.

Gender and Constitutional Change: Transforming Politics in the UK?, web site, http://www.pol.ed.ac.uk/gcc.

Gordon, E. (1991), *Women and the Labour Movement in Scotland 1850–1914*, Clarendon Press, Oxford.

Hughes, A. (1999), ' "The Politics of the Kitchen" and the Dissenting Domestics: The ILP, Labour Women and the Female "Citizens" of Inter-War Clydeside', *Scottish Labour History*, no. 34, pp. 34–51.

Lovenduski, J. (1999), 'Sexing Political Behaviour in Britain', in S. Walby (ed.), *New Agendas for Women*, Macmillan, Basingstoke.

McCrae, R. (1991), 'Women in the Scottish Labour Party', in Woman's Claim of Right Group (ed.), *A Woman's Claim of Right in Scotland*, Polygon, Edinburgh, pp. 47–55.

McDonald, R., Alexander, M. and Sutherland, L. (2001), 'Networking for Equality and a Scottish Parliament: The Women's Co-ordination Group and Organisational Alliances', in E. Breitenbach and F. Mackay (eds), *Women and Contemporary Scottish Politics*, Polygon at Edinburgh, Edinburgh, pp. 231–40.

McRobbie, A. (2000), 'Feminism and the Third Way', *Feminist Review*, 64, pp. 97–112.

Mackay, F. (2003), 'Women and the 2003 Elections: Keeping Up the Momentum', *Scottish Affairs*, 44, summer.

Mackay, F., Meehan, E., Donaghy, T. and Brown, A. (2002), 'Gender and Constitutional Change in Scotland, Northern Ireland and Wales', *Australasian Parliamentary Review*, 17 (2), spring, pp. 35–54.

Mackay, F., Myers, F. and Brown, A. (2003), 'Towards a New Politics? Women and Constitutional Change in Scotland', in A. Dobrowolsky and V. Hart (eds), *Women Making Constitutions*, Palgrave, Basingstoke.

Mitchell, J. (2000), 'New Parliament, New Politics in Scotland', *Parliamentary Affairs*, vol. 53, no. 3.

Perrigo, S. (1996), 'Women and Change in the Labour Party', *Parliamentary Affairs*, vol. 49, no. 1.

Russell, M. (2000), *Women's Representation in UK Politics: What Can Be Done Within the Law?*, The Constitution Unit, University College London, London.

Russell, M., Mackay, F. and McAllister, L. (2002), 'Women's Representation in the Scottish Parliament and National Assembly for Wales: Party Dynamics for Achieving Critical Mass', *Journal of Legislative Studies*, 8 (2), pp. 49–76.

Scottish Labour Party (2003), *Annual Report 2003*, Scottish Labour Party, Glasgow.

Smyth, J. J. (1992), 'Rent, Peace, Votes: Working-Class Women and Political Activity in the First World War', in E. Breitenbach and E. Gordon (eds), *Out of Bounds: Women in Scottish Society 1800–1945*, Edinburgh University Press, Edinburgh, pp. 174–96.

III

Scottish Labour, State, Nation and Autonomy

CHAPTER 8

New Labour, New Parliament

Douglas Fraser

In October 2000, in the week of Donald Dewar's death, Scottish Labour moved to its third headquarters in as many years, using part of the AEEU office on Glasgow's West Regent Street. No longer was it Keir Hardie House, or the corporate chrome temporary accommodation of Delta House. The new office would be called John Smith House.

There was a message being sent out with the location and name of the new home. Here was Scottish Labour living cheek by jowl with a trade union, the very part of the Labour movement from which Tony Blair was distancing himself. And here, with the naming ceremony, was a reminder that Scottish Labour was closer to the values of Tony Blair's predecessor.

That was particularly significant at a time of turf wars between Labour ministers at Westminster and those at the year-old Parliament in Edinburgh. This chapter will argue that with devolution very much the legacy of Blair's predecessor, it created tensions with the Blairite 'project'. While setting up the home rule institutions must be seen as a major constitutional achievement, Labour still managed to inflict damage on itself in selecting those members it wished to have elected to the new Parliament. Three leaders and First Ministers within thirty months, the novelty of coalition government along with external pressures, were to test the inexperienced Labour MSP group. This chapter analyses what went wrong for Labour's selection, some of the things that also went right, and the changes that have been forced on it with the arrival of Scottish home rule. It concludes with the home rule challenges which Scottish Labour faces next.

JOHN SMITH, TONY BLAIR AND UNFINISHED BUSINESS

John Smith had left a number of legacies with his untimely death in 1994. In the light of Blair's revolutionary zeal in reforming the party, it was the

127

devolution project which was the part of that legacy which would stick permanently. John Smith had effectively locked it into the Labour programme for government, and for Blair to have ditched it would have been a disrespect too far, both to Smith's memory and to Scottish Labour voters, who were seen as deserving a reward for keeping the party faith in increasing, tactically voting numbers through eighteen Tory years.

Smith had been a junior minister under Jim Callaghan's premiership, working with Michael Foot on the 1970s devolution project. While the party had been split over devolution, that job associated Smith with the pro-home rule side of the debate, even though there are doubts about him having been a believer before then. By contrast, Neil Kinnock, his predecessor as leader, had been strongly opposed to Welsh home rule in the 1979 referendum campaign and was tetchy when questioned about the project as leader between 1983 and 1992. Kinnock was among those converted to the cause by the experience of watching the exercise of the Thatcher government's untrammelled, large majority power. In opposition, Labour used the argument that devolution would never again allow Scotland to be the test bed for policies such as the poll tax.

By the time of Smith's death, a new generation had risen up the political ladder with a long-held personal commitment to home rule. Foremost among them was Gordon Brown, effectively guardian of Smith's legacy for Scotland. Blair also had an admiration for Donald Dewar, with whom he had shared a Westminster office. Dewar was a close friend of Smith's from Glasgow University debating days, and a pro-devolutionist from the days it had been a marginal concern, treated with strong suspicion by mainstream Scottish Labour under Willie Ross.

In 1993, in his first leader's speech to the Scottish party conference, Smith spoke of his ambition to attend, as a Labour Prime Minister of the UK, the opening day of the Scottish Parliament. A few weeks before his death, at the party's conference in Dundee, he declared that devolution was 'the settled will of the Scottish people' and would be 'the cornerstone of our plans for democratic renewal' in Britain (*The Herald*, 3 June 1994). As leader, Blair could take on the party on Clause Four as a symbolic break with the past. He could even take a chance on imposing a two-question pre-legislative devolution referendum on the party, as he did in July 1996, sparking a furore which should have warned him this was dangerous territory for him. Significant also was that the Scottish Constitutional Convention had locked Labour in with Liberal Democrats on the issue, and Blair at that time was working secretly with Lib Dem leader Paddy Ashdown on his dream of an alliance which would keep Conservatives permanently out of power. Rolling back on devolution would have undermined that project. The fundamentals of Scottish home rule, whatever his doubts about it, were effectively off-limits.

The impact of the Constitutional Convention on shaping Labour's future should not be underestimated. As Shadow Scottish Secretary and therefore Scottish Labour leader, Dewar had in October 1988 committed the party to the Scottish Constitutional Convention with Liberal Democrats, the STUC, church representatives and groups sharing a growing collective consciousness as 'civic Scotland', made up of individuals and institutions which were becoming increasingly anti-Conservative government and, by extension, pro-devolution (Harvie and Jones 2000). Dewar and his successor as Shadow Scottish Secretary, George Robertson, along with McConnell as General Secretary from 1992 to 1998, were getting used to a new type of politics which involved tricky deal-making with a party in opposition to them, and elements within Scotland which required compromise. The agreement to secure proportional voting for the new Parliament was hesitantly approved by a Scottish Labour Party being led into very unfamiliar alliances. So too with the pressure exerted through the Convention which would be important to Labour's adoption of equal representation for women. This was a good training ground for coalition government.

There was another significance behind the choice of West Regent Street as the party's new Scottish headquarters. Here was a signal that, however much Scotland's political and commercial balance was tilting east to Edinburgh, the dominant party was going to keep itself rooted where its heartlands have long been, on the Clyde. This has caused practical problems in the early days of devolution. Under First Ministers Donald Dewar and Henry McLeish, headquarters staff appeared to be in the dark, at fifty miles' distance, about the political messages emanating from St Andrew's and Bute Houses in Edinburgh. But with two former general secretaries in place as First Minister Jack McConnell and Scotland Secretary Helen Liddell, communications between government and party appeared to improve markedly by the 2003 election campaign.

McConnell belonged to a generation and a movement within the party which had allied its loyalties more closely than before to Scottish cultural and political identity and to the home rule cause. He was a leading member of Scottish Labour Action, a group formed in 1988, in the frustrated wake of the 1987 Tory election victory. This was a new generation pushing for modernisation before the Blairites took ownership of that word. From the Scottish Labour Action group, who together had come through the anti-Militant battles as student activists, eight became MSPs, six of them as ministers and four in the Cabinet: Jack McConnell; Susan Deacon; Wendy

Alexander; and Sarah Boyack. They, at least, had the advantage over many others of having known each other for years, though subsequent events were to show that could be a disadvantage. When Jack McConnell went for the leadership in succession both to Donald Dewar and, successfully, to Henry McLeish, those former Scottish Labour Action comrades joined forces to block him. Six months after Jack McConnell became First Minister, none of them were left in the Cabinet.

CAN THE CANDIDATES?

The Tory Government years running up to devolution did much to close down the debate on the issue within Labour. There is a credible argument that Margaret Thatcher did more than anyone to bring about Scottish home rule. Critics remained within, however. Tam Dalyell would continue to argue the plans were 'a motorway to the break-up of Britain without any exits'. Once formed, the Parliament and Executive would take the brunt of off-the-record sniping from Westminster MPs resentful at its powers, profile and pretensions, as in the January 2001 put-down when it was suggested the Executive change its name: 'They can call themselves the White Heather Club if they want, but they will never be the Scottish government' (quoted by Iain Macwhirter, *Sunday Herald*, 12 January 2003). But with the institutions of home rule in place, the debate had moved on. What mattered for Scottish Labour was first who would represent it, then how it would work and what the party would do with it.

The new Parliament brought with it a clean slate for candidacies and the challenge to all the party machines of how to choose those candidates. Labour faced an enviable position of holding fifty-six out of seventy-two constituencies at Westminster, but that meant the stakes were all the higher for Scottish Parliament candidate selection. The choice for the top-up regional lists was of far less importance, at least outside the Highlands and Islands. What was a golden opportunity for Labour, particularly at a time of modernisation, turned out to bring out the worst in it. Because selection processes say much about the ways in which power is distributed within any party, this exposed the tensions the party would prefer hidden. One outcome, as planned, was gender-balanced candidacies and results, which enjoyed widespread support. But in other respects it was mismanaged and it damaged the party internally and in the eyes of the public. At least as significant as those who were elected were those who were not. Realising the danger of unwanted people getting through to constituencies for selection, and that this was a one-off opportunity to shape the Labour group for many years to come, it was decided between London and Glasgow headquarters that control should be exercised by tight control of the list allowed into such constituency selections. This took place against a backdrop of factionalism, which has since faded, and a perception of New Labour as being run by 'control freaks'. It also owed much to the unhappy experience of locally controlled candidate selection, which had reached a low point with a poor-quality candidate in the 1988 Glasgow Govan by-election.

In 1997–8, the party was still embroiled in a series of scandals in Glasgow Govan, Glasgow Council Labour Group, following the suicide of Paisley MP Gordon McMaster in 1997, and with local councils in North Lanarkshire and East Ayrshire beleaguered by mismanaged direct labour organisations. The latter blocked the prospects for two council leaders who wanted to make the transition to the new Parliament. One analysis (Bradbury et al. 2000) asserts that the divisions were along a nationalist–unionist cleavage within the party, which became loosely allied to left–right splits. But the divisions may have been both more complex and cruder, in terms also of a test of loyalty and discipline, of New versus Old Labour, of Blairites versus Brownites. A group known as The Network had been formed to drive the Blairite New Labour agenda in Scotland, in the belief that it faced tougher internal party resistance than in England. One of the foremost Network members was Rosemary McKenna, elected in 1997 as the MP for Cumbernauld and Kilsyth, who would chair the committee vetting candidates for the Scottish Parliament, with Dundee West's Ernie Ross as her deputy. 'The Scottish Parliament has to be different. There's a wealth of new talent coming forward and we are going to choose the best, no matter whose nose may be out of joint,' said McKenna (*Daily Record*, 15 May 1998).

That vetting process was where most of the problems were encountered. It was set up to include five representatives of the Scottish Labour Party Executive, five nominated from the London-based National Executive Committee, five 'experienced party members', along with five independent advisers, including Edinburgh University politics professor Alice Brown, and Nigel Smith, who had chaired the Yes-Yes referendum campaign in 1997. This committee split into sub-groups of four for the interviewing of 208 candidates sifted from the original 500-plus who submitted applications. The form had required a 500-word essay on what they wanted to achieve in the Scottish Parliament and the long-list would be interviewed on their knowledge, experience and commitment, the latter described by disgruntled participants as 'thinly disguised loyalty-test questions'. Only 166 made it to the final approved list, 69 of them women. Either Labour had a shallow talent pool, or it had placed particularly high hurdles in the way of approval. Constituencies were left with little choice. A third of those approved would be elected.

Reports that the process would be used to block several prominent MPs started surfacing in the media in early March 1998, five days after the selection panel first met (*The Herald*, 5 March 1998). Tony Blair's speech at the Scottish Labour conference in Perth that week was interpreted as giving a strong hint that the vetting procedure would be in line with the New Labour project under the guise of quality control: 'This isn't about stopping any particular person – it is about ensuring high-quality candidates. No one has an automatic right to selection. Scotland deserves the best from Labour at local and national level. That is what it will get.' (*Daily Record*, 7 March 1998)

The *Herald*'s initial story may have been a warning to MPs Maria Fyfe and Norman Godman, both named as certain to be barred if they sought an MSP seat. Neither did so, and both stood down from Westminster in 2001. By mid-May, the story of loyalty tests blocking prominent figures moved on in *The Herald*, with pictures of MPs Michael Connarty, Dennis Canavan and Ian Davidson as if mug shots of the condemned (*The Herald*, 13 May 1998). In addition, one of Donald Dewar's friends and special advisers at the Scottish Office, Murray Elder, was reported to be excluded. Denied at the time, the reports turned out to be accurate. Connarty quickly grasped that a knock-back from the vetting panel – saying that he was unsuitable to represent the party and his constituents in the Scottish Parliament – would undermine his claim to represent Labour at Westminster. He withdrew from the process. Ian Davidson kept going, but was not on the final, approved list. He would later attack the criteria used, having faced criticism in his selection panel interview for having gone to the interview informally dressed. This treatment helped alienate him from the Westminster leadership. Whereas he had, as a Strathclyde Region councillor, been at the forefront of Labour's drive for electoral credibility, his rejection turned him into a thorn in the Government's flesh, with his opposition to joining the euro-zone among other issues. As he told *The Herald*:

> One peculiar feeling I have is a sense of liberation, because I now feel free to speak and act any way I wish. Despite never having voted against the Labour whip in six years, I have not made the panel, therefore I need feel no inhibitions now. (15 June 1998)

The selection experience of two left- and nationalist-leaning Labour MPs, Dennis Canavan and John McAllion, was very different. The party gambled on Canavan taking his rejection on the chin, but got it badly wrong. He would go on to stand in Falkirk West as an independent in the 1999 election, winning not only the biggest majority in Scotland but a large share of Central Scotland list votes. John McAllion was reckoned to be a more potent threat in more marginal Dundee East if he were to follow in the direction Canavan was heading. McAllion was allowed through and was later to be useful to the Labour leadership, as a sign of its claimed willingness to tolerate dissent. Meanwhile, Donald Dewar's bad grace in handling Canavan's electoral success kept the Falkirk West MP and MSP at bay until the Labour leader's death in 2000. After that, there were discussions about Canavan coming back into the Labour fold as a means of heading off his threat of forcing an unwanted Westminster by-election, but the talks stalled and the by-election went ahead anyway.

These were only the high-profile MPs. Also omitted from the approved list were several who were well known within the party, whose only reason for disqualification could be that they were too independently-minded or perhaps that they did badly at interview. Excluded were Tommy Sheppard, former deputy general secretary, Esther Roberton and Isobel Lindsay, who had both been able and prominent members of the home rule movement, Jeanne Freeman, who would become Jack McConnell's right-hand woman as special adviser, Susan Deacon, who would get back in on appeal to become the first devolved Health Minister, Elizabeth Maginnis, former Cosla education convener, and Mark Lazarowicz, who may not have been good enough for Holyrood but was later deemed adequate to the task of being Labour's MP for Edinburgh North and Leith. Nigel Smith, an independent member of the selection panel, would later say that he was unaware if some candidates had been steered to appear before particularly tough panels and that there had been no cross-checking between the four panels (*The Herald*, 16 June 1998). Whatever the reason, Tony Blair's promise of 'the best' and a system to select only 'high-quality candidates' came to look suspect when some of those who didn't make it were set against those who did.

On the approved list was the daughter of the woman chairing the selection process, and others with eye-catchingly unorthodox backgrounds for Labour (though they would subsequently fail to become candidates), such as Richard Holloway, Episcopalian Bishop of Edinburgh, Doug Maughan, an airline pilot, and Anwari Din, the only member of an ethnic minority on the approved list. Ian Welsh was held up as an example of business experience (he was Kilmarnock FC chief executive), who fought and won the marginal Ayr seat, only to resign after a few months because he reckoned his talents were not being used.

By the time the battle over Labour's approved list was complete, the fight for candidacies did less damage to internal party relationships or its external perception. One notable exception was in Motherwell and Wishaw, where a tussle between Bill Tynan, a seasoned trade union official, and Jack

McConnell, who had recently resigned as party general secretary, led to a margin in McConnell's favour of only two votes. That left a residue of resentment within the local party which returned to cause him trouble. As McConnell publicly acknowledged after becoming First Minister, dissident elements in the local party leaked information about its fundraising as a means of discrediting the MSP.

Also casualties in this process were several prominent men who fell foul of the twinning arrangements introduced to ensure gender balance, such as Ian Smart and Bob McLean, both leading lights in Scottish Labour Action. The membership strength of Midlothian's twin seat, East Lothian, was such that incumbent MP John Home Robertson would secure that candidacy, meaning Midlothian had to go to a female candidate and not Bob McLean who could expect it otherwise. So too with Smart in Cumbernauld and Kilsyth, twinned with Strathkelvin and Bearsden, which was always going to win Sam Galbraith the most votes on the men's side of the ballot. At a time when Labour in England was running scared of a legal challenge to women-only shortlists for candidates, and the Welsh twinning process was in trouble, there was privately some consideration of legal action to challenge the twinning process, but it came to nothing. There remained grumblings in some seats about having female MPs whom party members would prefer not to have, but the threat of deselection for the 2003 election only came close to unseating Glasgow Rutherglen's Janis Hughes. The twinning process soon gained a perception as having successfully achieved what was intended. And because it was men who suffered the brunt of the 2003 knock-back at the polls, women were left in the majority within the Labour group in the second Parliament, having twenty-eight out of Labour's fifty seats.

One consequence of the selection war was to create a media-fuelled public perception of Labour control-freakery which did much to ensure Dennis Canavan's electoral success in Falkirk West. The reporting in the media was of a Blairite purge. Tom Brown in the *Daily Record* referred to Scotland's new scientific breakthrough when he called the Parliament 'Dollywood', full of cloned, sheep-like MSPs without minds of their own: 'Enemies within are using the rigorous New Labour selection process for the parliament to fuel fears that it is giving birth to a flock of lookalikes and think-alikes' (*Daily Record*, 15 May 1998). In the twenty months between overwhelming media support for devolution at the time of the referendum and the powerfully negative reporting of the first parliament once elected, the media and public mood changed. Contempt for future MSPs was being sown early, not least because of Labour's tactics.

It was not only the media and public who disapproved of the process. An academic survey of those approved for the Labour list – both successful and unsuccessful in the selection system – subsequently found that a quarter of them found the system for selecting the panel and then selecting constituency candidates to be undemocratic. Nearly a third thought the constituency candidate selection to be unfair. Fully 83 per cent thought the regional list candidate selection was undemocratic and 76 per cent thought it unfair. The sense of dissatisfaction was felt as strongly by those who made it as candidates as it was among those who aspired and failed. And that does not include the dissatisfaction which can be expected from those not even allowed onto the list and not included in the survey (Bradbury et al. 2000).

The blocking of Westminster MPs meant a significant lack of experience coming north. Only six of Labour's fifty-six MPs risked the selection process successfully – Donald Dewar, Sam Galbraith, Henry McLeish, John McAllion, Malcolm Chisholm and John Home Robertson – while all six SNP MPs made the switch. McLeish in Central Fife was slow to decide, publicly hesitating while he talked with the Prime Minister and Chancellor over his prospects as a minister in Whitehall (*The Herald*, 2 March 1998). Other MPs would later complain that, although they had talked to Dewar about it, he refused to ease their way into the Scottish Parliament with any assurances of jobs if they risked moving north, or even his support in winning their own constituency selection. In any case, their experience and seniority might not have carried them far: after the second set of elections in 2003, Malcolm Chisholm and John Home Robertson would be the only former Labour MPs still sitting as Labour MSPs.

Dewar, in particular, was not given to such conspiracies, and may have been over-keen to avoid charges of cronyism, which had become commonplace within the Scottish party. But one outcome of that decision would be a defining characteristic of the Labour group that would be elected to Holyrood: it owed little to its leader. There was respect and affection for him, but in seeking to avoid those charges of being a control freak, he therefore lacked control. Dewar did little to shape an experienced and loyal team with which to lead the transition to devolution. Sam Galbraith, as pre-devolution Health Minister, was the closest colleague moving with him, while Wendy Alexander was a special adviser and loyalist who won a berth in Paisley North. Murray Elder, another special adviser, tried but did not even make it to the approved list. Lord John Sewel, then a Scottish Office minister, was also politically close to Dewar and made it to the approved party list, but Dewar either did not try or could not succeed in securing him a candidacy in his Aberdeen base, where he had been council leader.

The only MSP who would owe his position to Dewar would be Peter Peacock, who had been leader of Highland Council's ruling independent group, and who had toyed with running as an independent for Parliament.

Dewar's influence swung it for him to join Labour in 1998, and secure top position on the regional Highlands and Islands' Labour list. The leader also forced through Glasgow advocate Brian Fitzpatrick as second choice after Dewar on the Glasgow top-up list, though he was not elected from that position, instead being appointed Dewar's head of policy. Overall, however, the result was a First Minister elected in May 1999 who knew remarkably little of the group from which he would pick his ministerial team.

The group which gathered in early May 1999 on the steps beside John Knox's statue – including Labour's new 'monstrous regiment of women', as the Protestant preacher had it – was the result of a strange process of selection. Was this the Dollywood of clones? On-message cronies? The result of a conspiracy and ruthless purge? Yes. And no. An attempt had clearly been made to sift out those whose faces did not fit. In some cases it worked, yet other awkward elements got through. Left-wingers might not be of the most rebellious variety, but they would become prominent. And apart from a few voices, the group as a whole would distance Scottish Labour in the Scottish Parliament from the Blairite modernising agenda in Whitehall. If there was an attempt at a secret purge to get top-quality, on-message candidates, it was not a very good one – both because it failed to achieve the desired result, and because it was not very secret.

PLUGGING IN TO POWER

The results on 6 May 1999 were good for Labour. Of the fifty-six out of seventy-two constituencies they held at Westminster, they won fifty-three in the Scottish Parliament, topped up by three regional seats from the Highlands and Islands. That pattern was to have a significant effect on the group in the first Parliament: a frustration about list MSPs from other parties encroaching on constituency business, quickly manifested by voting them lower allowances. Because so few Labour MSPs depended on proportional voting for their seats – after the 2003 election, there were four out of fifty – they were less likely to sympathise with Lib Dem demands that councils also have voting reform.

The most striking novelty about the new group was that it was 50 per cent female. It was also, inevitably, inexperienced. Many were little known to each other. An assessment of their backgrounds (Shephard et al. 2001), comparing them with MPs, found them to be relatively young, averaging 45 on first being elected in 1999, and five years younger than the average Scottish MP. But they were five years older, on average, than MPs at the time of MPs being first elected, and the academics warned of an effect from the same intake growing older and staying in place together, without space for newcomers.

More significant for Labour was the background of its new MSPs. The research found that they had only two out of fifty-six new members (3.6 per cent) who were from the traditional blue-collar/industrial background that was the traditional base for the party. That compares with 25 per cent of Scottish Labour MPs, with a further 39.3 per cent of the Westminster group defined as having trade union careers.

Of Labour MSPs, the dominant career paths were from education (37.5 per cent), social welfare/health (23.2 per cent), trade unions (21.4 per cent) and equal numbers from finance/business and from local government (19.6 per cent). While 10.7 per cent had been MPs, 41.1 per cent had been local councillors – a factor which would have a significant impact on the 'municipalist' style with which the group tended towards (or was whipped into) group cohesion. That recruitment from the ranks of councillors was also significant in depriving local authorities of some of their most able leaders. The public sector dominance among MSPs led to criticism that the Parliament generally lacked an understanding of commerce and business.

For the Labour group, the 1999 election led them into new territory, requiring them to forge a new identity, and a new role within the party as well as the new Parliament. There were two obvious but no less significant effects for Labour. One, which had been anticipated in the 1999 election campaign, was that its main opponent across much of Scotland, the SNP, had a new platform, thirty-five representatives, and a level of state-funded support staffing which represented a major lift from the party's previously meagre resourcing. The SNP's status as main opposition party meant a new parliamentary fault line from the one with which Labour was familiar at Westminster.

The other key effect was that Labour had to look to at least one other party for support if it was to win votes. The naturals for that were the sixteen Liberal Democrats, having worked with Labour in the Constitutional Convention and sharing a commitment to making devolution work. Jim Wallace, the party leader since 1992, knew Dewar well from the Commons. He would speak later of the first coalition talks casting the Lib Dems as supplicants (*Sunday Herald*, 11 May 2003). Labour's programme was already in place since its 1997 election win, there was momentum behind the reforms being driven by the pre-devolution team, and the only question was what extra had to be done to secure Lib Dem support. That was how Lib Dems first required abolition of up-front student tuition fees, which had only just been introduced by Westminster for the whole of the UK. Here was the first sign of how the electoral arithmetic from devolution was going

to drive Scottish government in different directions from the UK administration, creating tensions with other parts of the Labour movement. It led
to awkward questions for Labour ministers at Westminster about how they
could justify Scots having a less onerous student finance regime. But that
was what could be expected of devolution: Scots choosing their own
priorities.

Much more tension was caused in late 2000 into early 2001 over long-
term care of the elderly. Dewar had agreed, weeks before his death, to pursue
the same line as Whitehall, in a partial implementation of the Sutherland
report into long-term care, to which Lib Dem partners also agreed. But on
taking over, Henry McLeish indicated that he aspired to go further. Once
the issue was open again, Lib Dems decided this time to push Labour to full
implementation. The means by which that could be achieved were at times
chaotic, particularly when it became clear that McLeish faced the opposition of key members of his own Labour Cabinet team. While splitting his
own party, McLeish got his way. But one price Labour paid was that its
disarray would hand credit for the policy to Lib Dems, who were proving
adept at attaching their names to populist measures while Labour was slow
to do so. Only with the rise of McConnell to the premiership did Labour
move to claim policies for itself rather than the two-party Executive, most
notably in tackling youth crime.

So the first tensions were, predictably, between the Labour-led coalition
in Edinburgh and Labour in government in Westminster. Further tensions
would erupt involving other layers of the party after the 2003 election, when
Lib Dems forced their Labour partners into acceptance of voting reform for
local councils. Labour policy, against such a reform, had been reinforced
during a party consultation over the previous year, but McConnell's arm was
forced by parliamentary arithmetic which showed that if he defied the Lib
Dems, he would be leader of a minority administration and yet still lose out
on the policy. Most Labour council leaders were incensed, their spokesman
threatening a 'four-year war' over the issue, while there was anger also at the
new partnership agreement encroaching on several areas of council responsibility. Scottish Labour MPs at Westminster were also angered that they
were being forced to abandon party policy, particularly when it was because
of Lib Dem leverage, and there was talk of Labour MSPs facing deselection
challenges if they voted for electoral reform.

It would be wrong to overlook the significance of Labour having three
leaders and First Ministers in the first four years of devolution. That created
instability, plus a high turnover of ministers and of special advisers. Donald
Dewar's death helped the group to bond more closely, while other events
helped Labour MSPs adopt a bunker mentality against the media in

particular. For example, there was the experience of Jack McConnell through the Lobbygate inquiry into newspaper allegations concerning his former lobbying company. Others included Wendy Alexander's problems over repealing Section 28/2A banning teachers from 'promoting' homosexuality; Sam Galbraith at bay over the meltdown in the Scottish Qualifications Authority; and Henry McLeish's political demise over his 'muddle, not a fiddle' in sub-letting his constituency office. The frequent sense of crisis in the first two years could have torn the group apart, but seemed instead to bind it more closely together.

Its voting record was remarkably cohesive, probably owing much to the high value placed on loyalty in the selection process, but perhaps also due to the first chief whip, Tom McCabe, the Hamilton South MSP, whose demeanour was not one given to indulgence of those colleagues with rebellious spirits. He came from a municipalist experience, where the practice is of councillor groups reaching common lines collectively and binding every member, unlike the Westminster tradition where ministers agree a common line, and expect back-benchers to follow it, while leaving room for dissent.

Some commentators are particularly scathing of this mindset, telling a story of devolution which is a battle between new, enlightened politics and a descent into small-minded, parochial factionalism with which Labour in its West of Scotland strongholds has become synonymous. Iain Macwhirter has written of the rise of McConnell to the party leadership and his subsequent reshuffle as:

> an exercise in the crudest form of council factionalism. It was a Lanarkshire lock-out, the kind of politics that flourishes in the badlands of Labour local government in west central Scotland. The summary execution of five out of six of the original Labour ministerial team established by Donald Dewar was a numpty purge which cast Jack McConnell in a new paranoid light. (Macwhirter 2002: 31)

Ross Martin, a one-time Labour councillor, argues that the mindset required for local government lacks the big-picture skills of the next level up:

> Many of our first crop of MSPs came from a municipalist background with a dominant culture of local politicians acting as, for a host of historical reasons, nothing much more than 'political clerks of works', dealing in a very direct way to ensure that a constituent's problem is sorted. Moving up to the strategic level was always going to be a challenge for many. (Martin 2003)

That strand of criticism of Labour has been largely from outside, and mainly in the media. It is one which has had little impact on the MSP group, though the early stages of the second Parliament in 2003 showed signs that local government in particular could expect a tougher, more reformist approach to it from the Executive. Concerns inside the parliamentary group have been more about ministers being remote, over-protected by civil servants, and failing to consult. Mike Watson, MSP for Glasgow Cathcart, noted in his record of devolution's first year that this made for tense group meetings, citing one time when SNP MSPs found out about a concession to the Section 28/2A anti-repeal campaigners before Labour MSPs were informed (Watson 2001). Such problems tended to be sorted out in private. There were periods in the first Parliament when formal back-bench liaison mechanisms were tried, but without lasting. Only with the partnership agreement of May 2003 did the Lib Dems force on Labour a new way of working, drawing back-bencher representatives into consultation with ministers at a much earlier stage than Labour MSPs had been used to. Only occasionally did disagreements within the Labour group break into the open through media reporting. The experience of the Parliament and the Executive in hostile media coverage meant that many Labour MSPs preferred not to be seen mixing with journalists. The Black and White Corridor of the temporary Parliament would fill up at times with spin doctors and opposition MSPs briefing journalists, but the only Labour MSPs likely to pass through it were those on their way to the customary location for a mid-debate cigarette.

Committees offered a platform for MSPs to distance themselves from party leaders, as Andy Kerr did while convener of the Transport and Environment Committee, voicing strong criticism of the Executive's policy of contracting out two, large, trunk-roads maintenance contracts. The new committee system was intended to be different from Westminster, and the extent to which it has achieved that much has been widely under-appreciated. Policy is increasingly driven by the committees' in-built tendency towards finding consensus, pushing both the Executive and parties' manifesto-writers onto common ground. This was the means by which the only significant defeat of the first term was inflicted on the Executive front-benchers, as a result of a bill introduced and piloted by Tommy Sheridan, leader of the Scottish Socialist Party, which was to abolish poindings and warrant sales. Ministers argued against it, but did not reckon on the effect of Labour MSPs sitting in committee, who had heard the arguments in favour of the bill, backed it in three committees which had considered the evidence, found themselves pulled to the left by the presence of the SSP, and rebelled against the Labour whip on the crucial vote in April 2000. An unnamed Labour MSP was quoted as explaining the vote:

140

This was a line drawn in the sand. People here in Scotland are more rooted in traditional Labour. Traditional Labour was saying to New Labour, 'No, we're not doing that.' It was a poverty issue and a class issue. The new dynamic of this parliament is that if the committees hang together, they can be effective. (*The Herald*, 27 April 2000)

That was a warning to ministers of the leverage committees could give to swing back-benchers against ministerial positions. But it was exceptional. MSPs were all at the start of their Scottish Parliament careers, many wanting to win preferment and get ahead. Left-winger John McAllion, with twelve years' experience of Westminster and little hope of ministerial office, was the only Labour MSP with the confidence to be a regular rebel, but his style was not to gather support and lead a left-wing faction. His revolts were usually joined by only one or two others, and the problems he caused the leadership disappeared with the loss of his seat to the SNP in the 2003 election. For others who had aligned themselves with the Left, the cohesion of a potential faction was weakened by several of those who could have taken leadership roles being drawn into ministerial responsibility, particularly with Jack McConnell's reshaping of the Cabinet in November 2001. Indeed, the Left itself was not as it has been in the Westminster parliamentary party, not least because of the selection process. Rather than an ideological Left, there is a less rigid outlook which can be called 'community Left', made up of people, many of them women, whose radicalism is based on their experience of living and working in deprived communities and is perhaps more pragmatic than the traditional Left. That different dynamic of the SPLP was shown with the creation of a deputy group leader's post in November 2000, which went uncontested to then back-bencher and later Cabinet minister Cathy Jamieson, who had been aligned both with the traditional Left and, as a social worker and children's services campaigner, with that community Left outlook. Her new role demonstrated that women could demand such senior posts for their own (male MSPs recognised unquestioningly that the post would go to a woman), that the hierarchy was less formal than Westminster in that the deputy's post did not go to a minister, and that the control-freak days were over when such an established Leftist could be allowed to hold such a post.

By the end of the first four years, a new rebellious dynamic was becoming clearer – one which is commonplace at Westminster. MSPs who had served as ministers and left or lost their jobs had combined elements of resentment, frustration, experience, profile and independence to make problems for the ministerial team. Former Health Minister Susan Deacon was one of those to rebel against the party line on the lead-up to war in Iraq, in February 2003. Even though it was not a devolved issue, it demonstrated her ability to rally dissenting MSPs. Jackie Baillie, sacked by McConnell as Social Justice Minister, did likewise in forcing the pace of charity law reform immediately after the 2003 election.

DEVOLUTION'S LABOUR PAINS

So what has been Scottish Labour's experience of devolution? The Parliament has created a new focus of power within the party, just as it has within Scotland. The leader's position in particular is strengthened by being directly elected, as Donald Dewar was, unopposed, in September 1998, giving him a legitimacy only shared with the leader and deputy leader at Westminster. The Labour leader has a government to head, which requires compromise with his coalition partner, forcing the centralised London leadership and headquarters to loosen their grip. The turf wars between John Reid, as first post-devolution Scotland Secretary, and Donald Dewar, when he was First Minister, are reduced now that the role of Scotland Secretary has been downgraded. The leader of the Scottish Parliament Labour Group is now the dominant figure within Scottish Labour, having no need to court the approval either of the Prime Minister or other big beasts in the Whitehall Cabinet, such as Chancellor Gordon Brown.

A realisation this was likely may have been behind the concerns in Westminster at what devolution could bring. As Bradbury et al. suggest, there may have been a fear that a genie was being released from the devolution bottle, enhancing the conservatism of the 1998 selection processes, but, as they argue, it 'clearly backfired. The façade of enlightened central approval panels and the democratisation of selection was too thin to mask the machinations going on behind.' (Bradbury et al. 2000) The same lesson of relaxing central control was learned a much harder way in Wales, with the replacement of Tony Blair's imposed choice for First Secretary, Alun Michael, by Rhodri Morgan, whom the Prime Minister had opposed. Blair's approach to the London mayoral election backfired even more embarrassingly. The party would do well to remember these lessons when setting up regional assemblies in England.

The selection process did the party and Parliament a great disservice, coming at a time of heightened factionalism, excluding some of the more able activists from candidacies, and thus diminishing the Parliament's potential to develop an innovative style of politics. What Scottish Labour has yet to address is how to revisit its candidate selection, both to winnow out under-performers and also to open up opportunity for others. Only one constituency MSP was forced out during the reselection process ahead of 2003 – Henry McLeish, because he was under the cloud of a police investigation. The party also needs to address its system for prioritising its regional list candidates. That has not been taken particularly seriously, as so few are elected from them, but it will become more important if, as seems likely, Labour comes to depend more heavily on having its MSPs returned from those lists. It needs, at least, to revisit the party's self-imposed rule which is supposed to ban candidates from standing for both constituencies and regional lists. There were several exceptions to the rule in 2003, one of them leading to Richard Baker being elected as a North East Scotland list MSP, and the party may come to regret applying the rule elsewhere if it unnecessarily loses them one of the party's more senior figures.

The traditional background of blue-collar/industrial career paths of Labour's representatives have all but disappeared in the Scottish Parliament, in contrast with the Scottish Labour group at Westminster. However, the Labour group has become a new forum for women to flex their muscle within the party. Their impact is still becoming clear, but shows signs of a more community-orientated approach to politics. Anecdotal evidence also suggests the high proportion of women provides a base from which they exercise a significant loyalty to each other. The drive to gender balance in representation is being taken forward at council level. However, Labour has not addressed one of the inadvertent results of success: if positive discrimination can be used with such successful results for women, why not for other groups, starting with ethnic minorities?

The selection process created a cautious and loyal group, notable for being cohesive in its voting. They could have been weakened by the crises and two changes of leadership within three years, but appear instead to have been strengthened. Dissent, rebellion and independent-mindedness have been slow to emerge, though the power of the committees has offered a vehicle for divergence from the ministerial line. A high turnover of ministers in the early years has led to a problem for the leadership – one which is familiar in Westminster – of having to contend with back-benchers who have little reason to maintain loyalty.

Perhaps the most interesting and significant devolution dynamic for Scottish Labour has been the changing way it relates to its opponents in other parties. The Parliament has opened up informal links and friendships between MSPs, and requires members to work more closely together than Labour has been used to doing before – not only with Lib Dem coalition partners but with Nationalists and Tories whose committee posts give them a new locus in policy. That is being mirrored in local councils. Whereas Labour had majority control of twenty out of thirty-two councils when the unitary authorities were first elected in 1995, that has fallen to fifteen, some on knife-edge majorities, forcing the party in much of Scotland to work in a variety of coalitions and partnerships. No more than five councils are likely to remain in (narrow) majority Labour control after 2007, under the Executive's proposed single transferable vote system.

This process was begun through the Scottish Constitutional Convention, and ever since Donald Dewar in 1988 gambled on 'living a little danger-ously', his party has gradually lost its dominance of Scottish politics through both concessions and erosion of its base at the ballot box. It now rules only with the agreement of the Liberal Democrats, who have forced Labour to accept that its role in local council politics will be dramatically altered from the next election. It sits in a Parliament which has seven parties represented, six of them in significant blocs. In 2003, it lost six seats to its three main rival parties plus an independent hospital campaigner. As *The Guardian* concluded in a post-election editorial in 2003, 'The idea of Labour hegemony in Scotland has been blown to the winds . . . the old ways are weakening' (20 May 2003).

So having achieved the goal of Scottish home rule for which Keir Hardie argued, and which had split the party in the 1970s, what next? The results of the 2003 election suggest that Labour's wish that devolu-tion would stop the momentum of nationalism may be coming true. Now it faces new questions. How does it refresh itself, its representatives and its membership while adjusting to its reduced dominance of Scottish politics? How should it continue aligning itself with Scottish identity in a way it successfully did in the 1980s and 1990s? How distinctive and different does it wish to become in policy terms from Labour at Westminster? Does the electoral success and continuing threat from the far left and Greens mean it should fight to its left? How does it handle the inevitable challenges of having to amend the reserved and devolved powers set out in the Scotland Act? How does it handle the equally likely move to a new, needs-based assessment of Scotland's share of UK Government spending? And, most intriguing for the development of devolution, how will it respond when it does not have the lead in both Edinburgh and London, whether it be a Conservative-run Westminster or a Scottish Executive controlled by its opponents?

While responsibility for the content is that of the writer, thanks go, for their advice and help, to MSPs and others in the Scottish Labour Party, plus Professor Lindsay Paterson and Dr Nicola McEwan of Edinburgh University.

REFERENCES

Bradbury, J., Mitchell, J., Bennie, L. and Denver, D. (2000), 'Candidate Selection, Devolution and Modernisation: The Selection of Labour Party Candidates for the 1999 Scottish Parliament and Welsh Assembly Elections', in P. Cowley, D. Denver, A. Russell and L. Harrison (eds), *British Elections and Party Review*, vol. 10, pp. 151–72.

Harvie, C. and Jones, P. (2000), *The Road to Home Rule*, Polygon at Edinburgh, Edinburgh.

Macwhirter, I. (2002), 'The New Scottish Political Classes', in G. Hassan and C. Warhurst (eds), *Anatomy of the New Scotland: Power, Influence and Change*, Mainstream, Edinburgh, pp. 27–36.

Martin, R. (2003), *Social Democratic Soup – the New Scotch Broth?*, background paper for the Scottish Forum for Modern Government, Edinburgh.

Shephard, M., McGarvey, N. and Cavanagh, M. (2001), 'New Scottish Parliament, New Scottish Parliamentarians?', *Journal of Legislative Studies*, vol. 7, no. 2, summer 2001.

Watson, M. (2001), *Year Zero: An Inside View of the Scottish Parliament*, Polygon, Edinburgh.

Chapter 9

Scottish Labour and British Politics

Iain McLean

Scottish Labour and British Politics: Awkward Partners

Ever since Keir Hardie won 617 votes in Mid-Lanark in 1888, Scottish Labour and British politics have been intertwined. Ramsay MacDonald wrote as follows to Hardie from the offices of the Scottish Home Rule Association, for which he worked. It was the first letter between the two Scots co-founders of the Labour Party.

> I cannot refrain from wishing you God-speed in your election contest . . . The powers of darkness – Scottish newspapers with English editors . . . , partisan wire-pullers, and other etceteras of political squabbles – are leagued against us. But let the consequences be what they may, do not withdraw. *The cause of Labour and of Scottish Nationality* will suffer much thereby. Your defeat will awaken Scotland, and your victory will re-construct Scottish Liberalism. (Quoted in Stewart 1921: 40; my emphasis)

The cause of Labour and of Scottish Nationality. Would that be one cause, or two? In 1888, MacDonald thought they were one. So, probably, did Hardie. The first generation of Scottish Labour politicians were instinctive nationalists. The Red Clydesider George Buchanan promoted a Scottish Home Rule Bill in 1924, and the non-Red but Labour MP the Rev. James Barr promoted another in 1928. But the same George Buchanan went on to become the first chairman of the National Assistance Board after World War II. The same James Barr, in the same year, was one of the Scottish MPs who formed the Commons majority to throw out the proposed Church of England Prayer Book.

National Assistance was a UK-wide programme, where benefits entirely depended on how poor an applicant was, not where she lived. This was the model for Labour's approach to health and welfare spending from the first

Labour government in 1924 until, at least, the grant of devolution to Scotland and Wales in 1998. Some of Labour's most egalitarian politicians have been her most anti-devolutionist. Above all, Aneurin Bevan was bitterly hostile to any devolution to his native Wales or any other part of the UK, on the grounds that devolution would interfere with the tax and expenditure transfers needed to establish a truly National Health Service.

As to the Rev. James Barr, there is no evidence that he thought through the delicious inconsistency of his position. Not many purely English matters come before the House of Commons, but the Church of England Prayer Book was one such. It was none of Scottish MPs' business. But the House of Commons defeated a measure that the majority of English MPs who voted supported. It was defeated twice. Certainly on the first occasion, and probably on the second as well, the net number of votes against from Scottish, Welsh, and Northern Irish MPs exceeded the margin of defeat. Barr demonstrated by his actions that what became known as the West Lothian Question when Tam Dalyell MP (then for West Lothian) raised it persistently in the 1970s long pre-existed Tam Dalyell. I return to the West Lothian Question below.

Hardie, MacDonald and Barr were nationalists partly because all Scots have been nationalists of a sort since a separate national, compulsory, education system was created beginning in the 1870s. Scottish education has always differed from English. The famous promise in the 1707 Act of Union to protect Scottish universities is not there because the Scots feared that some future Funding Council would demand a uniform research assessment exercise. It is there because the universities produced ministers, and ministers must continue free to teach Presbyterian truth. In the eighteenth century, Presbyterian truth implied Roman Catholic error. The assimilation of Catholic education in the Education (Scotland) Act 1918 is therefore remarkable, and has not been studied as much as it should have been. Its effect was that there arose two publicly funded educational systems in Scotland, each of them free to develop its own brand of cultural nationalism. In the 1960s, when I sat at the next desk to Robin Cook at the Royal High School, we learnt how Scots, wha had wi Wallace bled (Scots, wham Bruce had aften led), were welcome to their gory bed, or to victorie. From such a schooling it was hard to emerge untouched by cultural nationalism.

Consider the careers of Labour's two outstanding Scottish politicians – outstanding in Scotland, I mean – namely Tom Johnston and Donald Dewar. Both were bitter and effective enemies of Scottish Nationalism. Before World War II, Johnston founded the London Scots Self-Government Committee 'with the aim of converting the [Labour] Party to the need for Scottish Home Rule and producing a scheme which would reconcile this with the planned economy' (Keating and Bleiman 1979: 126). But being a Home Ruler did not make him a political nationalist. He used the (alleged) Scottish Nationalist threat as a lever to prise substantial extra public spending per head for Scotland throughout the Churchill wartime government. Similarly, Dewar spiked the SNP's guns with the Scotland Act 1998. But after 1945, Johnston turned down all manner of UK or international posts to become chairman of the 'Hydro Board' (the North of Scotland Hydro-Electric Board) – and get his long-delayed revenge on the Highland lairds he had denounced in *Our Scots Noble Families* (Johnston 1909). Dewar, an expert on the Scottish Colourists and the Highland Clearances, turned out not to have a passport when, as shadow Scottish Secretary, he first had to go abroad. Johnston and Dewar were alike cultural nationalists but political unionists.

Ever since 1924, then, Scottish Labour politicians have had to resolve the tensions between their Scottishness and their Labourness. Some have been tempted to resolve it in a Gramscian way. Could Scotland be a red base, an outpost of socialism (as Antonio Gramsci hoped for Turin) in a capitalist world? At different times, but especially the eras of 'Red Clydeside' (1914–31) and now, it has been commonplace to argue that Scottish socialism is well to the left of British socialism. Hence, a socialist Scotland would stand to the left of a less socialist (perhaps a New Labour) UK.

The evidence base for the Gramscian strategy is weak. I have long argued that, for the most part, Red Clydeside was pale pink (McLean 1999). Although my views remain controversial, I have not seen an evidence-based case against them. There were certainly some socialist revolutionaries on the Clyde during World War I, and some robust, or panicky, government repression of them. But their mass support arose from day-to-day grumbles about rents, working conditions, or housing. There is no strong evidence that Scottish Labour voters, or Scottish Labour MPs, were more left-wing *en bloc* than English Labour voters, or English Labour MPs. After four years of wartime excitement, Glasgow produced a lower Labour vote in the 1918 general election than English working-class cities.

For more recent years, there is survey evidence comparing the views of the Scottish public with those of the UK public as a whole. Journalists and politicians often claim that the Scottish people are more left-wing, or more sympathetic to Scottish nationalism, than the British people as a whole. In the mid-1990s, William Miller and colleagues undertook a massive research study to test this hypothesis. Their results (Miller et al. 1996) give it no support at all. Table 9.1 summarises their results. Like all other researchers who have studied the question from survey evidence, Miller and associates conclude that differences between Scottish and general British social attitudes are minuscule.

Table 9.1 Differences between Scottish and British political attitudes

Subject	Average British score	Average Scottish score	Difference
Liberty	−25	−25	0
Equality	55	61	+6
Respect for authority	39	39	0
Respect for traditional values	37	39	+2
Wealth creation	53	58	+5
Tolerance	3	2	−1
Limited government	1	1	0
Right to speak out	35	34	−1
Right to protest and rebel	31	35	+4
Self-reliance	13	9	−4
Economic equality	46	53	+7
Caring	79	84	+5
Equal rights	40	45	+5
Protection	53	52	−1
Right to know	87	90	+3

Source: Adapted from Miller et al. (1996), table 11.1. The scores summarise answers to a large number of attitude questions (for question wording see Miller et al. 1996, pp. 480–98). A positive value means support for the property shown. The range of possible scores is from −100 to +100.

So where did the idea that the Scots were more left-wing than the English come from? As recently as the 1955 general election, the Conservatives won more votes, and more seats, in Scotland than did Labour. A tradition of working-class authoritarianism, allied to anti-Irish and anti-Catholic xenophobia, probably accounts for Scotland's pro-Conservative deviance until then. Since 1959, Conservative fortunes in Scotland have rapidly declined. However, table 9.1 shows that this cannot be because Scotland is more socialist than England. Rather, it can be put down to Labour's success in capturing the cultural nationalist vote, and portraying the Conservatives, especially during the Thatcher era, as anti-Scottish. The Labour vote in Scotland is a product of weak cultural nationalism rather than of strong socialism.

It is also true that Scotland has supplied many of the leaders of the Labour (and Communist) left: from James Maxton and William Gallacher in the 1920s to Tommy Sheridan MSP now. But their brightness in the socialist sky has always hidden the dimmer light of the much larger number of

Labour politicians who were not distinctively left-wing. There really is no evidence for the claim, however often it is made, that Scottish Labour politics is to the left of British Labour politics.

Are they more separatist? That is trickier. Socialist devolutionists should find Nye Bevan a hard nut to crack. Bevan wanted the National Health Service to be a truly national command-and-control service – reportedly saying that if a bedpan were dropped in Tredegar the Minister ought to know. Such a vision is incompatible with Welsh (or Scottish) devolution. Why then have so many Scottish Labour politicians, from Keir Hardie to the present day, welcomed home rule or devolution for Scotland? To answer that, I take a detailed look at the most dramatic year in Scottish Labour's history, 1974. I then enquire how far Scottish Labour and national (especially Labour) politics need each other, concluding with an analysis of the two points where the shoe has always pinched: representation at Westminster and financing public services in Scotland.

The Dalintober Street Devolutionists

The Scottish National Party (SNP) first gave Labour a really nasty shock in November 1967, when Winifred Ewing took the safest Labour seat in Scotland at the Hamilton by-election. In response, Prime Minister Harold Wilson set up the Royal Commission on the Constitution: a characteristically Wilsonian device to appear to be doing something without committing himself to anything. In the 1970 general election, the threat seemed to subside: Ewing lost Hamilton and the SNP's only consolation was to snatch the Western Isles in the very last (and smallest) seat to declare. The Royal Commission under Lord Kilbrandon reported in 1973, recommending devolved assemblies for Scotland and Wales. By then the SNP was rising fast again, because it had discovered its most effective slogan ever: 'It's Scotland's Oil . . . '. One version of the poster, featuring a haggard-looking old lady, went on: 'so why do 50,000 people in Scotland a year die from hypothermia?'. International lawyers gravely disputed whether it was in fact Scotland's oil. Should Scotland declare independence, the international boundary would run north-east, not due east, from Berwick-upon-Tweed, thus putting a third of the North Sea oilfields into the English sector. Another third was off Shetland, which was then making the same demands for separation from Scotland that the SNP was making for separation from England. These subtleties did not spoil a great slogan. The SNP won another by-election in 'safe Labour' Govan within a week of Kilbrandon reporting.

Labour politicians started to panic. At this point, there were few principled devolutionists in the national party, although one influential one was the Oxford academic Norman Hunt (Lord Crowther-Hunt), a member of the Kilbrandon Commission who was to be Wilson's key adviser in the events that followed. The rest of the UK Labour leadership were like the Tory peers in 1911: divided into hedgers and ditchers. The hedgers, led by Harold Wilson, believed that making some gestures to devolution would head off the Scottish Nationalist threat. For them, devolution was a purely pragmatic move, to be taken with no deep thought as to its constitutional implications. The ditchers, led by Labour's once and future Scottish Secretary Willie Ross and (in a quite different mode) by the MP for West Lothian Tam Dalyell, believed that any concession to the SNP was dangerous. For them, devolution was a dangerous precedent, a slippery slope, the start of the break-up of Britain.

In the February 1974 general election, the SNP held Western Isles and gained six more seats, four from the Conservatives and two from Labour, while just failing to hold its by-election gain in Govan. It won 22 per cent of the Scottish vote. Astute politicians knew that, while the electoral system had protected Labour by giving the SNP only 10 per cent of the Scottish seats for its 22 per cent of the vote, it would swing round viciously if the SNP vote share were to rise by another 10 percentage points or so. On a vote share of somewhere between 30 and 35 per cent, the SNP would flip from victim of the electoral system to its beneficiary. With an evenly distributed 35 per cent of the vote, it could win more than half of the seats in Scotland (Labour had just won forty out of seventy-one seats – that is, 56 per cent – in Scotland on 37 per cent of the vote). Were it to do so, it would start to negotiate for Scottish independence. Bang would go the United Kingdom and (more importantly for national Labour politicians) Labour's chance of forming a governing majority, which utterly depended on its forty Scottish seats.

Through the year 1974, Labour's national elite focused on these governing realities, while its Scottish elite focused more on the pros and cons of devolution per se. This led to the confused events of June to August. On June 22 1974, Scotland were playing Yugoslavia in the World Cup. A thinly attended meeting of the Labour Party's Scottish Executive was evenly divided between hedgers and ditchers when, in Tam Dalyell's account:

> all eyes turned to . . . the petite and comely Mrs Sadie Hutton of Glasgow, who had drifted in after doing her morning's shopping. Loyal to her [ditcher] Chairman, and resentful of the pressure that was being put on him from Transport House, she raised her hand . . . So, by six votes to five, the Scottish Executive of the Labour Party reaffirmed their policy that an Assembly was 'irrelevant to the real needs of Scotland'. (Dalyell 1977: 101)

Pandemonium ensued. To reverse this embarrassing decision, the national leadership of the Labour Party called on their trade union shock troops. In July, the national executive of the party resolved that it 'recognise[d] the desire of the Scottish people for the establishment of an elected legislative Assembly within the context of the political and economic unity of the United Kingdom'. The shock troops were sent with their card votes to a special Scottish conference on 17 August in the Dalintober Street Co-operative Halls in Glasgow. (Note that this entire sequence of events happened during the summer holidays.) This duly reversed the Scottish Executive's position. By command of the National Executive, the uncertainly devolved Scottish Executive announced that it was now in favour of devolution.

Tam Dalyell's bitter but entertaining diary account of this meeting records John Smith as having said that devolutionists 'could not have their cake and eat it, by insisting that they keep the office of Secretary of State for Scotland, and all seventy-one MPs'. But that was precisely the position the party adopted. In Keating and Bleiman's words (1979: 167), 'the difficulties over which devolutionists had agonised for years were solved at a stroke by incorporating in the successful propositions the principal demands of both devolutionist and unionist factions'. John Smith, the most successful and only committedly devolutionist Labour minister in the ensuing struggle to legislate, helped to enact the Scotland and Wales Acts 1978, which provided precisely for devolved assemblies in each country while retaining its Secretary of State and its full slate of Westminster MPs.

In the October 1974 general election, the SNP advanced further, to eleven seats and 30 per cent of the Scottish vote. Then the most extreme pro-devolutionists in Scottish Labour split off to form the Scottish Labour Party. It seemed that the ditchers had been right, and that the Union was not to be saved by these card vote manoeuvres in the school holidays. In the next four years, they turned out to be wrong. During the Parliament of 1974–9, the SNP message became confused – notably on whether they would concede to Shetland the same autonomy for 'Shetland's Oil' as they claimed for 'Scotland's Oil'. The Scottish Labour Party fizzled out. As the 1979 general election approached, the SNP-backed confidence motion that precipitated it was ridiculed as 'turkeys voting for Christmas'. The SNP was reduced from eleven seats to two. The Scottish Labour Party lost its two sitting MPs. After the election, Mrs Thatcher immediately repealed the Scotland and Wales Acts, which had failed to gain the referendum support that hostile amendments to the Government bills had inserted. The Scots failed to rise up in wrath, and devolution went to sleep until the creation of the Scottish Constitutional Convention in 1989.

Tam Dalyell gets to the heart of the issue when he records the following conversation with Lord Crowther-Hunt on the night of Dalintober Street:

> The real trouble is that he thinks that the SNP exists because people want a different constitutional set-up; Ronnie [TD's agent] and I know the SNP flourishes on account of the greed of the people for North Sea Oil revenues, disgust at local council corruption scandals, stirring up Rangers supporters' clubs by Orangemen because there are too many Catholics in the Labour Party, and a host of other matters, which are well known to those of us who struggle along in the gutter of political life, but which are somewhat novel, if known at all, in Oxford University Common Rooms frequented by Norman. (Dalyell 1977: 108)

Dalyell exaggerates, but he was closer to the truth than Crowther-Hunt. The coming of devolution has shown that people did want a different constitutional settlement. Devolution is, after all, the settled will of the Scottish people. But it is a low-salience issue. On the whole, the Scots do not want independence; they want more. The devolution settlement has entrenched that, but it leaves unresolved strains which I discuss below.

DOES SCOTTISH LABOUR NEED BRITISH POLITICS? DOES BRITISH POLITICS NEED SCOTTISH LABOUR?

As Scottish Labour is not a separatist party, it is self-evident that it does need to be involved in British national politics. From 1707 until 1999, all legislative decisions affecting Scotland were taken in London. The executive was the Government of the UK, taking UK-wide decisions on some matters that affected Scotland and Scotland-only decisions that affected others. The decisions were always taken in London, but usually implemented in Edinburgh. There has always been a Scottish executive minister (originally the Lord Advocate; from 1885, in response to Irish nationalism and the first calls for Home Rule All Round, a Secretary for Scotland; since the 1920s a Secretary of State for Scotland). The Scottish administration has been located in Scotland since the 1880s, and in the twentieth century it has had complete administrative autonomy for the matters within its province.

It made sense for Scottish Labour figures such as Hardie and MacDonald to call for home rule before 1924. But, from MacDonald's first Labour Government in that year until the events leading up to Dalintober Street, it made little or no sense, for the reasons already analysed. The levers of power lay in London: those who wanted to control them must go there. If Scottish

Labour politicians wanted to make a difference, it was in London that they must make it. From the (very different) careers of Ramsay MacDonald and John Wheatley in the 1920s to those of Robin Cook and Gordon Brown today, Labour's most successful Scots have operated in non-Scottish ministries. The only exceptions, as already discussed, are Tom Johnston and Donald Dewar, with Willie Ross a rather pale third to that pair.

The answer to the second question is less self-evident. Most British politicians have been Unionists since 1707. There are principled Unionists and pragmatic Unionists. Principled Unionists value the Union of the United Kingdom in and for itself. Pragmatic Unionists value it as a means to achieving something else, such as socialism (or at least a Labour government). Since the first great challenge to Unionism in 1885, the centre of gravity of principled Unionism has lain in the Conservative and Unionist Party (which has been its official title for most of the time since then; in Scotland indeed it was named the Unionist Party, *tout court*, from 1912 until 1965). The Labour Party contained the centre of gravity of pragmatic Unionism.

Gladstone's conversion to Irish home rule in December 1885 shocked principled Unionists to the core. The Union and the British Empire hung together. To grant home rule to Ireland would be taken all over the Empire as a sign of weakness. Hence the bitterness with which Unionists blocked home rule for Ireland until 1914. Meanwhile, Unionist politicians wondered what would have to be done to stop the Scots (and, later, the Welsh) from going the way of Irish disaffection. They decided that they must do two things: protect Scottish representation, and protect Scottish public spending.

The Liberal Government of 1880–5 created the post of Secretary for Scotland and the Scottish Office (the previous Liberal Government having created the Scotch Education Department in 1872). The Unionist Government of 1885–6 appointed the first Secretary for Scotland. A Secretary (of State) for Scotland saved UK ministers from getting involved in things they did not understand (a notable example being the Disruption of the Church of Scotland in 1843, badly mishandled by an otherwise competent minister, Sir James Graham). And it might head off Scottish demands for home rule.

Once a Secretary for Scotland was established in the Cabinet, he (there has been no female incumbent until Helen Liddell) could protect Scotland's financial, legal and representational position. As to finance, formula funding for Scotland and Ireland arrived with George Goschen, Chancellor of the Exchequer in the Unionist Government of 1886–92, which had come into office on the defeat of Gladstone's Home Rule Bill.

The Goschen Formula (or Proportion) was simply 80:11:9 for England and Wales, Scotland, and Ireland respectively. The ratio of 80:11 was approximately the population ratio between England and Wales and Scotland in 1888, but from 1914 onwards it became more favourable to Scotland as the Goschen Proportion remained constant and Scotland's relative population declined. The Goschen Formula never covered the whole of Scottish public expenditure, but the Secretary for Scotland could always argue for at least the Goschen proportion of any new spending programme in Cabinet. Where circumstances permitted, he could argue for more. He need never concede less. So Goschen became a floor for Scottish public spending, which is the main reason why Scotland was about 25 per cent above the per capita level for England and Wales when devolution hove on to the scene in the 1970s. Unionist politicians, notably Stanley Baldwin, argued against disturbing the Goschen Proportion despite Scotland's population decline, on the grounds that to do so might awaken the demons of home rule or independence (Levitt 1999).

A similar story can be told about parliamentary representation. I have given the detail elsewhere (McLean 1995); here is a summary. There is a myth, propagated notably by Tom Johnston, that the Act of Union guaranteed Scottish over-representation in Parliament. It did not; it guaranteed representation. Scotland's forty-five MPs in 1707 were fewer than Scotland's population proportion, and her sixteen representative peers were far fewer. The first redistribution Act to guarantee even approximately equal-population constituencies was that of 1884. Scottish representation in the Commons then gradually became more favourable as Scotland's population share declined but her seat share in the Commons did not. Her over-representation (and that of Wales) was entrenched by the Speaker's Conference which sat during World War II. Its minutes, only recently released, record:

> it would be very desirable, on political grounds, to state from the outset quite clearly that the number of Scottish and Welsh seats should not be diminished. The absence of any such assurance might give rise to a good deal of political feeling and would lend support to the separatist movements in both countries. (Speaker's Conference 1944, minutes of the 9th meeting. House of Lords Record Office.)

Accordingly, the number of Scottish seats was set at a floor of seventy-one, and of Welsh seats at thirty-five. These numbers have now crept up to seventy-two and forty respectively. As the relative population of both countries has continued to decline, they have become substantially over-represented. By the time of the Boundary Commission review that created the set of constituencies currently in force, the average electorate in England was 68,626, in Scotland 54,569, and in Wales 55,569 (Rossiter et al. 1999: table 4.13). On an equal population basis, Scotland would have only fifty-seven seats rather than seventy-two. If, as happened in Northern Ireland between 1920 and 1972, her number of seats was further reduced by a third to allow for the existence of the Scottish Parliament, she would have only thirty-eight seats in the House of Commons. The Scotland Act 1998 provides for the number of Scottish seats in the Commons to come down to (but not below) her population proportion. Even this is controversial, as it would bring in its train a consequential reduction in the number of MSPs, which the Scottish Parliament can complain is an improper interference in its autonomy, even though electoral arrangements are 'reserved' to Westminster under the Scotland Act.

PINCH POINTS: REPRESENTATION AND FINANCE

Thus the Unionist devices to keep the Scots happy over many decades were disproportionate representation and disproportionate public expenditure. As we have just shown, these initiatives originated from Unionist (i.e. Conservative) or wartime coalition governments. But the pragmatic Unionists of the national Labour Party favoured them as well. Above all, Labour needed those seventy-one Scottish seats (and the thirty-six Welsh ones). Without them, it could not normally form a governing majority. Of left-wing governments over the last century, only those of 1906, 1945, 1966, 1997, and 2001 have held more seats in England than the Conservatives. That is why the Dalintober Street 'compromise' (as Keating and Bleiman quaintly call it) was that Scotland should have an elected Assembly *and* retain a Secretary of State *and* retain seventy-one seats at Westminster.

As already noted, the Dalintober Street deal seems to have saved Labour's bacon in Scotland. But it caused serious trouble in England, trouble which persists. Politicians in the poorer regions of England noticed that a century of Goschen had given Scotland considerably higher spending per head than they got, although their unemployment and social deprivation was no less bad (NRST 1976). And Scotland was to be offered all three elements of the Dalintober Street compromise. To politicians in Newcastle and Liverpool, it seemed that the Labour Government was rewarding the Scots for threatening to vote SNP, while punishing the Geordies and Scousers who had only Labour to vote for. Accordingly, a back-bench revolt co-ordinated in Newcastle defeated the flagship Scotland and Wales Bill in February 1977 (Guthrie and McLean 1978).

The Labour Government could not tackle the inequality of representation. To do that would be to defeat its sole purpose in the devolution legislation, namely to retain its capacity to govern the UK by retaining access to all these Scottish and Welsh seats. It could, however, tackle the inequality of finance. Its response to the 1977 defeat was the Barnett Formula. In place of the static Goschen Proportion, Chief Secretary Joel Barnett and his officials devised a dynamic formula whereby Scotland's spending per head would in the long run converge to the same level as England's (McLean and McMillan 2003). Lord Barnett now says that he believed that his formula would not last 'six months or even twenty minutes' but it continues to govern the relationship between the UK government and those of Scotland, Wales, and Northern Ireland.

Thirty years after Dalintober Street, the shoe pinches in the same places as it always did. The Barnett Formula satisfies nobody. To the Scots, it is a 'Barnett squeeze', whereby public spending in Scotland grows more slowly than in England. To the northern English it is a device which has so far failed to reduce the persistently more favourable public spending position of Scotland. They are both correct. The Barnett squeeze is real and in due course it will bring Scottish public spending per head down below the point that would be justified by Scotland's greater spending needs. But there is no consensus on what should take its place. Treasury ministers and officials have taken a vow of *omertà* about what might replace it.

The fundamental problem of representation faced Gladstone in 1886. The Rev. James Barr cheerfully ignored it in 1928. Tam Dalyell drew such noisy attention to it in the 1970s that it has become known as the West Lothian Question (WLQ, to anoraks) from the name of his then constituency. It is this: *When you have asymmetric devolution, how many seats, with what voting powers attached, do you give to the territories that have devolved government?* There is no logical answer to the WLQ. You cannot deny the devolved territory any seats at all. That would be to impose taxation without representation. You cannot work the 'in and out solution' as Gladstone called it in 1893, namely that MPs from the territories with devolved government should have powers to vote on 'reserved' matters but not on 'devolved' matters. William Hague revived this idea in 1999, but its fatal flaw is that the Commons majority for devolved matters might be of a different partisan complexion to the Commons majority for reserved matters. So who would then comprise the UK Government? You cannot just leave things as they are, for that is to give the devolved territories a double advantage (seats and a Secretary of State) over the non-devolved territories. The nearest to a coherent solution is that which operated in Northern Ireland between 1920 and 1972, namely to reduce the numbers but not the powers of MPs from the territory with devolved government. And, as the Lords Committee on the Constitution bluntly pointed out in January 2003, there no longer exists a rationale for separate Secretaries of State for Scotland and Wales, with substantial staffs, now that the Scottish Parliament is responsible for all law-making and execution in the Scotland Office's domain (Norton of Louth 2003).

The Labour Party of the 1970s could not contemplate any of the rational solutions to the dilemmas of finance and representation, because those solutions would cut away the Labour Party's very power to govern the UK. The hegemonic New Labour governments of 1997 and 2001 have much more freedom. They do have a majority of seats in England. Conservative revival remains a remote prospect. A definitive solution to the problems of Scottish Labour and British politics lies in their grasp. However, they may not grasp it.

References

Dalyell, T. (1977), *Devolution: The End of Britain?*, Jonathan Cape, London.

Guthrie, R. and McLean, I. (1978), 'Another Part of the Periphery: Reactions to Devolution in an English Development Area', *Parliamentary Affairs*, 31, pp. 190–200.

Johnston, T. (1909), *Our Scots Noble Families*, 'Forward' Publishing, Glasgow.

Keating, M. and Bleiman, D. (1979), *Labour and Scottish Nationalism*, Macmillan, Basingstoke.

Levitt, I. (1999), 'The Scottish Secretary, the Treasury, and the Scottish Grant Equivalent, 1888–1970', *Scottish Affairs*, 28, pp. 93–116.

McLean, I. (1995), 'Are Scotland and Wales Over-represented in the House of Commons?', *Political Quarterly*, 66, pp. 250–68.

McLean, I. (1999), *The Legend of Red Clydeside*, 2nd edn, John Donald, Edinburgh. (Originally published 1983.)

McLean, I. and McMillan, A. (2003), 'The Distribution of Public Expenditure across the UK Regions', *Fiscal Studies*, 24, pp. 45–71.

Miller, W. L., Timpson, A. M. and Lessnoff, M. (1996), *Political Culture in Contemporary Britain*, Clarendon Press, Oxford.

Northern Region Strategy Team (NRST) (1976), *Public Expenditure in the Northern Region and other British Regions 1969/70–1973/74*, Technical Report no. 12, NRST, Newcastle-upon-Tyne.

Norton of Louth, Lord (Chairman) (2003), *House of Lords Select Committee on the Constitution: Session 2002–03, 2nd Report: Devolution: inter-institutional relations in the United Kingdom*, HL 28, The Stationery Office, London.

Rossiter, D. J., Johnston, R. J. and Pattie, C . J. (1999), *The Boundary Commissions: Redrawing the UK's Map of Parliamentary Constituencies*, Manchester University Press, Manchester.
Stewart, W. (1921), *J. Keir Hardie: A Biography*, Keir Hardie Memorial Committee, London.

CHAPTER 10

Pragmatic Nationalists?
The Scottish Labour Party and Nationalism

Nicola McEwen

Is the Scottish Labour Party a nationalist party? This may seem like an odd question to observers of Scottish politics, for whom nationalism is often equated with the independence objective of the Scottish National Party. But within the academic literature, nationalism is more broadly defined. It is not the preserve of a minority nation within an existing state, but may be practised at the level of the state as well. This chapter examines the extent to which the Scottish Labour Party has engaged in the politics of Scottish and British nationalism.

Nationalism has two interrelated components. It is a doctrine which holds that nations have the right to be self-determined, to determine their own affairs as they see fit. This need not imply that the objective of all nations is independent statehood. Often, national minorities resolve that their self-determination can be adequately exercised as part of a larger state (Keating 1996: 18–22). Nationalism may also be understood as the politics of nation-building, a form of political behaviour that seeks to reinforce identification with and belonging to the national community in question.

Understood in this way, nationalism can be identified both in nations without states, like Scotland, Quebec and Catalonia, and among established nation-states, such as the United Kingdom, Canada and Spain. In the case of sub-state nationalism, political actors engage in nation-building to emphasise the sense in which the nation they purport to represent is distinct from those with whom they share statehood, and invoke the language of self-determination to make political demands on their nation's behalf. These demands range from policy concessions to enhanced political autonomy and, ultimately, independence (Rudolph and Thompson 1989). As such, it is possible to be a nationalist while remaining opposed to independence. In the case of state nationalism, political actors at the state level also engage in the politics of nation-building, in an effort to strengthen the state's legitimacy and maintain national unity. State nationalist politics

160

is usually most evident when the state in question faces internal or external challenges to its political legitimacy and territorial integrity.

This chapter explores the Scottish Labour Party's engagement with the politics of nationalism. The first section considers the Scottish party's evolution from the Scottish nationalism of its early years towards the adoption of a British strategy. The chapter then discusses the resurgence of an autonomist Scottish nationalism within the Labour Party during the Thatcher years, voiced in the demand for Scottish home rule. The establishment of the Scottish Parliament transformed the terms of the Scottish constitutional debate. Having discarded its nationalist rhetoric, Labour in Scotland now largely shares in the discourse of their British colleagues in aiming to emphasise the values, interests and objectives which are deemed to hold the peoples of the United Kingdom together.

Scottish Labour and the British State

The Scottish Labour Party was not just born in 1888 with a commitment to home rule. Scottish home rule was an integral part of its character (Keating and Bleiman 1979: 51–2). Although home rule survived as a policy commitment following merger with the Independent Labour Party, its importance diminished as the emphasis shifted towards developing the British movement and increasing Labour's representation in the House of Commons. Scottish Labour's nationalism underwent a resurgence in the wake of the First World War, amid confidence in the Scottish labour movement and an expanding Scottish economy, and when the right to self-determination was in vogue across much of Europe. It receded once more in the mid-1920s, the combined effects of economic recession, declining confidence in Scotland's economic self-sufficiency, and a renewed focus on British electoral success. Scottish Labour's British focus reflected the wider party's embrace of the institutions of the British state and parliamentary system. Since its early experiences of government, Labour's priority has been to maximise its electoral strength in the competition for government and control of the British state.

While Labour's focus on the British state confirmed its status as a state party rather than a class party, it has historically shied away from embracing British nationalism. Jones and Keating suggested this was because the symbols of British nationalism (the Union Jack, the monarchy, and so on) were also the symbols of British imperialism, and were thus more easily absorbed by the Conservative Party (Jones and Keating 1985: 7; see also Keating and Bleiman 1979: 15–17). Yet there has been a more subtle British nationalism to Labour's discourse, linked to the social (class and national) solidarity embodied in the institutions of the post-war welfare state. Indeed, the first majority Labour Government entered office in 1945 on the pledge to build a 'New Britain', with a comprehensive welfare state at its core. Labour's New Britain would reflect the solidarity of the 'people's war' in building the 'people's peace' (Morgan 1990). The 1945 manifesto insisted that to build the welfare state would require 'the spirit of Dunkirk and of the Blitz sustained over a period of years' (Labour Party 1945; reprinted in Craig 1975). As Aughey put it, 'the Labour nation was to be sustained by the social democratic state' (Aughey 2001: 90). Welfare institutions, especially the National Health Service, thus represented national solidarity, while the social and economic security they promised reinforced a sense of belonging to and consent for the British system of government (Bennie et al. 1997: 5–6; McEwen 2002).

Labour in Scotland fully endorsed this British project. Although a token commitment to Scottish home rule was maintained until the late 1950s, and reiterated with some force during the Second World War,[1] the priority was the election and re-election of Labour governments at Westminster. The home rule cause was voiced more vociferously outside of the party political arena, most notably by John MacCormick's Scottish Convention (Mitchell 1996: 87–97; Harvie 1998: 169–73; Levitt 1998). The Convention mobilised political and popular support for a Scottish Assembly, and caused some anxiety within the Labour Government. In a memorandum to the Cabinet in 1947, the Labour Secretary of State for Scotland, Arthur Woodburn, warned of a widespread feeling that Scotland was neglected by central government, a feeling that may 'break through the party loyalties and become a considerable national movement' (PRO, CAB 129/22, para. 4). Fearing the impact the issue may have on the 1950 election, he later advised his Cabinet colleagues to guard against 'any action which can be represented as imposing on Scotland decisions in the making of which she appears to have had no real voice, or as being designed to primarily meet conditions south of the Border' (PRO, CP (49), 251, paras 7–9). However, as Scottish Convention's influence waned, the issue fell off the agenda of both government and party.

Notwithstanding the latent British nationalism of those on the left who sought to maintain the unity of the British working class, Scottish Labour's abandonment of the home rule commitment did not signal a conversion to British nationalism. Rather, the institutions and economic resources of the British state came to be viewed as the best means of addressing Scotland's social and economic ills. The 1958 report *Let Scotland Prosper*, which accompanied the Executive statement that formally rejected home rule, noted: 'the Labour Party in Scotland today realises that Scotland's problems can best be solved by socialist planning on a United Kingdom scale' (Labour Party [Scottish Council] 1958: 1). This view was reiterated in subsequent documents. The 1963 report *Signposts for Scotland* insisted that Scotland's needs would only be met 'within the framework of a national [British] plan' (Labour Party [GB] 1963: 13). The party's evidence to the Royal Commission on the Constitution (Kilbrandon Commission)[2] noted:

> The Scottish Council of the Labour Party has never been in any doubt that the enormous problems which we face can only be tackled by firm government from Westminster . . . The idea that the Scottish economy alone is strong enough to solve our social problems in the foreseeable future is quite absurd. (Labour Party [Scottish Council] 1970: 4)

The party feared that a change in the structures of government would weaken Scottish influence at Westminster, threaten the economic unity of the UK, and fail to address the economic and social problems facing Scotland (Keating and Bleiman 1979: 162–3). Keating suggested that this strategy could and did work as long as the system succeeded in delivering benefits for Scotland (Keating 1989: 98). Yet by emphasising the advantages of membership of the United Kingdom state in gaining access to the resources required to cure Scotland's social and economic ills, it reinforced the idea that continued support for the state structure was contingent upon the capacity of the state to deliver. The rise of the Scottish National Party amid British economic decline and, later, the promise of an oil-rich Scotland, forced Labour to reconsider its position on devolution. The home rule commitment was re-established between the elections of 1974, albeit with considerable pressure from the leadership in London (Wood 1989: 100–19), culminating in the rocky road to the Scotland Act (1978) and the ill-fated 1979 referendum (Bochel et al. 1981). Wood suggested that the Labour Party in Scotland never fully rejected the idea that Scottish grievances would only be resolved by radical economic policies on a UK scale (Wood 1989: 117). However, the experience of Thatcherism, and especially of years in opposition, did give rise to a marginalisation of this centralist perspective within the ranks of the Labour Party in Scotland, and encouraged the party to take the pragmatic road towards an autonomist Scottish nationalism.

Labour and Scottish Nationalism

If Labour in Scotland was a reluctant supporter of devolution in the 1970s, the party was significantly more enthusiastic in the 1980s. The years of

Conservative dominance at Westminster saw Labour in Scotland rediscover its nationalist roots. There were two different dimensions to Labour's Scottish nationalism, evident in the substance of and rationale for the devolution proposals, and in the discourse of popular sovereignty and self-determination.

In the first case, home-rulers called for a devolution scheme which would take Scotland beyond the proposals set out in the 1978 Scotland Act. Some amendments were made to strengthen Labour's devolution policy, but the bigger changes were in the symbolism and rationale used to advance the home rule cause. The 'Assembly' of the 1970s eventually gave way to demands for a constitutionally entrenched 'Parliament' which would enjoy wider powers, including economic and revenue-raising powers. After the re-election of the Conservative Government in 1983, Labour in Scotland increasingly regarded devolution as a means of resisting Thatcherism. The 'Green Paper' on devolution argued that rising unemployment, falling living standards, a loss of civil liberties, and 'savage' rent and rate increases, amongst other developments, 'could have been avoided if policy had been controlled by an Assembly which fairly reflected opinion in Scotland' (Labour Party [Scottish Parliamentary Group] 1984: 3). The most cogent expression of this argument came after the introduction of the poll tax, a flat-rate charge imposed on individuals without reference to their ability to pay. Introduced in Scotland a year earlier than elsewhere in the UK, the poll tax was widely condemned across the opposition parties, and came to symbolise the 'anti-Scottish' nature of the Conservative Government, and the need for a Parliament in Scotland (Labour Party [Scottish Council] 1988: 28–43).[3] While it is open to debate whether a Scottish Parliament could have resisted many of these policy developments, this combination of working-class politics and nationalist politics provided a powerful rationale for self-government (Denver et al. 2000: 29–32). Where Labour's post-war British nation had been sustained by the social democratic state, the party's Scottish nationalism in the 1980s was defended as a means of preserving the institutions, social services and jobs the social democratic state had created.

The second dimension of Labour's nationalism may be identified in the language of popular sovereignty and self-determination. In particular, a view emerged that elections in Scotland produced a separate 'Scottish mandate', which legitimised the case for Scottish autonomy and gave rise to the view that the Conservatives, decisively rejected by Scottish voters, had 'no mandate' to govern Scotland. There is some debate as to the extent to which the party fully endorsed the idea of a 'Scottish mandate' (Geekie and Levy 1989: 400–2; Naughtie 1989: 162–3). Certainly, the 'no mandate' view, endorsed by Labour's 1984 Scottish conference (Mitchell 1998), was expressed more vocally as the decade progressed. After the 'doomsday scenario' of the 1987 general election, when Labour won an overwhelming majority of Scottish constituencies but lost heavily to the Conservatives south of the border, a more explicitly nationalist tone emerged. Robin Cook, an opponent of devolution in the 1970s, accused Malcolm Rifkind, then Secretary of State for Scotland, of 'governing Scotland without a shred of mandate for what he's doing . . . to all intents and purposes, Scotland is an occupied country in which the ruling power depends for its support on a power-base which is outside the country' (Radical Scotland 1989: 10–11). In a bid to counteract the SNP's 'independence in Europe' slogan, Donald Dewar, then shadow Scottish Secretary, began to describe devolution as 'Independence in the UK' (Macwhirter 1990).

In demanding separate recognition of Scotland's political preferences, the 'Scottish mandate' did not sit well within a political system in which governments were elected by voters from across the UK. This justified demands for an array of strategies similar to those adopted by Scottish and Irish nationalists in earlier periods (Geekie and Levy 1989; Mitchell 1996) in attempts to force the Government to bow to the will of the Scottish people and set up a devolved assembly. Such strategies included the call for a national plebiscite, direct action and parliamentary disruption, the setting up of an alternative forum of Scottish MPs to sit in Scotland and deliberate and vote on Scottish issues, and a cross-party constitutional convention. Only the latter was seriously taken up by the Scottish Labour leadership.[4] Labour's official backing for and participation in the Scottish Constitutional Convention overcame its earlier scepticism and, in the view of Susan Deacon, 'marked a watershed in its attitude to the question of Scottish Home Rule' (Deacon 1990: 62). The language of self-determination also permeated the Scottish Constitutional Convention, at least in its early days. Its founding declaration, the Claim of Right, recognised 'the sovereign right of the Scottish people to determine the form of Government best suited to their needs'. It was endorsed by every Labour MP, except Tam Dalyell (Mitchell 1998: 489).

Although the discourse and substance of a social democratic, autonomist nationalism was evident at times within Labour's Scottish leadership, it was most clearly articulated among the home rule wing of the party. In March 1988, home-rulers set up an internal pressure group, Scottish Labour Action, to urge a revision and strengthening of Labour's devolution policy. Scottish Labour Action explicitly drew upon the language of nationalism and self-determination in reinforcing the 'no mandate' argument and championing Scottish home rule (see Deacon 1990: 66–7). Its nationalism was also evident in the substance of its proposals, which included the

demands for a stronger Scottish Parliament with financial independence
and control over economic and social security powers (Scottish Labour
Action c. 1989). Although many of its leading members, most notably Jack
McConnell, eventually melted into the mainstream of the Labour Party,
Scottish Labour Action played an influential role in boosting the discourse
of social democratic nationalism within the party. However, its success in
changing the substance of the devolution policy was more limited, particularly with respect to the powers that Parliament would enjoy.[5]

With Scottish Labour MPs, including John Smith, Gordon Brown and
Robin Cook, acting as leading members of the Shadow Cabinet, a UK
strategy was never abandoned, and increasingly came to the fore in the
1990s. Although the Conservatives won the 1992 general election –
producing doomsday scenario II in Scotland – it was not long before John
Major's party found itself deeply divided over the European Union, and
facing numerous allegations of sleaze. For Labour, its first general election
victory for over twenty years was now within reach, and winning it became
the party's central concern, with several implications for the home rule
issue. The predominance of the UK strategy was behind the controversial
decision to hold a two-question referendum, to test whether devolution was
indeed the 'settled will'. At the UK level, Labour was attempting to discard
its 'tax and spend' image and the proposed tax-varying powers of the
Parliament – the so-called 'tartan tax' – left the party vulnerable to
Conservative attacks. A referendum, with a separate question on taxation
powers, muted these attacks (Denver et al. 2000: 41–6). At the same time,
the nationalist wing of the Labour Party in Scotland was marginalised.
Almost all of those who had opposed the leadership's decision to hold a
devolution referendum had lost their places on the party's Scottish executive, while many prominent home-rulers failed in their efforts to stand as
Labour candidates in the 1999 Scottish Parliament election (Denver et al.
2000: 44; Mitchell 1998: 493–4). With New Labour in the ascendancy,
devolution was no longer an assertion of an autonomist Scottish nationalism. Rather, it was to be part of a comprehensive package of constitutional
reforms designed to revitalise British democracy. For New Labour, a
devolved Scottish Parliament was but one element in the birth of 'New
Britain'.

LABOUR AND NATIONALISM
IN THE DEVOLUTION ERA

Devolution in Scotland, and elsewhere in the UK, has coincided with a
reassertion and reinvention of Britishness at the centre. Although the

strategy to redefine Britishness has at times been given a rather superficial airing in initiatives such as Cool Britannia and Britpop, it has been treated with greater sophistication, in particular, in speeches and writings by Gordon Brown. In a lecture delivered in November 1997, two months after the successful devolution referendum, Brown underlined the need for a renewed sense of Britishness: 'We should be clear that our sense of being British matters as much as ever' (Brown 1997: 15). The idea of 'New Britain' has underpinned not just New Labour's constitutional reforms, but also its welfare reform agenda and its more positive attitude towards the European Union. However, the promotion of Britishness has been given particular emphasis in Scotland.

Indeed, since the demand for self-government in Scotland emerged from a dissatisfaction with the old British state and a desire to enhance Scottish autonomy, the success of devolution may be dependent upon generating among Scots a renewed sense of loyalty to the UK as a whole (Aughey 2001: 102–3). Gordon Brown has sought to redefine Britishness in a way that renders it more palatable to Scots. Reclaiming Britain as a multicultural, multinational state, Brown noted:

> People in Scotland reacted very strongly against the Thatcher view of Britishness, but more widely the old Britain of unreformed structures was ill-suited to deal either with new nationalities, that is people who have come into this country, as well as the old nationalities. (quoted in Richards 1999: 18)

In a booklet entitled *New Scotland, New Britain*, published in advance of the 1999 Scottish Parliament election, Gordon Brown and Douglas Alexander contrasted 'separation' with a new form of 'coming together' which they suggested devolution represented. The challenge of devolution was in acknowledging the UK's diversity 'without breaking the bonds of cohesion, common ideals, common political institutions, common language and common values that hold the country together' (Brown and Alexander 1999: 37). The idea of shared values has been particularly prominent. For Brown, the new constitutional arrangements reflected 'a new covenant of common purpose . . . a shared political endeavour where the underlying commitment to the values of democracy and fairness, binds Scotland and Britain together' (Brown 1999). This view was reiterated by Blair in the 2003 Scottish election campaign:

> there are still those who question whether there are still values around which Britain can unite. Those who would argue that the values of the people of Scotland are so different from the rest of Britain that they must choose between them as if national identity was some zero-sum game, when in truth, there is no

need to choose at all . . . Ours is a vision of a country united by common purpose and derived from shared values that make Scotland stronger with Britain, and Britain stronger with Scotland. (Blair 2003)

The idea that shared values, a common purpose, and a common political endeavour exist throughout the UK is intended to reinforce feelings of Britishness among Scots, and generate a greater sense of fraternity with citizens in the rest of the UK. As Mitchell observed, Labour's emphasis upon shared values as a means of sustaining a common British identity contrasts with the Conservatives' emphasis upon shared institutions. For Conservatives, a shared British identity is founded upon shared political institutions. Challenging these institutions by devolving power undermined that identity and thus represented a threat to national unity. For Labour, by contrast, a common British identity founded upon a community of shared values and a shared political culture can accommodate distinctive political institutions at the regional level (Mitchell 2003: 34). It is no accident that this discourse of shared values has been asserted in the wake of devolution. The idea of shared community values is commonly expressed by centre-left parties in other multinational states when their territorial integrity is challenged (Henderson and McEwen, forthcoming). In this respect, it is an example of nation-building politics, aimed in this case at strengthening British national unity and sustaining Scots' commitment to the British state.

The evidence as to whether this has been a successful strategy is mixed. On the one hand, both support for independence and support for the Scottish National Party has been contained since the establishment of the Scottish Parliament. On the other hand, there is little sign of a recovery in feelings of Britishness in Scotland. Scottish national identity remains the prevailing identity in Scotland.

This creates a challenge to the Labour Party in Scotland. The Scottish Labour Party has remained closely integrated within the British party, and supportive of the UK strategy. It has reiterated British Labour's insistence that Scotland and the rest of the UK are 'stronger together, weaker apart', a mantra oft-repeated in speeches, party publications and broadcasts. In a recent speech, Scottish Labour leader Jack McConnell echoed the discourse of UK Labour ministers when talking of 'the strength of our partnership within the UK. A partnership based on shared values and shared experiences' (McConnell 2003a: 2). Yet the predominance of Scottish national identity demands that the Scottish Labour Party must also appeal to, and be seen to reflect, Scottish national distinctiveness (Paterson et al. 2001: 115).

Indeed, McConnell frequently expresses his pride in Scotland, and celebrates the country's achievements in science, sport and culture. In his New Year message, he declared: 'I am proud to be a Scot because of who we are, what we do – and most important of all – what Scotland is capable of today' (Scottish Executive News Release, 29 December 2002). These sentiments were reiterated in a speech delivered a week before election day, when he declared: 'I love Scotland. I care deeply about the future of our country' (McConnell 2003b: 1). His discourse is of 'a new Scotland – with policies for Scotland and made in Scotland' (2003a: 1). Policy pledges are couched within the aspiration of building 'a Scotland we can all be proud to call home' (2003b: 5).

Labour's 2003 election manifesto may have been 'made in Scotland', but its contents would have given British Labour few causes for concern. Many of the Labour-led Scottish Executive's public policy goals, and the rhetoric surrounding them, have borne a strong resemblance to those articulated by the New Labour Government at Westminster (Bradbury and Mitchell 2002). The promotion of, and appeal to, Scottish national identity is clearly evident, but it has been separated from its association with territorial politics or ideological objectives. Far from being a reflection of Scottish nationalism, this discourse represents an explicit attempt to de-politicise Scottish national identity, to dissociate expressions of national identity from debates over Scotland's constitutional and political future.

Moreover, the Scottish Executive appears reluctant to assert itself as Scotland's 'Government', the embodiment of the nation and champion of the new Scottish democracy. The ill-fated administration of Henry McLeish had tentatively pursued a strategy of asserting greater Scottish national distinctiveness within the UK, and greater willingness to pursue a distinctive policy agenda, creating tensions with the UK Labour Government throughout much of his short tenure. This was notable in McLeish's decision to adopt the package of free personal care for the elderly, in the face of considerable pressure not to do so from his colleagues in London. It was also evident in his attempt to replace the term 'Scottish Executive' with the designation 'Scottish Government', a move heavily criticised and ridiculed by Scottish Labour MPs.

Thus far, McConnell has refrained from any similar strategy of asserting Scottish distinctiveness, or pushing the boundaries of devolution (Bradbury and Mitchell 2002: 300–3; Mitchell et al. 2003: 124–5). His administration has shied away from any issue that could give rise to a territorial dispute with the UK Government, even where issues of tension have arisen. For example, the Executive backed away from conflict with the Department of Works and Pensions when the UK department refused to transfer a proportion of funds from its Attendance Allowance programme, now redundant in Scotland under the Executive's free personal care scheme.

Similarly, Executive ministers, especially Labour ministers, remained subdued following negotiations within the EU Council of Ministers over reform of the Common Fisheries Policy, when the UK Government agreed to a settlement which will almost certainly have a devastating impact on the Scottish fishing industry. During the inevitable drift towards British involvement in the US-led war in Iraq, Scottish Labour's leadership was reluctant to engage in debates on the issue, let alone take a distinctive stance, on the grounds that the issue was constitutionally reserved to the Westminster Government. This was in spite of the depth of popular dismay, and the dominance of the issue in the Scottish and British media. This tendency to take refuge behind the constitutional division of powers was also evident in the recent case of the Ay family. Labour MSPs and ministers refused to be drawn into or even comment upon the treatment of a Kurdish woman and her four children, held in Dungavel Detention Centre in Lanarkshire for over a year, on the grounds that asylum and immigration are matters reserved to Westminster.

Scottish interests may be voiced in behind-the-scenes lobbying by ministers and civil servants, but the examples above highlight the reluctance on the part of Scottish Labour leaders and the Scottish Executive to *publicly* voice distinctive Scottish interests and concerns, where this may create friction with the Labour Government at Westminster. While this may be defensible on constitutional and legal grounds, and an understandable consequence of Labour Party unity, it does carry political risks. Home rule was not only about devolving legislative power over domestic policy. Advocates of devolution also argued that the establishment of a Scottish Parliament would enhance Scotland's voice within the UK. The Executive's reluctance to take a stand on reserved matters, or to stage a territorial defence of Scottish interests in its relations with the UK government, risks rendering Scotland's post-devolution voice somewhat ineffectual. Indeed, the survey evidence strongly suggests that an increasing majority of Scots feel that the Parliament has done little to enhance Scotland's voice in the UK (McEwen 2003).

Thus Labour's earlier flirtations with an autonomist Scottish nationalism at the height of the home rule movement have been cast aside in the era of devolution. Following the death of the first First Minister and the demise of the second, McConnell's primary focus has clearly been on stabilising devolution. The party in Scotland continues to promote Scottish national identity, but in a way that seeks to extract it from the arena of territorial politics. Instead, the focus has been upon the pursuit of practical policy objectives, well within the boundaries of the existing constitutional settlement.

CONCLUSION

This chapter began by asking whether the Scottish Labour Party could be characterised as a nationalist party. It would be unreasonable to characterise the party in this way, but Scottish Labour has periodically engaged in the politics of nationalism, while remaining steadfastly opposed to political independence.

For much of its history, Scottish Labour has been content to comply with the UK strategy of the British party. This is in part because of the strong degree to which the Labour Party in Scotland remains an integral part of the British labour movement. The UK strategy also provided opportunity for Scottish Labour to exercise influence at the centre and gain access to the resources of the British state to alleviate Scottish social and economic grievances. The party's flirtation with Scottish nationalism in the 1980s was during the long years of Conservative dominance, when such access to the centre was denied. For Labour, Scottish home rule came to be seen as a means of resisting Thatcherism and of enhancing Scotland's – and Labour's – voice in the UK. The party increasingly invoked the language of self-determination in voicing its demands for Scottish home rule, and was at the forefront of the broad-based nationalist movement whose players sought varying degrees of Scottish self-government.

It was inevitable that this nationalist movement would fragment once a devolved Parliament was set up. Indeed, Labour's Scottish nationalism had been discarded long before the Parliament's establishment, re-joining their colleagues in Westminster in their drive for election victory and the invention of 'New Britain'. Labour now seeks to emphasise the commonality between Scotland and England in a defence of British unity, rather than assert Scottish national distinctiveness.

Yet, even before devolution arrived on the political agenda, all political parties in Scotland had to find ways to 'play the Scottish card', to demonstrate their capacity to give voice to Scottish interests within the UK. A failure to do so may have carried a price on polling day. In the post-devolution context, Scottish Labour has yet to resolve how to play the Scottish card whilst maintaining support for the UK Labour Government and defending the constitutional status quo against the new nationalist challenge. This time, a failure to assert a distinctive Scottish voice may not only have repercussions for the party. It risks undermining the credibility of the Parliament Labour helped bring into being.

The research for this chapter was undertaken in 2002–3, when I was an ESRC postdoctoral fellow at the University of Edinburgh. I am indebted to the ESRC for the financial and other support offered by the fellowship (award no. T026271402).

NOTES

1. At the 'All Scotland Conference' in 1941, the Party had called for the establishment of an executive authority with legislative powers (to be staffed by Westminster MPs) to prevent Scotland from 'being left behind in post-war reconstruction or, at best, treated as a "region" of Britain' (Labour Party Scottish Council 1941). The 'Plan for Post-War Scotland' emerging from this conference embodied a commitment to Scottish self-government but it met with the wrath of Labour's National Executive Committee and was kept at a distance from the formal party policy programme (Harvie 1989: 73–4). The 1945 conference passed a resolution demanding the establishment of a committee to consider the necessity and desirability of devolution, while the devolution commitment was reiterated in principle in the 'Notes to Candidates' booklet during the 1945 election campaign (Labour Party Scottish Advisory Council 1945).

2. The Royal Commission on the Constitution (commonly referred to as the Kilbrandon Commission) was established by the Labour Government of Harold Wilson in 1969, in response to rising support for the Scottish National Party. It reported in 1973, recommending (by a majority) the establishment of a Scottish Assembly with legislative responsibility covering the administrative functions of the Scottish Office (Kellas 1989: 144–7).

3. The poll tax issue also caused considerable difficulties for Labour, however. As well as highlighting the party's impotence in the Westminster context, Labour allowed the initiative to be taken by their opponents, especially the SNP, whose 'Can't Pay Won't Pay' campaign contrasted with the Labour leadership's refusal to endorse non-payment and other forms of civil disobedience. In both respects, Labour's weakness was exploited by the SNP in the landmark 1988 Govan by-election, when one of the safest Labour seats in Scotland was lost to the SNP candidate, Jim Sillars.

4. The cross-party nature of the Convention was limited by the SNP's decision not to participate. For a review of events leading up to the SNP's self-exclusion from the Convention, see Macwhirter (1990: 27–30).

5. Scottish Labour Action did enjoy greater success in securing Labour's commitment to proportional representation in elections to the Scottish Parliament, and in nurturing the party's commitment to gender equality in its parliamentary representation.

REFERENCES

Aughey, A. (2001), *Nationalism, Devolution and the Challenge to the United Kingdom State*, Pluto Press, London.

Bennie, L. , Brand, J. and Mitchell, J. (1997), *How Scotland Votes*, Manchester University Press, Manchester.

Blair, T. (2003), *Now is the time to pull together, not pull apart*, speech delivered at the Burrell Collection, Glasgow, 15 April 2003.

Bochel, J., Denver D. and Macartney, A. (eds) (1981), *The Referendum Experience: Scotland 1979*, Aberdeen University Press, Aberdeen.

Bradbury, J. and Mitchell, J. (2002), 'Devolution and Territorial Politics: Stability, Uncertainty and Crisis', *Parliamentary Affairs*, no. 55, pp. 299–316.

Brown, G. (1997), 'Spectator/Allied Dunbar Lecture', *Spectator*, 8 November 1997, pp. 15–16.

Brown, G. (1999), speech on Britishness delivered to the London School of Economics, London, 15 April 1999.

Brown, G. and Alexander, D. (1999), *New Scotland, New Britain*, Smith Institute, London.

Craig, F. W. S. (ed.) (1975), *British General Election Manifestos 1900–1974*, Macmillan, London.

Deacon, S. (1990), 'Adopting Conventional Wisdom: Labour's Response to the National Question', in Brown, A. and Parry, R. (eds), *The Scottish Government Yearbook 1990*, pp. 62–75.

Denver, D., Mitchell, J., Pattie, C. and Bochel, H. (2000), *Scotland Decides: The Devolution Issue and the Scottish Referendum*, Frank Cass, London.

Geekie, J. and Levy, R. (1989), 'Devolution and the Tartanisation of the Labour Party', *Parliamentary Affairs*, vol. 42, no. 3, pp. 399–411.

Harvie, C. (1989) 'The Recovery of Scottish Labour', in I. Donnachie, C. Harvie and I. S. Wood (eds), *Forward! Labour Politics in Scotland 1888–1988*, Polygon, Edinburgh, pp. 7–29.

Harvie, C. (1998), *No Gods and Precious Few Heroes*, Edinburgh University Press, Edinburgh.

Henderson, A. and McEwen, N. (forthcoming), 'Do Shared Values Underpin National Identity? Examining the Role of Values in National Identity and the UK', *National Identities*.

Jones, B. and Keating, M. (1985), *Labour and the British State*, Clarendon Press, Oxford.

Keating, M. (1989), 'The Labour Party in Scotland, 1951–1964', in I. Donnachie, C. Harvie and I. S. Wood (eds), *Forward! Labour Politics in Scotland 1888–1988*, Polygon, Edinburgh, pp. 84–98.

Keating, M. (1996), *Nations Against the State*, Macmillan, Basingstoke.

Keating, M. and Bleiman, D. (1979), *Labour and Scottish Nationalism*, Macmillan, Basingstoke.

Kellas, J. (1989), *The Scottish Political System*, 4th edn, Cambridge University Press, Cambridge.

Labour Party (GB) (1963), *Signposts for Scotland*, policy statement prepared by working party of representatives of NEC, SCLP and the Scottish Group of Parliamentary Labour Party.

Labour Party (Scottish Advisory Council) (1945), *Notes for Labour and Co-operative Speakers in Scottish Constituencies*, 1945 general election.

Labour Party (Scottish Council) (1941), *Plan for Post-war Scotland*, August.

Labour Party (Scottish Council) (1958), *Let Scotland Prosper: Labour's Plans for Scotland's Progress*, document prepared by working party of representatives of NEC, SCLP and the Scottish Group of Parliamentary Labour Party.

Labour Party (Scottish Council) (1970), *The Government of Scotland*, evidence presented by Labour Party (Scottish Council) to the Royal Commission on the Constitution, March.

Labour Party (Scottish Council) (1988), *Labour, the Assembly and the Poll Tax*, Labour Briefing Paper.

Labour Party, Scottish Parliamentary Group of Labour Members (1984), *Labour's Green Paper on Devolution: A Consultative Document*.

Levitt, I. (1998), 'Britain, the Scottish Covenant Movement and Devolution, 1945–50', *Scottish Affairs*, no. 22, winter, pp. 33–57.

Macwhirter, I. (1990), 'After Doomsday . . . The Convention and Scotland's Constitutional Crisis', in A. Brown and R. Parry (eds), *The Scottish Government Yearbook 1990*, pp. 21–34.

McConnell, J. (2003a), *The Labour Choice is to build on what we have started*, speech delivered at the Burrell Collection, Glasgow, 15 April 2003.

McConnell, J. (2003b), *Only Labour – on your side*, speech delivered in Stirling, 24 April 2003.

McEwen, N. (2002), 'State Welfare Nationalism: The Territorial Impact of Welfare State Development in Scotland', *Regional and Federal Studies*, vol. 12, no. 1, pp. 66–90.

McEwen, N. (2003), 'Is Devolution at Risk? Examining Attitudes towards the Scottish Parliament in Light of the 2003 Election, *Scottish Affairs*, vol. 44, pp. 54–73.

Mitchell, J. (1996), *Strategies for Self Government*, Polygon, Edinburgh.

Mitchell, J. (1998), 'The Evolution of Devolution: Labour's Home Rule Strategy in Opposition', *Government and Opposition*, vol. 33, no. 4, autumn, pp. 479–96.

Mitchell, J. (2003), 'Devolution and the Future of the Union 1', in J. Fisher, D. Denver and J. Benyon (eds), *Central Debates in British Politics*, Pearson Education Ltd, Harlow, p. 35.

Mitchell, J. and the Scottish Monitoring Team (2003), 'Third Year, Third First Minister', in R. Hazell (ed.), *The State of the Nations 2003: The Third Year of Devolution in the United Kingdom*, Imprint Academic, Exeter, pp. 119–42.

Morgan, K. (1990), *The People's Peace: British History 1945–1990*, Oxford University Press, Oxford.

Naughtie, J. (1989), 'Labour 1979–1988', in I. Donnachie, C. Harvie and I. S. Wood (eds), *Forward! Labour Politics in Scotland 1888–1988*, Polygon, Edinburgh, pp. 156–70.

Paterson, L., Brown, A., Curtice, J., Hinds, K., McCrone, D., Park, A., Sproston, K. and Surridge, P. (2001), *New Scotland, New Politics*, Polygon, Edinburgh.

Radical Scotland (1989), 'Pragmatic Politics: An Interview with Robin Cook', *Radical Scotland*, no. 36, December 1988/January 1989, pp. 10–12.

Richards, S. (1999), 'Interview: Gordon Brown', *New Statesman*, 19 April 1999, pp. 18–19.

Rudolph, J. R. and Thompson, R. J. (eds) (1989), *Ethnoterritorial Politics, Policy and the Western World*, Lynne Rienner, Boulder.

Scottish Labour Action (undated, c. 1989), *Real Power for Scotland: Scottish Labour Action's Response to the Constitutional Convention's Consultative Document, 'A Parliament for Scotland'*.

United Kingdom Government Publications (1947), *Scottish Demands for Home Rule or Devolution*, PRO, CP (47) 323, CAB 129/22.

United Kingdom Government Publications (1949), *Scottish Affairs*, memorandum by the Secretary of State for Scotland, 12 December 1949, PRO, CP (49) 251.

Wood, F. (1989), 'Scottish Labour in Government and Opposition, 1964–1979', in I. Donnachie, C. Harvie and I. S. Wood (eds), *Forward! Labour Politics in Scotland 1888–1988*, Polygon, Edinburgh, pp. 99–129.

CHAPTER 11

The Autonomy and Organisation of Scottish Labour

Peter Lynch and Steven Birrell

In November 1997, Tommy Sheppard, the former Assistant General Secretary of the Scottish Labour Party, published a Scottish Labour Action (SLA) discussion paper entitled 'A New Scottish Labour Party'. The paper included a supportive foreword from SLP chair, Jackie Baillie, who was later to serve as a Scottish Executive minister under both Donald Dewar and Henry McLeish. The paper, though one of the last activities of SLA, proposed a range of measures to prepare the Scottish Labour Party for devolution, largely through giving it autonomy over policy, organisation and campaigning in devolved areas. The paper offered an alternative menu to that proposed by the rather anodyne 'Partnership in Power' document produced by the National Executive in London in 1996 and used as a blueprint for organisational modernisation across British Labour. 'Partnership in Power' introduced such ideas as the National Policy Forum to discuss policy in detail between annual conferences. This form of rolling policy review was adopted by British and Scottish Labour as a more efficient mechanism to discuss policy rather than badly worded composite motions discussed at conference which were amalgams of motions from different Constituency Labour Parties (CLPs), unions and affiliated organisations. However, 'Partnership in Power' said nothing about devolution – as if it did not exist, even though it was appearing rapidly on the political horizons of both government and party.

What Sheppard and SLA sought was the level of constitutional devolution given to Scotland under Labour's plans to be mirrored in the devolution of policy and organisational powers to the Scottish Labour Party. This suggestion might sound uncontroversial as a natural outcome of devolution itself, but the internal politics of Scottish and British Labour are not that simple. Historically, Scottish Labour has had two versions since the First World War. The first organisational version of Scottish Labour from 1915 to 1994 was known initially as the Scottish Advisory Council and was an attempt to improve Labour's organisational weakness in Scotland (Keating and Bleiman 1979: 56). In the second half of the twentieth century, Labour in Scotland was known as the Scottish Council of the Labour Party or the more familiar Labour Party – Scottish Council. However, as the terms indicate, this was an organisational unit rather than anything political even with the emergence of devolution as an issue in the late 1960s. Indeed, despite supporting devolution (reluctantly) in the 1970s and producing the first Scottish Labour manifesto at the October 1974 general election – 'Powerhouse Scotland' – the undevolved party remained a reality until 1994. At the Scottish Labour conference in Dundee in 1994, the party officially altered its name to the Scottish Labour Party – in spite of the Sillarsite connotations – and altered its rulebook to prepare for devolution. However, whilst such changes enabled it to stress a higher degree of autonomy, more accurately it gave Scottish Labour room to stress a more distinctive identity, while leaving most other things unchanged, meaning centralised in the British party in London. Finance, staff and membership all remained heavily centralised, which severely circumscribed Scottish Labour autonomy in spite of Labour's devolution plans for Scotland. Four years on from devolution this position remains unchanged and the root of some of the party's organisational problems in Scotland.

Moreover, a number of internal developments within Scottish Labour – including its election to power – have brought fundamental changes to the internal life of the party. For example, the party has experienced defactionalisation at all levels, loss of members and activists as well as the migration of many within the party to government. Many key modernising figures in the party are now concerned with running the government system as opposed to campaigning for more autonomy or democracy within Scottish Labour and the party is suffering from this. Internally, Scottish Labour has experienced something of a political vacuum similar to British Labour. The organised factions of the 1970s and 1980s have disappeared, but nothing has replaced them. As these factions are often responsible for party reforms such as one member one vote (OMOV), membership selection of MPs and MSPs, equal gender representation and devolution itself, their contemporary absence has negative implications for Scottish Labour. As shall be argued below, electorally and in policy terms, Scottish Labour may appear in good health, but its organisation and membership is weak, which has fundamental implications for its future as the hegemonic party of Scotland.

LABOUR ORGANISATION IN SCOTLAND

Labour organisation in Scotland can be conceived in three different ways: the *party in public office*, the *party on the ground* and the *party in central office*

(Katz and Mair 1994). A health-check of each of these different components of the party would lead to quite different diagnoses about the party's current condition. For example, an examination of the *party in public office* would indicate a healthy Scottish Labour Party. At the electoral level Scottish Labour appears strong. Despite a relatively poor Scottish election in 2003, Scottish Labour retained fifty MSPs and a leading role in the Scottish government. It had three MEPs, fifty-five MPs and numerical dominance at Westminster as well as continued strength in local government in Scotland. The semi-permanent nature of Scottish Labour's electoral dominance was exactly what made it an institutionalised party (Hassan 2002). However, beneath the electoral level, Scottish Labour is not so healthy. The *party on the ground* has declined significantly, with a loss of members and shrinking local organisations in areas of electoral strength as well as weakness. This situation is not uncommon in Western democracies, especially for incumbent parties, but it does present a picture of hegemonic decline. In terms of organisation, funding and membership, Scottish Labour appears much less institutionalised and stable. The *party in central office* has expanded, with more staff and resources than ever, but it lacks even the most basic powers over organisation and control of its own funds. Therefore there is a paradox about the party in central office, because, despite devolution, the Scottish Labour Party remains a regional section of a highly centralised British Labour Party. Some of these features raise questions about the health of party democracy whilst others illustrate the difficulties with any autonomous SLP: lack of members, money and organisational capacity. Indeed, as will be argued below, electoral reform of local government combined with a declining party membership has the capacity to deinstitutionalise Scottish Labour and weaken its role as Scotland's hegemonic party.[1] However, one striking feature of these difficulties is that Scottish Labour lacks the organisational powers to address them and reverse the organisational fortunes of the party in Scotland.

Scottish Labour has traditionally had a very small central organisation, with a focus on administrative functions as opposed to campaigning, fundraising, policymaking or political communications. Part of the reason for this weak central capacity is a result of the legacy of centralisation within British Labour that designated the Scottish Labour Party as a regional unit. Throughout the 1920s, Labour established regional organisations across Britain which existed as regional bureaucracies of the central organisation itself. In his study of the two main parties in Britain in the 1950s, Robert McKenzie (1964: 240) rightly dismissed the importance of these regional organisations to the overall distribution of power within the Labour Party. They had no role in policy and existed to 'manage' the party in the region.

In Scotland, for example, research staff were absent until the 1970s and then thin on the ground after that whilst political communications staff did not emerge until the 1990s. Scottish Labour's organisational peak occurred between 1995 and 1999, when the key seats strategy for the 1997 general election and the preparations for the first Scottish election in 1999 brought an expansion in party staff. Political communications, research and regional organisers and offices were all part of the expansion that took place under Jack McConnell's period as Scottish General Secretary. A further expansion took place in 1998–9 with a total staff complement of twenty-six at party headquarters. These included five research staff and five local organisers amongst a total of twelve organisational staff and five media officers (Scottish Labour Party 1999).

However, whilst the party's central capacity increased in terms of staff and resources, the finances available to Scottish Labour were and remain severely limited. Indeed, the funding of the Scottish Labour Party was something of a mystery until 2000 and the investigations of the Select Committee on Standards and Privileges. Monthly budgets for the party for the duration of the Scottish election campaign were published as annexes to the Select Committee on Standards and Privileges report into misuse of House of Commons funds by John Maxton MP and John Reid MP (House of Commons 2000). These budgets indicated the extent to which Scottish Labour lacked its own sources of funding and was reliant on British Labour to fund its campaigns and staff.[2] For example, the Scottish Labour Party fought the 1999 Scottish election on a total expenditure of £1,490,602, yet its estimated income from all sources was £180,000 (House of Commons 2000). Indeed, in the accounts provided to the Select Committee, one budget line was named 'subsidy required' – with the subsidy to the tune of £1,310,602 (House of Commons 2000).

Furthermore, the quarterly registration of donations to the Scottish Labour Party by the Electoral Commission from 2001 onwards revealed a clear picture of the limited number of donations made to the SLP. For example, in the first two quarters of 2001, with a June general election to be fought, the Scottish Labour Party received registered donations totalling £87,100 whilst its total expenditure at the 2001 election was recorded as £1,108,826 (Electoral Commission 2003a). Indeed, throughout the period of Electoral Commission monitoring available from 1 January 2001 to the end of March 2003, a total of £206,989 was donated to Scottish Labour with an additional £16,500 donated to the Scottish Labour–Trade Union Liaison Group (Electoral Commission 2003b). Most donations came from trade unions such as Amicus, MSF and the CWU, with some private donations from the *Daily Record* and *Sunday Mail* as well as Scottish Power. However, these sums were not substantial in the context of the amount of money Scottish Labour was spending on election campaigns and the party was and likely remains heavily dependent on British Labour for finance, with implications for Scottish Labour's autonomy. Given this pattern, it is highly probable that Scottish Labour's 2003 election budget was again heavily subsidised. The growth of the party in central office was therefore almost entirely a product of subsidies from British Labour. Therefore, if donations to the central organisation fell, especially from the trade unions, then there would be less available for the Scottish party to receive in subsidy. As membership has also fallen, as will be discussed below, then a politically acceptable source of alternative donations – as opposed to multimillionaire businessmen – has not come from party members either, generating a financial vicious circle for the party.

Whilst the money donated to Scottish Labour centrally was low from 2001 onwards, the money donated by trade unions to local Constituency Labour Party units was not substantial either. Over the period of available Electoral Commission reporting from January 2001 to the end of March 2003, CLPs received total donations worth £121,108 (Electoral Commission 2003b). The vast majority of these donations came through trade union sponsorship of MPs and MSPs and amounted to several thousand pounds over a year. However, as the case of Motherwell and Wishaw CLP showed in 2002, the legal registration of donations to Constituency Labour Parties cannot be guaranteed. Motherwell and Wishaw CLP came under investigation by both the Electoral Commission and the Labour Party because of non-reporting of donations. Regular donations came from the ISTC trade union as well as a number of local firms and individuals. There was also an issue over funds missing from the accounts of this same CLP. As the CLP was the constituency of the First Minister, Jack McConnell, the breaches in the law over funding were particularly controversial, especially as they followed the office expenses scandal in Central Fife CLP which brought about the resignation of First Minister Henry McLeish in November 2001. Neither of these experiences covered the Scottish Labour Party in glory, especially when they involved the party's most prominent figure in Scotland.

Whilst finance is clearly a weak point for the Scottish Labour Party, membership is another. The reason for this is twofold. First, Scottish Labour membership has fallen dramatically over the last five years. Quite simply, increases in membership whilst Labour was in opposition in the 1990s have been reversed in the post-1997 period. Electoral success and government status has been accompanied by falling membership, despite Labour's electoral popularity and devolution. Second, Scottish Labour does not control membership and one cannot actually join the Scottish party. British Labour in London controls membership recruitment, is responsible for managing membership and receives the membership fees from individual members. The Scottish Labour Party has no incentive for recruiting members nor is it in a position to mount membership recruitment campaigns. Membership recruitment initiatives are the province of the NEC in London and the Scottish party has a minimal role in membership. Therefore, the financial difficulties experienced by the party explained above cannot be addressed by increasing party membership in Scotland.

Of course, historically speaking, Labour membership in Scotland was never particularly impressive. Because of an NEC rule from 1963 to 1979 that required CLPs to affiliate 1,000 members to the party regardless of their actual membership (Whiteley 1982: 113), Scottish and British memberships were always highly inflated. For example, Labour in Scotland regularly reported membership of 72,000 or so – which was the number of Scottish constituencies multiplied by 1,000. However, the Scottish party was still applying the 1,000-member affiliation rule in 1989, when it reported a membership of 74,000.[3] When actual membership began to be reported in the 1990s, a much more realistic figure emerged of 19,708 in 1993, rising to a peak of 30,770 at the end of 1998 (Scottish Labour Party 1999) before falling to 22,153 at the end of 2002 (Scottish Labour Party 2003). This was an actual increase of twenty-nine members in the year from 2001 (Scottish Labour Party 2002), so membership may have stabilised after its 1998 peak. However, despite this stability the drop in membership since 1998 is worrying for the party. Membership in some CLPs showed signs of collapse as well as secular decline, which probably increased in 2003 with membership discontent over Labour's policy over the war in Iraq.[4] In 2002, three safe Glasgow seats had CLPs with under 200 members (Baillieston, Shettleston and Springburn), whilst Pollok recorded 218 members. Similar small memberships were found in Aberdeen North (127), Ayr (231), Central Fife (220), Dumbarton (217), Falkirk East (220), Greenock and Inverclyde (154), Paisley North (167), Western Isles (205) and West Renfrewshire (209). Whether these figures are entirely accurate is a matter of conjecture. It is not unlikely that these membership figures are inflated and that actual membership is smaller. Before 2000, Labour continued to count individuals as members until their payment subscription was fifteen months overdue. In 2000, this time period was reduced to six months (BBC News, 4 March 2000). Further changes were made in 2002–3 to move members onto monthly direct debits, which would give a more accurate measure of membership levels (Labour Party 2002: 12).

However, the six-month time period and the slow move to direct debits for each member make it probable that membership remains inflated.

There are a number of reasons why the decline in Scottish Labour membership is important. First, in terms of membership size, Scottish Labour's significance has fallen and its institutional hegemony is under threat. In membership terms, it is now a smaller and declining part of civil society in Scotland. Moreover, in spite of existing as the leading party and incumbent party at three levels of government in Scotland, membership has fallen. Meantime, it faces a more competitive electoral environment at Scottish and future local government elections, with fewer members from which to choose candidates and fight campaigns. Second, Scottish Labour is a relatively small component of British Labour. The British party reported a membership of 272,000 in 2001 (Labour Party 2002: 12) meaning that Scotland had 8 per cent of Labour members in Britain despite its electoral strength.[5] This fact might sound unimportant, but it means the SLP has a smaller voice within British Labour than its historical electoral success would suggest whilst also limiting the number of OMOV votes from Scotland available in any future leadership election; not a comforting thought for Gordon Brown. Third, a smaller party might mean a reduction in the number of activists and the decline of a tradition of activism. Party activists are important to an organisation at election time and can play a vital role in target seats (Denver and Hands 1997; Seyd and Whiteley 1992, 2002). Such activism has declined to be replaced by media-driven campaigns, telephone canvassing and the electoral efforts of the payroll vote within Scottish Labour such as MPs' and MSPs' researchers, party staff, local councillors, trade union activists, and so on, rather than ordinary party members. When voters complain of disengagement from parties and politics (with consequent falls in electoral turnout), it's not difficult to see some of the factors that have contributed to such complaints.

Fourth, the fall in membership raises questions about the health of democracy and participation in the Scottish Labour Party generally. Who is actually making decisions within the party at all levels? Are members involved or disengaged and what does this say about the party itself, particularly at the grass roots? One of Seyd and Whiteley's major conclusions about Labour in power (2002: 175) was that reductions in participation within the party were followed by a loss of members: loss of voice was quickly followed by exit, to paraphrase Hirschman (1970). This situation damaged Labour's electoral prospects in marginal seats by reducing its campaigning base locally: think of the first-past-the-post seats lost at the Scottish election in 2003 such as Aberdeen North, Edinburgh Pentlands, Edinburgh South and Strathkelvin and Bearsden. Also, what are the consequences of membership decline for the SLP over the longer term? Unless it receives serious attention, Scottish Labour's membership may continue to decline and decay as there are a lack of incentives for membership and reductions in participation across the party – evidence of a downward spiral that the party needs to break to maintain its position in Scotland, not least amongst core voters (Seyd and Whiteley 2002).

Of course, none of the parties in Scotland or indeed the UK as a whole can point to healthy membership figures. Party membership has been falling over several decades and there is something of a 'crisis of party' in relation to membership, activism and involvement that is found across all the parties (Mair 1994: 4–5). Short-term attempts to address this problem such as Labour's Red Rose campaign and the various initiatives led by John Prescott in the 1990s did succeed in increasing Labour membership but these seem to have been consigned to history. Membership peaked in 1998 and has fallen substantially since then. In the USA, the weakness of political parties led them to be dubbed as 'empty vessels' (Katz and Kolodny 1994). Has the decline in membership, activism and participation within Scottish Labour begun to render it as a party on the road to becoming an empty vessel or can it renew its grass roots to avoid such a fate? One thing is for sure: devolution and electoral success has not led to greater grass-roots involvement and increased membership.

POLICYMAKING IN SCOTTISH LABOUR

Since Labour came to power at Westminster in 1997, two modes of policymaking have been practised within the Scottish Labour Party: one exclusive and one inclusive. For example, the party's manifesto for the first Scottish election in 1999 was largely the product of Scottish Office advisers and the party leadership (Hassan 2002). The manifesto's contents did not follow the more democratic route outlined in 'Partnership in Power' whereby policies would be discussed through the medium of the Scottish Policy Forum before being voted on at party conference. The 1999 manifesto was therefore highly elite-driven. The manifesto for the 2003 Scottish election was more inclusive and followed the 'Partnership in Power' blueprint. The 2003 manifesto saw approximately 11,000 party members involved in discussing the contents of the manifesto through a series of meetings, amendments and cluster meetings, with 256 local policy forum meetings held to discuss the manifesto (Scottish Labour Party 2003). Thus around half the membership had some role in the policy process, which probably compares more favourably with the old conference amendment process. Party members, CLPs and affiliated organisations made submissions, amendments and then voted on the contents of the manifesto at the 2002 and 2003 conferences. Overall, the process took three years of discussion amongst party members and elites. Whether this discussion was meaningful is an open question. For sure the 2003 manifesto had much more inclusive roots than that of 1999. It also followed a much more logical and focused approach to policy than the bad old conference days of awkwardly composited motions and amendments. However, it would be interesting to see membership feedback about this process. Do they feel more engaged in policymaking as a result of the Scottish Policy Forum process or is policy-making still too elite-driven, in which ministers and party researchers dominate over secretive proceedings? Certainly, polling amongst the Labour membership at large found support for the policy forum approach compared to conference (Seyd and Whiteley 2002: 158). However, whilst participation in policymaking can be seen as one positive selective incentive for membership, it has not halted the decline in membership: the new, inclusive policy process has not persuaded members to remain within the party and its appearance has coincided with a large-scale exit of party members.

LEADING SCOTTISH LABOUR

Who chooses our leaders is a fundamental question for democracy, especially in relation to political parties in Scotland. However, it is not merely a question of democracy in the case of the Scottish Labour Party, but also one of autonomy because of devolution. After all, what would be the point of devolution if political leaders were still chosen in London? Before devolution, the leader of the Scottish Labour Party was effectively the Secretary of State for Scotland or Shadow Secretary of State for Scotland. Each was chosen by the UK leader at Westminster – whether Prime Minister or Leader of the Opposition. However, devolution brought about the election of Scottish party leaders by the party in Scotland rather than at Westminster, though the leader in the Scottish Parliament has shared the title of Scottish Leader with the Secretary of State for Scotland – a splendid confusion that existed between Henry McLeish and Helen Liddell (Hassan 2002: 36). The election of the party leader was one particular aspect of SLP autonomy that was instituted with devolution and supported by groups such as Scottish Labour Action. Donald Dewar was elected as Scottish Labour leader in October 1998. Following Dewar's untimely death in 2000, Henry McLeish became leader in October 2000, before his resignation in November 2001 and the election of Jack McConnell as Labour leader and subsequently as First Minister.

Before looking at the actual leadership selection processes, it is worth briefly considering the status of these leaders within the party. Whilst the media and indeed the electorate may view McConnell as the leader of the Scottish Labour Party, only Dewar was actually empowered with such authority. His two successors were appointed to the position of Leader of Labour in the Scottish Parliament.[6] Although McConnell's influence undoubtedly extends beyond the Holyrood group, this title implies a fairly limited leadership role that does not establish him as *the* leader of Scottish Labour. Indeed, ascertaining such a figure within the Scottish party hierarchy is no easy feat. Some argue that as a unitary party, the leader of the British party is also the Scottish leader whereas others have referred to Gordon Brown as 'the Godfather of Scottish Labour' using the Scottish party as his own personal fiefdom. What is certain is that following Blair's decision to downgrade the office of Scottish Secretary to a part-time role, this hitherto influential figure is unlikely to enjoy a prominent position within Scottish Labour. Also, by empowering McConnell and other future leaders with such a limited jurisdiction, it suggests that Labour is reluctant to embrace devolution whilst illustrating a lack of autonomy for the Scottish party.

The three leadership contests since 1998 have two things in common. First, they involved very limited opportunities for democratic decision-making by ordinary party members. The lack of ability of members to participate in basic party functions such as electing their leader seems to go hand in hand with declining party membership and limited opportunities for membership involvement in the internal life of Scottish Labour. Second, despite the lack of democracy, the selection processes were examples of Scottish autonomy, as it was Scottish elites who chose the leaders on each occasion. Dewar was elected by an electoral college in 1998. The college comprised elected politicians (MPs, MEPs, and so on), local party representatives and also affiliated trade unions. Each was given a third of the votes to select the Scottish leader, though only 500 people took part in the vote. Moreover, not only was Dewar the sole candidate elected with 99.8 per cent of the vote but mass membership involvement was limited to one-third of the electoral college – so much for one member one vote. However, though Dewar's election was not exactly a high point for intra-party democracy, worse was to follow. Only eighty people were involved in the vote to elect McLeish as Scottish Labour leader in 2000. Although an electoral college involving all Scottish party members and affiliate members – rumoured to total 412,000 – was proposed to elect McLeish's successor, this idea was quickly shelved when it became apparent that there was only one candidate with sufficient nominations. Subsequently, Jack McConnell's electorate comprised of only eight-four people in 2001. The electorate in each case was restricted to MSPs and members of Labour's Scottish Executive Committee.

The small numbers of party elites involved in selecting the Scottish Labour leaders raises major questions about party democracy in Scotland. Here after all is the main governing party of Scotland whose leader is selected by tiny groups of people, unlike the UK parties who had begun to use membership ballots to select their leaders. Direct democracy became prevalent within British Labour under the leaderships of Smith and Blair in the 1990s (Seyd and Whiteley 2001: 75–6). But in Scotland, delegate democracy remains strong. Moreover, whilst directly electing the party leader can be viewed as a positive selective incentive to be a Labour Party member, it is clearly not one which exists in the Scottish Labour Party. However, whilst this is a problem for democracy and membership recruitment/retention, it's not necessarily a problem for devolution. Labour leaders in Scotland have actually been chosen by Scottish elites without substantial interference from Westminster and No. 10 Downing Street; compare and contrast with Wales and London. So devolution has been successful in this regard even if democracy has not.

This theme of Scottish-elite dominance is reinforced when one considers the role of Labour MSPs in the nomination aspect of the selection process. In order to be considered for the leadership in 2001, interested candidates had to secure the nominations of seven parliamentary colleagues. The challenges of both John McAllion and, more surprisingly, Malcolm Chisholm ended at this stage, as neither was able to attract this level of support. McConnell achieved it comfortably with thirty-three nominations. Whatever their reasons for endorsing McConnell and failing to support the other candidacies, the Scottish Labour MSPs have assumed a monopoly over the nominations process. They have established themselves as 'gate-keepers', effectively being able to dictate who can and, just as important, who cannot be considered for the leadership with no direct role for the constituency parties or the unions. However, as mentioned above, although hardly an exercise in intra-party democracy, the nominations process is controlled by a Scottish elite, with little scope for UK party influence.

Power and Autonomy in Scottish Labour

The two most significant increases in the autonomy of the Scottish Labour Party following devolution involved the capacity to make policy through the medium of the Scottish Policy Forum as well as the role of the Scottish party in electing the party's leader in the Scottish Parliament. As discussed above, the Scottish party has effective autonomy over selecting its leader, even though this power is monopolised by party elites and grass-roots members are excluded: autonomy has been delivered in the absence of democracy. However, in many other areas of party life, the Scottish Labour Party lacks autonomy and the central organisation in London remains dominant. Areas such as finance, staffing, membership, party rules and discipline are still controlled by British Labour centrally. Such control is a constraint on Scottish Labour's autonomy and also deprives it of powers to modernise itself and rejuvenate its organisation and membership. Indeed, internally, the Scottish party appears becalmed. Since the 1980s Labour across the UK has undergone a process of defactionalisation. Formerly important groups within the party such as Tribune, the Labour Co-ordinating Committee (LCC) and the Campaign Group, which were organised amongst the Parliamentary Labour Party at Westminster in addition to across the CLPs, have all effectively declined (Seyd 1987). In Scotland, the 1980s saw the development of some distinct factions such as the LCC, Scottish Labour Action and the Scottish Labour Women's Caucus. However, by the late 1990s these factions had declined and disappeared. Part of the reason for the decline was programmatic success. Scottish Labour Action may not have created an autonomous Scottish Labour Party, but it did influence Labour's devolution policy. The Women's Caucus also saw success through candidate selection measures to ensure greater representation of women MSPs amongst the Scottish Labour group in the Scottish Parliament. Not only did these two groups achieve some degree of success, culturally, if not programmatically, but some of their leading figures – though by no means all as Douglas Fraser's chapter makes clear – were elected as MSPs and later became Scottish Executive ministers. The modernising faction, the Network, appeared to come to life in 1998–9 to influence the candidate selection processes for the Scottish Parliament, but has not been prominent since then. Labour Renewal Network, a network of modernisers around the influential journal *Renewal*, has had little impact north of the border. The only ideological or issue-based factional grouping which remains active at present is the Campaign for Socialism, which was formed in 1994 as part of the campaign to retain Clause Four of the Labour Party constitution. This organisation has grass-roots members and activists and a few MP and MSP members, but has had a minimal influence over Scottish Labour.[7]

Rather than issue or ideological factions, Scottish Labour's internal politics have become influenced by local family/personality factions in the constituencies and by the loose network of Blair and Brown supporters amongst parliamentarians. Locally, factions are influential over candidate selections for local authorities and the Scottish and Westminster Parliaments, especially when party membership in a CLP is small. Sometimes, local parties can be understood as power bases for MPs and MSPs, who are able to build and maintain a local machine to maintain their position. Local alliances and patronage rather than issues or ideology are prominent here, alliances that will be threatened by the use of proportional representation for local government. However, across Scottish Labour generally, the Brown–Blair competition has become the most important observable division within Scottish Labour, with MSPs apparently allied with one or other of Labour's two leading figures. But, again, this is a rather strange set of loose alliances that is more about personalities and their ambitions than issues or ideologies. Blair and Brown are both modernisers and their followers in Scotland are also modernisers with few ideological or policy divisions between them. Determining whether these divisions have any real substance within Scottish Labour is also difficult. Sure enough, certain prominent figures such as Douglas and Wendy Alexander can be associated clearly with Gordon Brown, whilst Jack McConnell can be associated with Tony Blair to some extent, but these simple facts do not actually tell us much about the policy or direction of Scottish Labour. Nor can we tell whether the apparent Blair–Brown divide has any great resonance at the grass roots of Scottish Labour. Certainly, there is no factional organisation associated with Blair or Brown similar to the LCC or Scottish Labour Action in the past, though any future Labour leadership contest may create one.

There are two ways of looking at the defactionalisation of Scottish Labour. First, it could be seen as a positive development as factionalism is often associated with internal divisions and serious splits in the party. The post-1979 experiences of Labour with the gang of four and SDP, the Bennites, the Militant Tendency, the 1983 manifesto, and so on, all point to the negative side of factionalism which made Labour unelectable. New Labour was a direct, moderate response to these factional divisions. Second, however, one can view the decline of factions as a negative development for healthy internal democracy. Factions provide ideas, policy alternatives, rotating party elites and strategic choices. Moreover, they provide internal debate, especially when a party is in opposition. They also provide a usual means of dissent for party activists when Labour is in government, though arguably this can be destructive too as outlined above. Within Scottish Labour, the leading figures associated with factions and internal groupings were also associated with modernisation of policy and organisation within the party. McConnell as general secretary helped encourage a party with over 30,000 members and at the minimum a party which was able to benefit from the Blairite upswing of 1994–7. Scottish Labour Action helped modernise Labour's devolution policy away from 1970s Assembly-style devolution and made the ground more conducive for a pro-autonomy, pro-distinctive Scottish agenda, but did not actually succeed in convincing the Labour Party of this argument. Nothing has replaced such driving forces within the party organisation and electoral success has transferred many leading figures from the party on the ground and the party in central office to the party in public office. This has resulted in stagnation at the grass roots and party central office becoming a primarily administrative organisation, though this could be seen as a natural consequence of governmental status: power migrates from the party organisation and membership to the parliamentarians, ministers and civil service. However, this raises questions about Scottish Labour's grass roots in relation to local campaigning, incentives for membership, development of policy and ideas outside government, and the potential for debate within the party at all levels. What is not being suggested here is a return to the early 1980s by any means, rather that the combined effect of multi-level incumbency, limited membership power in the party, the migration of power and influence to parliamentarians, decline of factions, decline in membership, and so on has negative effects on political parties that should be of concern to Scottish Labour at a time of voter disengagement from elections and political parties. Quite understandably, the party has become preoccupied with governing and with elections to the detriment of the grass roots.

CONCLUSION

Clearly, the prospect of an autonomous Scottish Labour Party envisaged by Tommy Sheppard and Scottish Labour Action has been only partly realised. Policymaking through the medium of the Scottish Policy Forum and the election of Labour's leader in the Scottish Parliament offer the clearest examples of Scottish Labour autonomy. However, in organisational terms, Labour remains a fairly centralised party that effectively limits the level of autonomy available to the Scottish party, especially in relation to finance, membership and organisation. Indeed, the weakness of Scottish Labour's organisation has become one of its most compelling features since devolution, with little organisational autonomy to address this problem. The decline in membership, if continued, offers the biggest challenge to Scottish Labour even as it enjoys electoral success. In England, the Conservatives' impressive election machinery in the constituencies disappeared with its mass membership throughout the long years of electoral success in the 1980s. A similar experience might come to haunt Scottish Labour – and British Labour too – despite the 1997 and 2001 landslides and the Scottish victories of 1999 and 2003. If Labour's local campaigning machine declines with membership losses, then losses of seats to its rivals in lower turnout elections appears likely. Some of this scenario came true in 2003 and more losses could follow unless the party finds new ways to incentivise membership and re-grow its organisation in Scotland. Even then, the tide may be turning against Scottish Labour with the onset of proportional representation for local authority elections in 2007, which will reduce the number of Labour activists and campaigners too. How Scottish Labour addresses its membership and organisational problems given the lack of organisational powers and the migration of key party figures into the government remains an open, though vital, question for its future electoral prospects.

NOTES

1. The argument over hegemonic status could be made in relation to Labour's electoral representation in Scotland, rather than its popular vote. For example, whilst 43 per cent of the Westminster vote in 2001 could be seen as potentially of hegemonic proportions, 35 per cent of the first vote and 29 per cent of the second vote in the Scottish Parliament elections in 2003 looks decidedly unhegemonic. What does give support to Scottish Labour's hegemonic aspirations is the 78 per cent of Scottish Westminster representation it won in 2001, counting Michael Martin, the Speaker.
2. Before the Select Committee's report, the nature of funding for Scottish Labour was difficult to determine from the party's annual report and accounts.
3. This was the last year in which Scottish Labour calculated its membership under the old rules.
4. The newspapers were filled with anecdotal evidence of a haemorrhaging of Scottish Labour members in the first half of 2003 in reaction to government policy on Iraq in addition to other areas of discontent such as the fire fighters' strike. Future membership figures in Scottish Labour's annual reports will reveal the extent of this decline.
5. Scottish Labour Party membership was 22,124 at the end of 2001.
6. In the manifesto for the 2003 Scottish elections, McConnell signed off as First Minister of Scotland and Leader of Labour in the Scottish Parliament. However, in other election material, he was referred to as Scottish Labour leader.
7. The formation of the internal pressure group Compass in September 2003 by a wide range of individuals associated with the Labour journal *Renewal* and the Labour-orientated think tanks the Fabian Society, Demos and the Institute for Public Policy Research perhaps indicated a new stage in Labour pressure group politics, but it seems unlikely it will have much of a Scottish profile. See their initial statement, 'Compass: A Vision for the Democratic Left', reported in *The Guardian*, 15 September 2003.

REFERENCES

Denver, D. and Hands, G. (1997), *Modern Constituency Electioneering*, Frank Cass, London.

Electoral Commission (2003a), *Register of Campaign Expenditure – The Labour Party, 2001 General Election*, Electoral Commission, London.

Electoral Commission (2003b), *Register of Donations to Political Parties*, Electoral Commission, London.

Hassan, G. (2002), 'The Paradoxes of Scottish Labour: Devolution, Change and Conservatism', in G. Hassan and C. Warhurst (eds), *Tomorrow's Scotland*, Lawrence and Wishart, London, pp. 26–48.

Hirschman, A. (1970), *Exit, Voice and Loyalty*, Harvard University Press, Cambridge.

House of Commons (2000), *Select Committee on Standards and Privileges, Second Report*, TSO, London.

Katz, R. and Kolodny, R. (1994), 'Party Organization as an Empty Vessel: Parties in American Politics', in R. Katz and P. Mair (eds), *How Parties Organize: Change and Adaptation in Party Organizations in Western Democracies*, Sage, London.

Katz, R. and Mair, P. (1994), 'The Evolution of Party Organisations in Europe: Three Faces of Party Organisation', *American Review of Politics*, vol. 14, pp. 593–617.

Keating, M. and Bleiman, D. (1979), *Labour and Scottish Nationalism*, Macmillan, Basingstoke.

Labour Party (2002), *Annual Report 2002*, Labour Party, London.

McKenzie, R. (1964), *British Political Parties*, Heineman, London.

Mair, P. (1994), 'Party Organizations: From Civil Society to the State', in R. Katz and P. Mair (eds), *How Parties Organize: Change and Adaptation in Party Organizations in Western Democracies*, Sage, London.

National Executive (1996), *Partnership in Power*, Labour Party, London.

Scottish Labour Party (1999), *Annual Report 1998/99*, Scottish Labour Party, Glasgow.

Scottish Labour Party (2002), *Annual Report 2002*, Scottish Labour Party, Glasgow.

Scottish Labour Party (2003), *Annual Report 2003*, Scottish Labour Party, Glasgow.

Scottish Labour Party (2003), *The Road to the Manifesto*, Scottish Labour Party, Glasgow.

Seyd, P. (1987), *The Rise and Fall of the Labour Left*, Macmillan, Basingstoke.

Seyd, P. and Whiteley, P. (1992), *Labour's Grassroots*, Clarendon, Oxford.

Seyd, P. and Whiteley, P. (2001), 'New Labour and the Party: Members and Organization', in S. Ludlam and M. Smith (eds), *New Labour in Government*, Macmillan, Basingstoke, pp. 73–91.

Seyd, P. and Whiteley, P. (2002), *New Labour's Grassroots*, Palgrave, Basingstoke.

Sheppard, T. (1997), *A New Scottish Labour Party*, Scottish Labour Action, Kilsyth.

Whiteley, P. (1982), 'The Decline of Labour's Local Party Membership 1945–79', in D. Kavanagh (ed.), *The Politics of the Labour Party*, Allen and Unwin, London, pp. 111–34.

IV

The Wider Movement,
Scotland and Internationally

Labour's Journey from Socialism to Social Democracy: A Case Study of Gordon Brown's Political Thought

Gerry Hassan

Gordon Brown has been a significant UK Labour politician for twenty years, from his election as MP for Dunfermline East in 1983, and has made a major contribution to Scottish Labour for at least thirty years. This chapter addresses the evolution of Brown's political thought, and examines his understanding of socialism and social democracy. It also looks at his thinking on economic and social policy, and devolution and constitutional change, and uses these to map out some of the key issues about the development of Labour over the period, the creation of New Labour, and the contribution of Scottish Labour to the wider British Labour movement. It is, of course, a 'work in progress', given that Brown is still, very much, an active politician at the height of his powers.

GORDON BROWN: THE MAN AND POLITICIAN

Gordon Brown was born in 1951 in Giffnock on the southside of Glasgow and moved to Kirkcaldy at the age of three where his father was a Church of Scotland minister. Growing up in an environment where politics were often discussed, Brown had a political conscience from an early age, and in 1963, at the age of 12, campaigned against Alex Douglas Home in the Perth and Kinross by-election. As a schoolchild he won a newspaper competition in the *Scottish Daily Express*, writing on Britain in 2000: 'A new generation is being born. By 2000, Scotland can, for the first time in history, have found her feet as a society which has bridged the gaps between rich and poor, young and old, intellectual and labourer.' (Routledge 1998: 36) This combination of Kirk, small-town Kirkcaldy and Labour was natural for Brown according to one commentator: 'Gordon Brown is a born member of a ruling elite. In the community into which he was born, his father was a member of the social and elite and the Labour movement represented the political class.' (Brivati 2002: 238)

Brown joined the Scottish Labour Party in 1969 and began to make a reputation for himself as a national figure from an early age, winning election to the Scottish Labour Executive in 1976 at the tender age of 25. Henry Drucker, an academic at Edinburgh University at the time, reflects that the effect of Brown on the atrophied culture of Labour was not exactly positive: 'All the older people hated him. Those over 50, old Labour, just couldn't stand him. He was too fast for them, too clever, too popular, too good with the press. But he was the future.' (Routledge 1998: 71) He was intensely disliked by the Labour right who saw him as an over-enthusiastic and ambitious Labour politician too impatient to get things done, and not sufficiently respectful of his elders. However, he was also not trusted by the left, as he did not uncritically embrace the then emerging programmatic certainties of the Bennite left; he was not even at any point a member of CND, whereas Tony Blair was. Brown was an old-fashioned Tribunite left-winger in the tradition of Michael Foot and Neil Kinnock.

Brown's commitment to Labour was underlined in the turbulent devolution decade of the 1970s when Jim Sillars set up the breakaway Scottish Labour Party. Drucker comments that Brown was a possible target for the fledgling party: 'Gordon was the key figure when Sillars set up the SLP. The person he most wanted to join was Brown. He knew if he could get Brown he could get the entire younger generation in Scotland.' (Routledge 1998: 74–5) Sillars disagrees: 'I don't think that it is in his nature in any event to take that kind of gamble. He had a fairly set course for the top.' (Routledge 1998: 75)

Brown remained in Labour and became Chair of Scottish Labour's Devolution Committee and campaign in the 1979 referendum. The party was badly split and Brown, young and eager, was taking on a poisoned chalice. Alf Young, then Research Officer of the party, 'kind of knew' what was coming. 'The campaign was left to the enthusiasts like Gordon Brown. It meant a hell of a lot of work devolving on a few shoulders. It was pitiful how much real effort was put into delivering the goods.' (Routledge 1998: 81)

Brown took a risk in the 1979 referendum and was part of a significant reverse for those campaigning for a Scottish Assembly, but it helped contribute to Brown's status as a national figure. Another important moment, although not public, was his definitive and personally brave break with the Bennite left. Labour at this point had just been rent asunder by the 1981 Benn–Healey Deputy Leadership contest, and the Bennites were out for revenge after Healey's narrow victory. At a meeting of the Scottish Labour Executive with Michael Foot in November 1981, the Bennites, led by George Galloway as chair, criticised Foot for excluding Benn from the

Shadow Cabinet, and Denis Healey for not supporting party policy on unilateral nuclear disarmament. Brown disagreed with the Bennites and according to a memorandum of the meeting said: 'We needed to win the support of the voters. Anything which prevents this and which puts the relationship between the party and the trade unions in jeopardy is not only needless but harmful.' (Allison 1995: 245)

Brown outlined that what Labour required was a Draft Manifesto which both left and right could sign up to and then 'we had to go and sell it in the country and start a moral crusade backed by the vast majority of party members.' (Allison 1995: 245) This was complete heresy to Bennite orthodoxy circa 1981: in acknowledging the realities of the external world and voters, when the Bennites were obsessed with the internal concerns of the party, and, as importantly, acknowledging the need to bring left and . right together. To openly accept that the right had a place in Labour's coalition in 1981 was an unusual and brave thing for a left-winger to say.

Brown had aligned himself with the evolving 'soft-left' in the party which was beginning to challenge the dogmas of the Bennites, and which would after 1983 coalesce around Neil Kinnock as leader (Seyd 1987). Elected as MP for Dunfermline East in the 1983 election, Brown immediately joined the Tribune Group and supported Kinnock for leader and deputy (so avoiding as a left-winger endorsing Roy Hattersley as deputy). In his Commons maiden speech in July 1983, he set out the human cost to his constituents of Thatcherism – with 4,000 'officially' unemployed and 6,000 more out of work: 'This is all because the government's philosophy is that the rich must get rich by way of tax cuts and that the poor must become poorer to ensure true prosperity.' (*Hansard*, 27 July 1983: cols 1226–44)

Afterwards one Tory MP congratulated Brown on his 'tour de force', while the then government minister, Rhodes Boyson, later called it 'the most effective speech' in the debate (Boyson 1995: 186). Later the same year, Brown and Blair drew the attention of Tory minister Alan Clark, who facing them in the Commons thought they were 'two bright boys . . . bobbing up all over the place, asking impossible, spastic, questions of detail' (Clark 1993: 53–4). Brown was clearly making his mark.

GORDON BROWN: THE THINKER

THE RED YEARS: CHAIRMAN BROWN

For the last thirty years, Gordon Brown has been a prolific writer contributing on a wide range of public debates about Labour and socialist politics.[1] His first significant venture was as editor of the famous *The Red Paper on Scotland*, published in 1975, that brought together twenty-nine contributors in a New Left analysis of contemporary Scotland. Originally planned as a Scottish contribution to critiquing the Heath government, it was overtaken by events in the form of the rise of the SNP in the two 1974 elections, and had two essays added at a late stage from an SNP perspective.

Brown in his introduction attempted to bring together in a convincing credo the return to a class politics under Heath, industrial unrest and the Scottish dimension. This was a bold intent, and if Brown tried to invoke the radical rhetoric of the age, a more measured, reformist politics clearly sat with them: 'a socialist society must be created', wrote Brown, 'within the womb of existing society', forming 'a coherent strategy with rhythm and modality to each reform to cancel the logic of capitalism', while he warned 'socialists must neither place their faith in an Armageddon of capitalist collapse nor in nationalisation alone.' (Brown 1975: 18)

Throughout the essay, Brown name-checks in eager manner the New Left icons of the age: Friere, Gramsci's 'Prison Notebooks', E. P. Thompson, the Institute for Workers' Control and many others. More tellingly he ends with a clarion-call of Labour-movement heroes, 'Scotland's socialist pioneers': Hardie, Smillie, Maxton, Maclean, Gallacher and Wheatley – with two of the six Communist, rather than Labour, politicians. It is also worth noting that all the New Left and Labour politicians were male (as indeed was *The Red Paper* itself, with no room in twenty-eight essays for feminist analysis or gender politics).[2]

Brown is revealing on the challenge of the SNP and the demand for devolution that was dividing Scottish Labour, which it entered the February 1974 election formally opposed to. His aim was an ambitious one:

> What this Red Paper . . . seeks to do is to transcend that false and sterile antithesis which has been manufactured between the nationalism of the SNP and the anti-nationalism of the Unionist parties, by concentrating on the fundamental realities of inequality and irresponsible social control, of private power and an inadequate democracy. For when the question of freedom for Scotland is raised, we must ask: freedom for whom? From what? For what? (Brown 1975: 8)

His politics were a very different kind of unionism to old-fashioned Labour or Tory unionism, or the 'new' unionism he was to invoke twenty years later:

> Scottish socialists cannot support a strategy for independence which postpones the question of meeting urgent social and economic needs until the day after independence, but nor can they give unconditional support to maintaining the integrity of the United Kingdom and all that entails – without any guarantee of radical social change. (Brown 1975: 9–10)

The Red Paper did not have any significant influence on the wider Labour movement, but it was an audacious attempt to influence ideas, and one unusual in a party and culture traditionally suspicious of intellectuals and theorists.

After the 1979 devolution débâcle, Brown co-wrote with Henry Drucker *The Politics of Nationalism and Devolution* which reviewed Scottish politics in the last century, the development of the Scottish Office and demand for home rule, assessed the previous decade and attempted to draw lessons for the future. Drucker and Brown argued that there could be no return to the flaws of the previous Scotland Act and any future legislation would have to address the following:

- There was no need for 71 Scottish seats at Westminster post-devolution, and this could be cut as Kilbrandon suggested to 57;
- Proportional representation would reduce fears of an SNP majority in an Assembly;
- Some form of taxation power could be devolved to challenge the centralism of the Treasury;
- The 'in and out' principle should be accepted where Scottish MPs did not vote on English and Welsh domestic matters. (Drucker and Brown 1980: 126–7)

They concluded that devolution in the 1970s in relation to Scotland and Wales was ad hoc with little grounding in political principle, leaving them open to the charge of opportunism: 'Devolution must be taken out of the relatively restricted confines of Scotland and Wales and seen as part of the attempt to make British government more acceptable to the British people.' (Drucker and Brown 1980: 129)

The following year, Brown finally submitted his Ph.D. thesis, *The Labour Party and Political Change in Scotland 1918–1929*, to Edinburgh University. This 545-page study looked at the politics of five elections in Scotland and the inter-relationship between the rise of Scottish Labour electorally and the failure of socialism to establish itself. Brown contended that the establishment of Labour as an alternative party of government was linked to its increasing lack of radicalism and the marginalisation of socialist ideas.[3] According to Brown: 'By 1929 the differences between Labour and Conservative parties may have appeared to the elector to be less matters of fundamental dispute than quantitative differences over how far economic and social reform should go.' (Brown 1981: 3)

'Labour was the home rule party of the twenties', asserted Brown (1981: 521), but it began to downplay its commitment because it 'wanted to be Scottish and British at the same time' and 'the fact that the sense of Scottish separateness was never sufficiently strong to force Labour into a more decisive stand.' (1981: 527) Brown concluded: 'It was not so much that Labour betrayed Scotland or vacillated on the Scottish issue: popular demand for home rule was secondary to the demand for action on unemployment, the poor law and other social and economic questions.' (1981: 527–8) And he drew a wider lesson from this:

> No theorist attempted in sufficient depth to reconcile the conflicting aspirations for home rule and a British socialist advance. In particular, no one was able to show how capturing power in Britain – and legislating for minimum levels of welfare, for example – could be combined with a policy of devolution for Scotland. (1981: 527)

1983 AND ALL THAT: THE ROAD BACK BEGINS

Brown was elected an MP in the Labour electoral disaster of 1983, and shortly afterwards published *Scotland: The Real Divide* with Robin Cook, which is seen as the origin of their bitter rift to this day. In his introduction, Brown began to acknowledge the very changed political environment from the one eight years previous in *The Red Paper* and the need for revisionism: 'making the case for social justice is not the same as solving the problem of poverty. If life is more complex than it seems to the ideologists of the New Right, changing circumstances force the left to reassess its social strategy.' (Brown 1983: 20) This meant that the left was going to have to face difficult choices:

> The era of automatic growth is not only over but unlikely to return in the near future. New principles for social security in a low-growth economy are badly needed. The first prerequisite for eradicating poverty is the redistribution of income and wealth from rich to poor. (1983: 20)

The Brown of 1983 is very different from 1975. There is not one mention of socialism in the 1983 essay, whereas the 1975 one was littered with references. More importantly, the 1983 Brown was grounded in an awareness of the left's weakness, the ascendancy of the right, and Labour's popular decline. He was prepared to acknowledge that 'the New Right have consistently won the argument that further moves towards equality are absurd . . . It is time for the left to argue the case for equality.' (1983: 20–1)

In 1986, following three years of work, Brown published his biography of James Maxton, Labour MP for Glasgow Bridgeton 1922–46 and leader of the ILP. He had access to private letters and correspondence, and according to Paul Routledge:

As a result, the book reads like the diary of a spiritual and political journey, as though Brown is torn between heart-felt admiration for the most charismatic socialist of his generation, and intellectual frustration with Maxton's compelling – but ultimately self-defeating – integrity. (Routledge 1998: 134–5)

Brown takes two major lessons from Maxton's life, one negative and one positive: his political failure and his understanding of socialism. He commented on Maxton and Wheatley, 'Their failure, the failure of the ILP and the Labour Party, foreshadowed the failure of a whole generation of British politicians to solve the problems of unemployment and poverty.' (Brown 1986: 21) However, Maxton's dream of identifying 'the third alternative' (1986: 192) between Bolshevism and MacDonald's timid reformism had longer-term consequences. His political philosophy was summarised:

Cold, bureaucratic, centralised state socialism held no attractions for him. For Maxton the only test of socialist progress was in the improvement of the individual and thus the community. Greater educational opportunities would not only free exceptional people to realise their exceptional talents but allow common people to make the most of their common humanity, and ordinary people to realise their extraordinary potentials. The social equality he supported was not for the sake of equality but for the sake of liberty. (1986: 315)

Thatcher won a third term in 1987 despite Labour's attempts to modernise under Neil Kinnock. Following the election, Brown stood for the Shadow Cabinet for the first time and was elected, finishing joint-eleventh with eighty-eight votes, being rewarded with the post Shadow Chief Secretary to the Treasury. The next year, after deputising for John Smith, recuperating from a heart attack, he enhanced his reputation, savaging Nigel Lawson; in the 1988 elections he came first and won 155 votes.[4]

The following year, Brown published *Where There is Greed*, his critique of Thatcherism and prognosis for how Britain could reverse its long-term economic decline. Brown was now attempting to challenge the free-market dogma of the right by reinventing government: 'Our competitors . . . recognise the purposeful role government can play as catalyst' (Brown 1989: 10). This meant shifting towards the Western European model of capitalism: 'Most of all they recognised that investment in education and training, and indeed in the personal well-being of their workforces, is more vital than ever to economic success.' (1989: 10) To Brown, 'Efficiency and fairness depend on each other' (1989: 10), words that were to become a mantra under New Labour. This was part of the emerging new credo under Neil Kinnock's leadership and the Policy Review process whereby the party was dumping many old shibboleths and embracing mainstream European social democracy. Brown was happy to be part of this: 'In this way a new supply side socialism for Britain is in the making. Its main themes are investment in skills and science, with teamwork, collective effort and the involvement of the workforce vital to a successful economy.' (1989: 10) It would only be a small shift from this to the 'Britain plc' of New Labour in power.

In 1992 Labour suffered a fourth election defeat which was a profound and unpleasant surprise for the party. John Smith emerged immediately as favourite to be leader, with Brown not prepared to stand against his friend for the post. The deputy leadership proved a harbinger of what was to come. Tony Blair urged Gordon Brown to stand, but Brown ruled himself out as he felt two Scots could not lead the party, and Blair felt it was too early for him to stand as the moderniser's candidate. Brown's failure to stand shifted the dynamic between Brown and Blair, so that in two years, Blair was determined not to miss his chance (Rentoul 2001: 178–81).

Smith's leadership was a frustrating period for the modernisers. Brown and Blair felt Smith too uncritically supported old Labour notions and gave sustenance to the 'one more heave' school. They found a receptive audience in the election of Bill Clinton as President as a New Democrat in 1992, and went out to visit Clinton's team in January 1993 to learn lessons for Labour, winning criticism from John Prescott and Claire Short about the Clintonisation of Labour.

LABOUR'S LOST LEADER: THE DEATH OF JOHN SMITH

John Smith's death in May 1994 was a traumatic shock to the party, and to Gordon Brown, who had worked closely with him for nearly a decade. With journalist James Naughtie, Brown produced a set of essays in memory of Smith – *John Smith: Life and Soul of the Party*. Brown's contribution was an essay, 'John Smith's Socialism: His Writings and Speeches', in which he offered the following view of Smith:

> the more he progressed in his political life the more he felt his actions closely bound up with his Christian beliefs – the desire to help others, to strive for a better and more just society, to seek to improve people's lives and opportunities through the power of the community. (Brown 1994b: 67)

Despite the essay's title, Brown offers no definition of Smith's socialism, but does paint a vivid picture of the man and his beliefs: 'It was when John talked of social justice, fairness, greater equality, that his words burned with passion.' (1994b: 62) No hint is given of the impatience Brown and others felt at Smith's slow approach to change in his period as leader, nor his silence on Labour malpractice in his own Monklands backyard which had become a major political controversy.

Values, Visions and Voices, an anthology of British socialism, came out the following year, with fellow Labour MP and prolific author Tony Wright. The opening words of the introduction by Brown and Wright locate the purpose of the book in the contemporary debate of the Labour Party and discussions on revising Clause Four: 'This book celebrates the socialist tradition in Britain. It seeks to show that fundamental socialist values endure and continue to inspire, which is why they should be clearly reflected in both the Labour Party constitution and Labour Party policy.' (Brown and Wright 1995: 18) 'All socialists', they argued, 'must be both radicals and permanent revisionists, constantly exploring how their enduring values can find fresh resonances and application.' (1995: 19) Given the intent to use the radical voices of the past to illustrate timeless values and the need to update these in a modern setting, the anthology was a narrow one, drawing from mainstream socialist voices, and omitting all kinds of difficult perspectives from areas such as feminism and other key social movements.

BROWN IN GOVERNMENT
PREPARING FOR POWER

Tony Blair became leader in July 1994 after John Smith's death in a period that has been incessantly dissected by New Labour Kremlinologists, keen to find out what really happened between Blair and Brown in the infamous meal at the Granita restaurant on 31 May 1994. The existence or not of a 'secret pact' by which Brown first supported Blair in return for Blair standing down in the future has been incessantly picked over (Rentoul 2001: 222–43; Routledge 1998: 189–210). Brown commented later to Paul Routledge about the manoeuvring after Smith's death, 'I was never part of the London scene' (Routledge 1998: 205) – a reference to the influence of Alastair Campbell and Peter Mandelson. What is not disputed is that the two men agreed in a briefing note the agenda and shape of the next Labour Government. This said:

> In his Wales and Luton speeches, Gordon has spelled out the fairness agenda – social justice, employment opportunities and skills – which he believes should be the centrepiece of Labour's programme and Tony is in full agreement with this

and that the party's economic and social policies should be further developed on this basis. (*The Guardian*, 6 June 2003)

This important historic document in the creation of New Labour, which turned up nine years after the event, has the words after 'Tony is in full agreement with this' scored out, and inserted in Gordon Brown's handwriting: 'has guaranteed this will be pursued'. This fairness agenda allowed Brown to see economic and social policy as under his tutelage. In *Fair is Efficient*, published one week before John Smith's death, Brown outlines this agenda: 'We must work hard at our own welfare system to ensure that it provides pathways out of unemployment and poverty rather than trapping people in persistent dependency . . . acting as a trampoline rather than as a safety net.' (Brown 1994a: 22) One month after Blair's election as leader and with the broad priorities of Labour in office agreed, Brown returned to the fairness theme: 'Fairness will be the theme, indeed the agenda of a Tony Blair administration. What people want in this country is a restoration of a sense of fair play and fair dealing. It's something that has gone missing.' (Routledge 1998: 212)

In an IPPR collection, *Reinventing the Left*, published to give impetus to a New Labour agenda, Brown contributed 'The Politics of Potential', addressing the theme that socialism was enabling individuals to realise their potential and his priorities for a fairness agenda:

- Tackling entrenched interests and unjust power and privilege which hold people back;
- An enabling state offering new pathways out of poverty: 'The welfare state should not just be a safety net but a springboard';
- A new constitutional settlement between individuals, communities and the state: 'to reinvent government we must first reconstruct the very idea of community';
- A new economic egalitarianism which accepts that people's potential and their labour is the driving force of the modern economy. (Brown 1994c: 114)

Brown was clear this was as inspiring a vision as any offered by the early socialist pioneers: 'My vision of a fair Britain means not just taking on entrenched interests that hold people back, and pursuing a modern social policy that offers pathways out of poverty, but a new economic policy – a new economic egalitarianism' (1994c: 122).

In the second John Smith Memorial Lecture in 1996, Brown posed that New Labour's idea of equality was more radical than Tony Crosland's:

Because this vision is grounded in a broader view of the diversity of human potential than a single type of academic intelligence, and because it recurs continuously throughout life, this view of equality of opportunity is not just stronger but more suited to the 1990s than that discussed by Anthony Crosland in his 'Future of Socialism', and by Professor Rawls in his 'Theory of Justice'. (Brown 1996: 2)

'Equality of opportunity', according to Brown, 'should not be a one-off, pass-fail, life-defining event but a continuing opportunity for everyone to have the chance to realise their potential to the full.' (1996: 2) In the Anthony Crosland Memorial Lecture in 1997, he made the distinction with Old Labour even more explicit:

> We cannot meet the challenge of creating both an educated economy and a just and more cohesive society without taking the idea of equality of opportunity seriously. Not hankering after an unrealisable equality of outcomes, as old Labour was accused of doing, advancing the wrong kind of equality, when the challenge is to make equality of opportunity real. (Brown: 1997a)

Thus, this was not a politics of retreat or dilution: 'We reject equality of outcome not because it is too radical, but because it is neither desirable nor feasible.' (1997a; also see 1999a) Neither desirable nor feasible to raise the higher rate of tax from Nigel Lawson's 40 per cent or increase Tory spending plans for the first two years of Labour in office.

DEAR PRUDENCE: GORDON BROWN AS CHANCELLOR

Brown in office proved an ingenious and imaginative, if over-active, Chancellor, who presided over the fruition of his fairness agenda with the New Deal, 25-year aspiration to eradicate child poverty, support for the working poor through the Working Families' Tax Credit, Children's Tax Credit, and increases in child benefit (Pym and Kochan 1998). There was also a sense of mission and purpose to Brown, his speeches filled with talk of 'making work pay' and rebuilding work around a 'revived work ethic'; there was a morally authoritarian strand to New Labour which in Brown spilled over to a puritan sense of self-discipline (*The Guardian*, 16 June 1997). 'The best form of welfare is work' (Brown 1999b: 52), wrote Brown, and his views are shaped by a Protestant work ethic, based on a belief in the goodness and salvation of work. There is a dullness and monotony to this world that seems without colour or song, and which does not recognise that there is more to life, let alone social democracy, than work.

He combined all this with endless talk of an 'end to boom and bust' and 'prudence with a purpose' which allowed him in July 2000 to unleash the floodgates of a Comprehensive Spending Review raising public spending by £68 billion over three years (Keegan 2003). Despite all this, many Labour members felt uneasy with aspects of Brown's politics: his centralism in the

Treasury via Public Sector Agreements, the diminution of Cabinet and Department responsibilities, his wider 'command and control' style, and the extent of PFI/PPP agreements across the public sector.

While doing all this, Brown still had the time to contribute to Scottish Labour's campaign for the 1999 Scottish Parliament elections, penning with Douglas Alexander 'New Scotland, New Britain'. This laid out the case for a new unionism, acknowledging that the old unionism based on empire and deference had gone for good. Instead, a new unionism should be based on such values as the NHS, national insurance and using public spending to pool and share resources. In an analysis far removed from *The Red Paper*'s reading of the SNP, Brown and Alexander did accurately identify that a Scottish Parliament changed the contours of Scottish politics from one defined by an anti-Tory ethos to one which was more anti-Nationalist: 'As long as Devolution was denied the SNP were able to conflate two distinct propositions – the majority wish for Devolution with the minority wish for separatism.' (Brown and Alexander 1999: 39)

Brown was seeking to do nothing less than redefine the idea of British-ness:

> I see Britain as being the first country in the world that can be a multicultural, multi-ethnic and multinational state. America, at its best, is a multicultural and multi-ethnic society, but America does not have nationalities within identifiable political units in the way that Britain does. We have a chance to forge a unique pluralist democracy where diversity becomes a source of strength. (quoted in Richards 1999)

Brown knew that a new idea of Britain was needed, and that the old progressive models would no longer do: the old social democratic state of Attlee centralism was discredited, while the old Labour devolution model of the 1970s was an ad hoc reaction to events. What Brown and others wanted was a 'New Labour Nation' which attempted to re-find 'a progressive British narrative' (Aughey 2001: 95).

A year later, Scottish Labour was hit by another tragedy when Donald Dewar, then First Minister, died in office, in October 2000. His funeral was a moving and fitting tribute to a man who had given his life to public service, and Brown's contribution was an apt one, informed by the feel of the manse he had grown up with as well as the Labour movement. Underlining the importance of public service, Brown commented:

> So when people say: 'What was special about Donald was decency', they tell you far less than half the story. What was special about Donald as a politician, was

that consistently, and tirelessly, he pursued the logic of his decency and worked for a just and more equal society. (Brown 2000: 40)

Dewar's legacy was one that Brown could identify with: a belief in social justice and a fair society, and the championing of a Scottish Parliament as a means to an end, not an end itself. 'Donald's achievement', commented Brown, 'is much more than a Parliament. Much more than the sum of his social reforms. It is that he ennobled the very idea of service and by his pursuit of a just society, he gave moral purpose to our public life.' (2000: 41)

Brown's relationship with Scottish Labour has always been a sensitive one, particularly since the deaths of John Smith and Donald Dewar. He is perceived and acts differently in Scotland. Faced with a more traditional Labour audience, Brown emphasises the common values and shared history that the party has. In return, Brown feels, as the most prominent UK Labour politician in Scotland since the death of Smith, that he can act as an old-style fixer which he would not dare do in the rest of the UK – in a way similar to Blair's actions over Ken Livingstone and Rhodri Morgan. Labour Party members have alleged that Brown has influenced party candidate selections and was involved in anointing Alex Rowley as Labour General Secretary. He also, it is alleged, played a key role in the Scottish Labour leadership elections of 2000 – trying to aid the succession of Henry McLeish without an election – and in 2001 supporting Wendy Alexander in her abortive campaign for the leadership against Jack McConnell, who subsequently became leader and First Minister. Whatever the rights and wrongs of such cases, what is important to note is that the reach of Brown into the Scottish party did have clear limits – McLeish did face a contest in 2000, and McConnell did become First Minister in 2001.

Brown saw one of his main missions in office as modernising Labour's sense of itself by protecting its traditional values, while engaging in pro-enterprise, pro-business ways of progressing them. This caused controversy in a number of areas: PFI/PPP and concerns over a two-tier workforce, and anxieties over the London Underground, which while accepting 'the moral limits of markets', went too far in terms of introducing private capital and competition into the public sector for most Labour members (Brown 2003c: 5) Brown attempted to assuage anxieties by presenting his New Labour message to Labour audiences in a way that emphasised their common bond. In his first speech to Labour conference as Chancellor, Brown invoked the heroes of Labour's past to justify the present:

It was because a century ago Keir Hardie looked at the world as it was and saw what a new world could be that he broke with the old order, set politics on a new, modern path and founded the Labour Party. It was because Aneurin Bevan looked at the old world of disease and deprivation, and saw what a new world could be, that he broke with the private healthcare of the past and established a National Health Service that still serves us today. And so now for our time, let the message go out. We govern and we seek to serve as a new generation. (Brown 1997b)

At the 2002 Labour conference, Brown articulated in semi-religious language and imagery the motivation of those who work in the public sector:

For them public service is a calling not just a career, far more about service than about self-interest. If we ever lose that ethic of public service, then we lose apart of what is unique about Britain that could never be replaced. (Brown 2002)

This was the more usual Brown approach, but he was also capable of selling a difficult message to a hostile audience. His address to the 2003 TUC conference – at the height of the Blair government's difficulties post-Iraq – was a difficult one for Brown which did not go down well with delegates:

there can be no return to inflationary pay rises, no return to loss-making subsidies that prevent the best long-term decisions for Britain, no resort to legislation from Europe or elsewhere that would risk jobs, no retreat from a pro-enterprise, pro-industry agenda and no retreat from demanding efficiency and value for money as well as equity as we renew and reform each of our public services. (Brown 2003a)

At the same time, in typical Brown style, he listed all the economic achievements and public sector new jobs in the manner that Matthew Parris once called 'an animated shopping list'. First came the economic achievements:

- Britain now has the lowest long-term unemployment since 1976;
- The lowest female unemployment since 1975;
- The lowest male unemployment since 1974;
- More lone parents in employment than at any time in our history;
- Where there used to be 350,000 young people long-term unemployed there are now just 5,000;
- Now lower unemployment than Germany, France, America and Japan; and
- More people in work in Britain today than at any time in the history of our country. (Brown 2003a)

And then, with only a brief pause to remind delegates of the spectre of the Tories, eighteen years and Michael Howard (prior to his becoming Tory leader), he listed the growth in public sector jobs:

- 50,000 more nurses;
- 10,000 more doctors and consultants;
- 25,000 more teachers;
- 88,000 more teaching assistants;
- 7,000 more policemen and women. (Brown 2003a)

This Brownite mantra is interesting on a number of levels because it appears in so many speeches to Labour audiences. The first part appears triumphalist, selling the success story of Britain in a way similar to Thatcherism at its height just before it imploded, but mixing it with a Labour chauvinism and self-satisfaction. The second element seems to be a politics without vision and values, reduced to 'schools and hospitals', as Labour ran its 2001 UK election campaign on, rather than the aspirations and hopes contained within them. Brown in these speeches appears trapped in a prison of his own creating: of New Labour's agenda which acknowledged the realities of Thatcher's legacy and globalisation, but which has bequeathed a party which is unsure what it stands for beyond managerialism, targets and assessments.

A History of the Future:
Brown in the Post-Blair Era

The Odd Couple: Blair and Brown and the Project

Gordon Brown has been the most successful Chancellor in Labour's history, able to banish memories of Labour Governments and economic crises which had destroyed the party's plans in 1931, 1967 and 1976. He was 'the most important and influential Chancellor since David Lloyd George' and 'the outstanding Labour figure of his generation' (Brivati 2002: 232, 237).

The dominant dynamic of New Labour in government has been the Blair–Brown relationship, seen by some as Blair-as-President to Brown-as-Prime Minister, to others, a Blair–Brown government of cohabitation or 'dual monarchy'. The analogy of a 'political marriage' has been used to describe the various stages of their relationship – the intimate early years when they were 'the young pretenders' under Kinnock and Smith, the defining point of 'the pact' and creation of New Labour, and now, a more formulaic and distanced relationship. The two men have very different styles:

> He [Blair] revels in his difference. In politics he is an outsider who has found his way in, and who seems determined not to be constrained within the usual boundaries. Brown, by contrast, has spent his life on the inside and is the politician who only steps out in his own terms. (Naughtie 2001: 266)

Both Blair and Brown have been significantly shaped as people and politicians by their Christian beliefs, and were from an early age influenced by the Scottish philosopher John Macmurray. He wrote extensively from a Christian socialist perspective of the importance of the community to individual worth, and of issues such as responsibilities and obligations being as important as rights. Blair was introduced to his writings at Oxford, while Brown's father, John, was hugely influenced by him (Rentoul 2001: 41–3; Routledge 1998: 19). From this shared source, the two men have developed very different types of Christian socialism, Blair being denigrated as a 'trendy vicar' always trying to appear young and hip to the point of near-ridicule, whereas there has always been something more rooted and old-fashioned in Brown; the former a very English type of Christianity, the latter, a very Scottish version (Craig 2003: 181–95).

Blair and Brown have been perceptively compared to a previous generation of Labour moderates – Roy Jenkins and Tony Crosland. Jenkins was the younger and the less Labour-orientated of the two; Crosland was the intellectual giant of the two and author of the revisionists' bible, *The Future of Socialism*. Jenkins' career went from strength to strength as he occupied some of the great offices of state (Chancellor, Home Secretary); Crosland belatedly became Education Secretary and briefly before his death, Foreign Secretary (Radice 2002: 330–1). An *Evening Standard* piece which originally made this comparison drew attention to Jenkins and Crosland's friendship being torn apart by jealousy and predicted the same fate for Blair and Brown. It has not happened yet. Jim Naughtie said of Roy Jenkins' relationship with Blair, 'Now and again when Jenkins and Blair meet, the Prime Minister gives a smile and says: "Tell me the Crosland story again."' (2001: 317)

UNDERSTANDING NEW LABOUR: ATLANTICISM AND LABOURISM

Brown and Blair's views are revealing in two key areas: the United States and their attitude and understanding of Labour and other progressive forces. Both politicians were fascinated by the success of Clinton and the New Democrats, and after Labour's fourth defeat in 1992 were eager to learn lessons from centre-left parties which won. There were differences between the two: Blair was more interested in Clinton the communicator whereas Brown felt an empathy for Robert Reich, Secretary of Labour in Clinton's first term, who talked the same language of skills, training and education. Brown has made annual pilgrimages to Wellfleet, Cape Cod, where he would meet with American academics and catch up on the latest thinking and books.

Something profound was at work in New Labour's attachment to

America. 'Its rhetoric is American', argued David Marquand, 'and the influences which have shaped its project are American, as is its political style.' (Marquand 1999: 239) This for a party which pledged itself to be 'at the heart of Europe', yet which also emphasised the traditional British role as 'a bridge' between the US and the continent, and during the Iraq war seemed to have become an apologist for American foreign policy. Marquand wrote several years ago with great prescience, 'When American and European interests diverge, New Labour can be relied on to show more tenderness to the former. Above all, it shares the prevailing American view of the new capitalism, and of the relationships between states and markets which it implies.' (1999: 239)

And while Brown remained mostly silent over Blair's decision to go to war side by side with George W. Bush in Iraq, his allegiance and enthusiasm for the American way is as great as Blair's. 'His approach, the approach of the government and the new political consensus, is based on a combination of new European social democracy and North American New Democratic ideology.' (Brivati 2002: 249) With Brown this was more about UK and US common ground on welfare, rather than warfare, 'seeking to achieve similar objectives and draw upon a similar range of policy instruments' in tackling welfare dependency, work requirements and making work pay (Deacon 2000: 16).

Where Brown and Blair display an even more obvious difference is in their relationship to Labour and what is called the politics of labourism. This is a complex set of historical and political forces by which the party 'has deliberately chosen to identify itself as the instrument of the labour interest rather than as a rationale for any ideology.' (Marquand 1999: 17) Blair is clearly from outwith the Labour tradition or beholden to labourism, impatient with much of its history and culture, and has constantly challenged the party to abandon some of its most outdated aspects. He has had for a decade as leader a semi-detached relationship with Labour, which in the popular years gave him freedom to appeal to moderate voters, but now he is less popular, this has shown the lack of support he has in the party. Brown is very different, and is a man imbued with the uniqueness of Labour and its ways, and who understands how it sees itself, its culture, values and history; in short, the importance of labourism. Martin Kettle once described Brown's politics as shaped by an 'awesome single-minded loyalty to Labour'.

This does make the feel of Blair and Brown very different: a Blair speech can name-check people outwith the Labour tradition – he once listed Lloyd George, Keynes and Beveridge as his heroes, none members of the Labour Party (along with Attlee, Crosland and Bevan) – while Brown can wrap up a modernising message by invoking the memory of Clement Attlee and Nye

Bevan (and, importantly, no one from outwith Labour). At the 2003 Labour conference, Brown argued that his economic record had happened because of Labour's values: 'Labour's values made it happen. Don't ever let people tell you this happened because we were lucky, it happened because we are Labour.' (Brown 2003b) 'Blair was wider but shallower. Brown was deeper but narrower', commented Rawnsley (2001: 154).

And yet it is easy to dwell on the difference, rather than the common ground. Paddy Ashdown found that his long journey with Tony Blair to realign the centre-left ended up nowhere; in these discussions Blair and Ashdown regularly worried about how to get Brown signed up to this agenda, but when Ashdown met Brown, the latter could not have been more friendly. 'The difference between Gordon and Tony', according to Ashdown, 'is that, while Tony is all about positioning, Gordon is a man whose head is literally bulging with ideas.' (Ashdown 2000: 484) Brown in typical labourist style has never grasped the politics of pluralism and democracy, but while Blair did, he did not succeed in championing them in office. One difference is that Blair wants people to like him and has a tendency to make people think he agrees with them, whereas Brown is more straight-dealing, which some see as being closed once he has made his mind up.

Brown is a much misunderstood person and politician, someone who is capable both of great self-confidence and sureness, and a sense of frailty and inner doubt. Colin Currie, a lifelong friend from university, portrays Brown in a way that adds credence to classic Scots stereotypes:

> If you can imagine an Edwardian cruise liner, the SS *Great Britain*, there is a charming captain, and deep down in the ship there is a hard Scots engineer who understands all the bits and pieces of the machinery and can wield a spanner in order to persuade people to do the difficult things. (Routledge 1998: 333)

And there is the Tory caricature of Brown as the full-blooded socialist who will if given the chance terrify children and Middle England. A classic example of this is given by the right-wing historian Andrew Roberts in a Centre for Policy Studies lecture in 2003. As Blair post-Iraq hit trouble, Roberts imagined a future where Brown became leader and Prime Minister before the next election, allowing the Tories to be returned and normal service in the British constitution resumed. Roberts does make the astute point that 'Brown will be anointed leader because of his past services to the New Labour revolution, for standing aside for Blair in 1994' (Roberts 2003: 4) and Labour have a track record of electing the wrong leaders for the wrong reasons, Michael Foot being the most obvious example.

However, Roberts falls for the Tories' own propaganda of believing Brown is shaped by 'the Politics of Chip', using the Oxford snubbing of Laura Spence as an example, seeing his championing of Maxton as support for extensive redistribution and belief in public spending as proof of Brown's Old Labour credentials. It is a comforting right-wing view of the world, and similar to the hard left-wingers who see New Labour as a conspiracy by which a right-wing coup captured the party. Roberts believes the millions of Tories who voted Labour in 1997 will come back to the Tories under Brown in 2005–6 'because they recognise in him the unmistakable outlines of an instinctive redistributionist, albeit a far more stealthy one than the original squeeze-'em-till-the-pips-squeak Old Labour type.' (2003: 7)

This is one version of the future: of Brown as a 'fag-end premiership' in Roberts' eyes or a brief interregnum before the second wave of modernisation to some Blairite loyalists. Another scenario would involve Brown becoming leader and Prime Minister and being a success with the party and public, and changing the contours of British politics. It is possible to imagine that a Brown mandate in 2005–6 could have much more vitality and impact than a diminished, demoralised 'fag-end' Blair premiership.

Gordon Brown has gained a reputation for being a determined, focused politician and he has commented on this:

> I was always concerned about issues of social justice, and I always felt that politics was the way to get them sorted out. My upbringing taught me to see things in terms of right and wrong, and the social conditions that appalled me have got to be sorted out. (Routledge 1998: 334–5)

One of Brown's favourite quotes according to Tom Brown is from the writer G. D. H. Cole's *The Simple Case for Socialism*:

> I ask no one to call himself a socialist unless he wants society to recognise other men's claims as no less valid than his own . . . The reason, the only valid reason, for being a socialist is the desire, the impassioned will, to seek the greatest happiness of the greatest number. (Brown, T. 2003: 13)

How does this measure against the performance of Brown and New Labour in office? New Labour's politics have been clearly shaped by 'post-Thatcherism', a step-change on from Thatcherism and the next stage on from neo-liberalism, while attempting to renew social democracy (Finlayson 2003; Driver and Martell 2002: 219). In this it has attempted to achieve a new synthesis while also negotiating an uneasy compromise between two competing traditions. Driver and Martell attempt to offer seven principles of Blairism:

- Inflation matters, competition is good;
- Work is better than welfare;
- Collective public services such as health and education promote social justice;
- Money is not everything: the public sector needs reforming;
- Delivery is all: it does not really matter who provides public services;
- Constitutional reform strengthens the UK;
- Britain should be an active player on the European and world stage, while European integration should be limited by national interests. (Driver and Martell 2002: 222)

If these are the seven crucial credos of Blairism, they really belong to New Labour, and are as much Brown's as Blair's. On another level, compared to Thatcherism, these are not exactly ideologically driven values, but more signposts for a post-ideological age driven by managers and administrators; the politics these principles define would only exclude unreconstructed Thatcherites and left critics of New Labour. They do in some sense amount to 'a new consensus', but are similar to Butskellism in the 1950s in taking its references from the previous political age. Blairism like Butskellism is a non-ideological ism.

Blair's politics have been deeply disrespectful of much of what is Labour tradition and culture – and a large part of this approach was refreshing and honest when it began. Brown has grown up immersed in the politics, culture and values of Labour. This has at points made them the perfect double act, with many shared objectives, but different styles and subtle nuances which hint at differing ways of seeing things. In the early years this strengthened their complementariness and chemistry, but the fault lines between the two are growing larger and larger. Labour after four election defeats had to reconnect with voters concerns and not be driven by activist concerns. However, after two Labour full terms, governing from the centre and ignoring party concerns, the time is right to change emphasis. New Labour's journey began twenty years ago, jettisoning the Old Labour British idea of 'socialism in one country', but has also abandoned the Kinnock era of Labour as a mainstream European social democrat party for a 'catch-all' party politics shaped by America and Atlanticism. This is not an appropriate place for developing a progressive politics.

Many parts of the Labour Party and wider movement are crying out for a little attention – activists, trade unions, councillors, MPs – and Gordon Brown has the capacity and gift to make these people feel special, unique and wanted – and part of something bigger and worthwhile. The challenge for Brown in the post-Blair era is two-fold. First, can he convincingly develop a politics of labourism with a politics of modernisation, or are the two mutually exclusive? This would involve recognising 'the progressive dilemma' whereby historically Labour has not understood the limited nature of its appeal to non-Labour centre-left Britain. Second, can he articulate a post-Blairite modernising politics which tackles some of the key issues facing Britain after two terms of Labour Government?

- 'The fairness agenda' of challenging widespread poverty, inequality and indefensible privilege;
- A public-sector reform agenda that involves people as citizens, not just consumers or producers;
- The lack of corporate responsibility and accountability;
- The deeply entrenched centralism which goes to the heart of the British state;
- And finally, the British dilemma in relation to European integration, and the continued obsession of the British political classes with Atlanticism.

Gordon Brown's place in the history books is already guaranteed as Labour's longest-serving Chancellor, as well as its most successful, attempting to develop a politics and practice of modernisation that is compatible with traditional Labour values. In this, he is a metaphor for Scottish Labour's journey from socialist transformation to a social democracy of reform and micro-vision, while unlike Blair trying to keep a sense of continuity. The challenges New Labour now has to address are issues that go to the heart of Labour's timidity both now and in the past, and on which Blair and Brown share responsibility. After a decade of New Labour dominance – an unprecedented event for Labour and British politics – the time for imagination and radicalism is running out, but has never been more needed. Change is needed, which amounts to more than one of style and culture.

Many thanks to Neal Lawson and James McCormick for comments on an earlier draft of this chapter.

Notes

1. Routledge's book quotes extensively from two of Brown's books – *The Red Paper* and *Scotland: The Real Divide* – which can be seen as much as political projects as publications, and to a lesser extent from a third – *Maxton* – which was a labour of love for Brown. It completely omits from history four books: *The Politics of Nationalism and Devolution*; *Where There is Greed*; *John Smith: Life and Soul of the Party*; and *Values, Visions and Voices*. Given Routledge's book is a semi-official account written with Brown and his friends' co-operation, these omissions are worthy of note.
2. 'The absence from *The Red Paper* not only of a gender politics, but also of any female voice, cannot be lightly dismissed as merely another feature of its time.' (MacDonald and

Cumbers 2002: 77)

3. Brown cites that in the 1929 general election, only 6 per cent of Labour candidates across the country mentioned socialism in their election addresses versus 43 per cent of Conservatives (Brown 1981: 476).

4. Brown finished first in Shadow Cabinet elections four times in the period up to 1997, although his popularity was in decline in the immediate period before the election due to his reputation as an 'Iron Chancellor'. Interestingly, Blair was never as popular in Shadow Cabinet elections, and never attempted to court such widespread popularity. He won 71 votes when he first stood in 1987 – failing to be elected – then 111 in 1988, elected in ninth place, and the following year secured 138 votes and fourth place.

REFERENCES

Allison, J. (1995), *Guilty by Suspicion: A Life and Labour*, Argyll, Glendaruel.

Ashdown, P. (2000), *The Ashdown Diaries: Volume One: 1988–1997*, Allen Lane, London.

Aughey, A. (2001), *Nationalism, Devolution and the Challenge to the United Kingdom*, Pluto Press, London.

Boyson, R. (1995), *Speaking My Mind*, Peter Owen, London.

Brivati, B. (2002), 'Gordon Brown', in K. Jeffreys (ed.), *Labour Forces: From Ernest Bevin to Gordon Brown*, Tauris, London, pp. 237–50.

Brown, G. (1975), 'Introduction: The Socialist Challenge', in G. Brown (ed.), *The Red Paper on Scotland*, Edinburgh University Student Publications Board, Edinburgh, pp. 7–21.

Brown, G. (1981), *The Labour Party and Political Change in Scotland 1918–1929: The Politics of Five Elections*, unpublished Ph.D., University of Edinburgh.

Brown, G. (1983), 'Introduction', in G. Brown and R. Cook (eds), *Scotland: The Real Divide: Poverty and Deprivation in Scotland*, Mainstream, Edinburgh, pp. 9–22.

Brown, G. (1986), *Maxton*, Mainstream, Edinburgh.

Brown, G. (1989), *Where There is Greed . . . : Margaret Thatcher and the Betrayal of Britain's Future*, Mainstream, Edinburgh.

Brown, G. (1994a), *Fair is Efficient: A Socialist Agenda for Fairness*, Fabian Society, London.

Brown, G. (1994b), 'John Smith's Socialism: His Writings and Speeches', in G. Brown and J. Naughtie (eds), *John Smith: Life and Soul of the Party*, Mainstream, Edinburgh, pp. 61–103.

Brown, G. (1994c), 'The Politics of Potential: A New Agenda for Labour', in D. Miliband (ed.), *Reinventing the Left*, Polity Press in association with the Institute for Public Policy Research, London, pp. 113–22.

Brown, G. (1996), 'Tough Decisions', *Fabian Review*, vol. 108, no. 3, pp. 1–2. Edited extract of Second John Smith Memorial Lecture.

Brown, G. (1997a), *Anthony Crosland Memorial Lecture*, 13 February 1997.

Brown, G. (1997b), *Speech to Labour Party Annual Conference*, Brighton, 29 September 1997.

Brown, G. (1999a), 'Equality – Then and Now', in D. Leonard (ed.), *Crosland and New Labour*, Macmillan in association with the Fabian Society, pp. 35–48.

Brown, G. (1999b), 'Enterprise and Fairness', in G. Kelly (ed.), *Is New Labour Working?*, Fabian Society, London, pp. 49–54.

Brown, G. (2000), 'Donald Dewar', in D. Steel et al., *Donald Dewar: A Book of Tribute*, The Stationery Office, Edinburgh, pp. 39–43.

Brown, G. (2002), *Speech to Labour Party Annual Conference*, Blackpool, 30 September 2002.

Brown, G. (2003a), *Speech to TUC Annual Conference*, Brighton, 9 September 2003.

Brown, G. (2003b), *Speech to Labour Party Annual Conference*, Bournemouth, 29 September 2003.

Brown, G. (2003c), *A Modern Agenda for Prosperity and Social Reform: Opportunity, Security, Prosperity*, Social Market Foundation, London.

Brown, G. and Alexander, D. (1999), *New Scotland, New Britain*, Smith Institute, London.

Brown, G. and Wright, T. (1995), 'Introduction', in G. Brown and T. Wright (eds), *Values, Visions and Voices: An Anthology of Socialism*, Mainstream, Edinburgh, pp. 13–29.

Brown, T. (2003), 'The Quiet Crusade', *Daily Mail*, 13 September 2003, pp. 12–13.

Clark, A. (1993), *Diaries*, Weidenfeld and Nicolson, London.

Craig, C. (2003), *The Scots' Crisis of Confidence*, Big Thinking, Edinburgh.

Deacon, A. (2000), 'Same Ingredients, Different Recipes? Comparing the British and American Approaches to Welfare Reform', paper to APPAM conference, Seattle, 4 November 2000.

Driver, S. and Martell, L. (2002), *Blair's Britain*, Polity, Cambridge.

Drucker, H. M. and Brown, G. (1980), *The Politics of Nationalism and Devolution*, Longman, London.

Finlayson, A. (2003), *Making Sense of New Labour*, Lawrence and Wishart, London.

Hansard (1983), 27 July, cols 1226–44, The Stationery Office, London.

Keegan, W. (2003), *The Prudence of Mr Gordon Brown*, John Wiley, London.

MacDonald, F. and Cumbers, A. (2002), 'When Brown was Red', *Soundings*, no. 20, summer 2002, pp. 64–78.

Marquand, D. (1999), *The Progressive Dilemma: From Lloyd George to Blair*, 2nd edn, Phoenix Giant, London.

Naughtie, J. (2001), *The Rivals: The Intimate Story of a Political Marriage*, Fourth Estate, London.

Pym, H. and Kochan, N. (1998), *Gordon Brown: The First Year in Power*, Bloomsbury, London.

Radice, G. (2002), *Friends and Rivals: Crosland, Jenkins and Healey*, Little, Brown, London.

Rawnsley, A. (2001), *Servants of the People: The Inside Story of New Labour*, 2nd edn, Hamish Hamilton, London.

Rentoul, J. (2001), *Tony Blair: Prime Minister*, 2nd edition, Little, Brown, London.

Richards, S. (1999), 'Interview with Gordon Brown', *New Statesman*, 19 April 1999, pp. 18–19.

Roberts, A. (2003), *The Gordon Brown Premiership and its Myriad Opportunities for Tories*, Seventh Keith Joseph Memorial Lecture, 8 April 2003, Centre for Policy Studies, London.

Routledge, P. (1998), *Gordon Brown: The Biography*, Simon and Schuster, London.

Seyd, P. (1987), *The Rise and Fall of the Labour Left*, Macmillan, Basingstoke.

CHAPTER 13

Scotland, Labour and the Trade Union Movement: Partners in Change or Uneasy Bedfellows?

Mark Irvine

The STUC is sometimes described, to its public denial and private delight, as the political wing of the Labour Party in Scotland. It was a joke which found particular resonance in the 1980s and 1990s, when Labour struggled determinedly to solve the riddle of electability, while the STUC led a fulfilling existence as genial paterfamilias to Scottish protest against the new Conservatism (Aitken 1997). Aitken's thoughtful history was written shortly before the 1997 general election, but his sentiments take on a more profound significance in the light of Scotland's new political settlement. The STUC has in Aitken's words been 'much more significant politically than it has been industrially: that it has often played a motive part in influencing public policy, but relatively rarely in affecting the outcome of industrial issues.' (1997: 2)

What is the nature of the relationship between Labour and the unions? How has it changed since the 1970s? Will Scotland's multi-party politics make a difference and can the unions learn to love New Labour, or will the party simply revert to its union roots once Tony Blair has had his day? Scotland's unions are at a turning point in history: they can be modern, forward-looking organisations that reflect genuinely the diverse views of their members, or just old-fashioned power brokers – prisoners of their Labour-dominated past. Scotland has a new Parliament, one that reflects all shades of opinion: Scottish Socialists and Greens both enjoy a place under the sun, alongside various independents. And yet the Scottish trade union leadership go on pretending that their organisations are monoliths and every union member supports Labour.

A mere 22,000 Scots are Labour Party members – less than half of one per cent of the population (1 in 227), yet trade unions are packed to the rafters with Labour clones. Impossible numbers are concentrated in all the top jobs, which can only happen, in equal-opportunity terms, if a hidden hand is at work. Unflinching support for equal opportunities is written into the

Scotland Act 1998. Scotland's new politics oppose discrimination of any kind, yet non-Labour union figures are as rare as snow in the Sahara. As employers, unions should accept that their recruitment practices encourage a culture that is openly hostile to Scots of a non-Labour persuasion.

Sadly, Scotland's unions now operate in a fundamentally anti-democratic way. A generation ago, many of Scotland's most able union leaders were members of the Communist Party of Great Britain (CPGB). Michael McGahey, George Bolton (NUM), Jimmy Airlie and Jimmy Reid (AEUW), James Milne and Doug Harrison (STUC), Hugh Wyper (TGWU) and many others were strong-willed and independent individuals, dialectical not dogmatic in their views.

Nowadays, the gene pool is a shallow puddle of its former self. Labour dominates union thinking in Scotland out of all proportion to its numbers, which is bad for the unions, but also for Labour because union democracy is being manipulated for political ends. So how, once the Scottish Communists bit the dust (a party which in its heyday could never claim more than 3,000 members), did things go so badly wrong?

1970s AND 1980s: How Things Went Wrong?

In the 1970s the British labour movement was alive with challenging ideas and fierce debate. The nature of democracy in a modern industrial state was a burning issue, as the post-war generation threw off its forelock-tugging past. A popular grass-roots work-in at Upper Clyde Shipbuilders in 1971–2 signalled new confidence, imagination and thinking, with the then Tory Government of Edward Heath conducting a spectacular U-turn to save the Clyde yards (Foster and Woolston 1986).

Marxist ideology and the Communist Party, in particular, had enormous influence on union politics. Structures had been built on the principle of 'representative' democracy with union delegates conveying rank-and-file views up and down the chain of command.

Many of the enduring industrial images from the 1970s portrayed trade unions in a negative light, such as the power cuts and three-day week of 1974. A decade of poor industrial relations culminated in the 'winter of discontent' in 1979 and split the unions over how to handle relations with a Labour government. A widespread belief developed that unions had moved beyond their legitimate, if narrow, self-interest to become the power brokers in UK party politics. But were they reflecting their members' views, or pursuing industrial militancy for political ends? A thumbnail sketch of the main players helps explain the industrial landscape, which was broadly similar across the UK.

The Stalinists, or 'Tankies' as they were affectionately known, were centred on the CPGB and believed trade unions and the organised working class were the key to political change. Classic Marxist–Leninist theory held that key groups or vanguards of workers with industrial muscle, such as the miners, were the key to challenging and changing the capitalist system. The industrial and class struggle would enlighten politically the mass of workers, who would then follow their leaders down a British road to socialism.

The Euro-communists – the CPGB's self-styled democratic left – favoured Gramsci over Lenin and a more inclusive style of politics. The emphasis was on individual as well as collective rights (such as one member one vote), broader democratic alliances with other groups, single-issue politics and rainbow coalitions that challenged gender and racial stereotypes. The defining difference was a rejection of old Marxist shibboleths about vanguards and 'top down' leadership.

The Labour Party had plenty of members supporting the Eurocom and Stalinist positions, but the most successful Labour group of all was the right-wing union bosses and their allies: Labour loyalists from the engineering, electricians and GMB unions. Resolutely anti-Communist and anti-Marxist, they ran the Labour Party, resisted the left and rescued Labour leaders repeatedly with block votes at TUC and Labour conferences (see Minkin 1991).

The fourth group comprised different ultra-left and Trotskyite parties and factions: the Socialist Workers' Party (SWP), Workers' Revolutionary Party (WRP) and, latterly, Militant, were all active and influential, especially during strikes and disputes. The traditional left and right hated the ultra left and Trotskyism worse than poison and held their fellow socialists in contempt, as dangerous adventurers, because of their trademark habit of pursuing impossible, unattainable demands, albeit with great passion and commitment.

By the end of the 1980s, union members expected much more than being treated as small cogs in a giant wheel – canon fodder in the increasingly bitter fight to control the Labour Party. The problem was that ordinary union members were no more left- or right-wing than were other voters who were growing restless of excessive union power and lack of democracy.

After the 'winter of discontent', anti-union sentiment played a part in Margaret Thatcher's election victory. The labour movement needed to respond subtly, but true to form the volume was turned up louder than ever. No one asked the obvious question: why were the biggest democratic gains in union history imposed from the outside by a hostile Tory government? The answer is, of course, that union democracy ground to a halt in the 1970s when small and unrepresentative groups of activists made all the key decisions and member-led democracy was a bad joke.

The days of union vanguards were about to end, but had a final, terrible death rattle in the miners' strike of 1984–5. The case for pre-strike ballots had been debated fiercely for years, but in the end union leaders lacked the courage to move from a position of strength by reforming internally. Ironically, the TUC condemned the Government for imposing 'anti-union' legislation supported by most ordinary union members. At the lowest point in 1984–5, Arthur Scargill took the once proud and powerful NUM out on strike without a ballot of members, and saw the union and industry crushed by the Tories (Crick 1985).[1]

Many on the left drew the obvious conclusion that industrial muscle on its own was no match for the forces of the state. Soon after, events in the Soviet Union dealt another hammer blow to the old 1970s-style socialism. The Soviet Union had been a touchstone for the Communist-dominated left: the existence of a Marxist state proved socialism could replace capitalism and market forces. Yet the Soviet Union collapsed politically in 1991 in the wake of Mikhail Gorbachev's ambitious programme of democratic reforms of glasnost and perestroika.

The miners' strike had shown the limits on union power in a modern democracy and the Soviet Union's abrupt demise demonstrated the hegemony of global capitalism. Together, these cataclysmic events precipitated the disintegration of the Communist Party of Great Britain and with it the intellectual cutting edge of the labour movement. The importance of informed consent, of winning people's hearts and minds, finally triumphed over the old ways of top-down, pseudo democracy where the leaders or a select group of cadres were always firmly in control.

Meantime, the Tories swept all before them, embarking on a massive programme of privatisation, shrinking further the old bastions of union power. The 1987 election saw another effortless Tory victory, but produced a much-needed reality check in the trade union movement: things were never going to change unless Labour and the unions changed themselves.

Suddenly, it was open season on policies that had been articles of faith a decade earlier. Out went a producer-focused socialism in favour of a more consumer-orientated approach, with policies abandoned such as any support for greater public ownership, public subsidies for failing industries and unilateral nuclear disarmament – as Labour reinvented itself. As old certainties began to blur and disappear, so too did many of the old divisions between left and right. Trade unions provided ballast for the party and were a major driver in refocusing Labour on getting back to power, but this would also have future implications for Labour's relationship with the unions.

In Scotland, the labour movement held together better and more cohesively than the rest of the UK, partly due to Labour's role as the establishment party north of the border, but also because of the STUC's ability to work on an all-party basis and with other parts of civic Scotland, notably the churches. Imaginative campaigns such as the Scottish occupation at the Caterpillar factory against the decision of the American multinational to close a profitable plant – similar in spirit to UCS the previous decade – failed to capture the public mood, and ended in defeat (Woolston and Foster 1988).

Iain Lawson commented wryly on his experience of an all-party campaign to save Gartcosh:

> The tactics are as follows:
> 1. Set up an all-party group made up of equal representation from all political parties. Top this up with representatives from all affected local authorities (usually Labour controlled), trade union members (usually Labour members), STUC (usually Labour members), a few ministers and a few representatives from other groups.
> 2. Have a main sub-committee made up of one representative from each group (inbuilt Labour majority).
> This ensures inbuilt Labour control. At the first and every meeting urge the need for a co-ordinated campaign with every move being made through the 'all-party' grouping. This effectively inhibits other political parties from taking separate measures which may embarrass the Labour party. Any suggestion of independent action results in accusations of 'rocking the all-party boat' to the detriment of the workers involved. (Letter to *The Scotsman*, 26 June 1986)

Lawson's telling insight exposed an all too common style of work: sharing power and influence was anathema to many in the Labour Party, and the STUC were happy at times to act as what to outsiders often seemed like little more than a 'front organisation' for the Labour Party.

THE WAY BACK

The Conservatives slowly began to implode post-1992, divided over Europe and their future direction. 'No beer and sandwiches' (Baslett 1991: 312) was already a policy under Neil Kinnock's leadership, which indicated no return to the cosy arrangements of the 1970s. Things shifted further under John Smith, and then under Tony Blair, who began to develop new policies which were pro-business and looking to encourage a new relationship with trade unions as partners.

The election of New Labour in 1997 under Tony Blair heralded a new relationship between Labour in power and the trade unions. Blair stated that there would be no 'special favours' and trade unions would be treated just like any other interest group. In response, the trade union movement began to think about how to adapt, survive and recruit members in the new environment. Three different perspectives arose:

- **Servicing** This involves a 'new bargaining agenda' around equal rights, flexible working and training. First adopted by the GMB in 1990, this approach was heavily influenced by independent research on what employees actually wanted from trade unions, placing greater emphasis on services to individual members and a more consensual approach as key to attracting women and professional workers.
- **Social partners** This co-operative model has been supported by government since May 1999 when Tony Blair endorsed the concept at a TUC conference, announcing the creation of a Partnership at Work Fund with up to £2.5 million of funds, including £1.2 million from government, to spend on projects to improve partnership at work.
- **Militancy** This approach comes from a newly resurgent left in the trade union movement which asserts that workers still retain the collective capacity for action because of widening injustice and inequality in work. Workplace union activists are increasingly using this sense of injustice to mobilise for collective action, shifting the emphasis from 'servicing' to 'organising'.

All three strategies have advantages and disadvantages. A 'servicing' model reduces unions to the role of a retail experience and members to consumers. Partnership has the potential to deliver new gains, but is restricted by the timidity of the Blair government on union issues, mistrust among some union leaders and the anti-trade union ethos of many employers. For example, Sir Clive Thompson, CBI President, commented:

> I believe strongly in partnership between a company and its employees, but I fail to see that a union is necessary to make it work. We mustn't fall into the trap of thinking partnership must mean unions. Of course it can, but what's right for one company is by no means right for all. By all means let's have partnerships – partnerships that really are between employers and employees. Let's have union involvement, but only where companies believe (this) can genuinely add value. (*Financial Times*, 24 June 1999)

And 'militancy' is silent on the changed composition of the trade union movement since 1979, with membership halved and trade unions effectively ghettoised in the public sector, with few members in the private growth sectors of the economy. Overall, 40 per cent of private sector workers were union members in 1979, whereas today it is 18 per cent (Taylor 2003).

In power, New Labour and Tony Blair were determined to hit the ground running, to be bold and at their best from day one. Immediately, the new

Chancellor, Gordon Brown, announced that the Bank of England would become independent and free from government control – a step too far even for Mrs Thatcher! The message to the unions was loud and clear – economic policy under New Labour would stick to public spending limits announced by the Tories before being ejected from office.

Labour's spending plans were a bombshell, but all the key decisions of the 1997 Parliament had already been taken. From the outset, government was committed to a wider role for the 'not for profit' and private sectors where union membership was relatively low. A public sector shake-up threatened what was left of traditional union power bases, which was the underlying cause for alarm.

Union bosses talked the talk of a new role for unions as social partners, as the friends of change not its enemy. But Labour insiders believed the internal union culture remained oppositional. New Labour advocates, who often had little empathy or understanding for trade union values and culture, feared weak leadership would result in the unions reverting to type at the first opportunity and that an upsurge in militancy would break out.

In Scotland also, New Labour was the only game in town despite the grumbling off-stage. Many Scottish union leaders privately denounced Tony Blair as a Tory, turning a blind eye to the fact that the Prime Minister and his Chancellor spoke with one voice on economic policy. Both were closer to the American Democrats, such as Bill Clinton and Al Gore, than Labour leaders of yesteryear.

True to his word, Blair set about John Smith's unfinished business of creating a Scottish Parliament in Labour's first term of office. The expectation and talk were of a new style of politics north of the border. Proportional representation (PR) for the new Parliament was the key along with power-sharing structures – all with the intention of nurturing a very different and consensual political culture to that of Westminster.

As Scotland's establishment party, Labour operated as a one-party state in its central belt heartlands, and it was to be a seismic shock when opposition parties were introduced to those areas via the regional list system of the Scottish Parliament. Donald Dewar, First Minister, even had the crazy idea of introducing PR to Labour's town halls – a death blow to the Old Labour ways of doing things. And through all the ups and downs since, this Scottish Executive commitment remained, with Jack McConnell declaring his support after the 2003 elections.

As the first Holyrood elections approached, a simmering row over using private finance to build schools and hospitals (PFI) brought a dull campaign to life. Predictably, Labour 'monstered' the SNP's 'Penny for Scotland' spending plans, cheered on by the mainly Labour-supporting press and the *Daily Record* in particular. The ugly aping of Tory tactics was the mirror image of what happened to Neil Kinnock and John Smith in 1992, but the irony was lost on voters.

Meanwhile, the PFI row was spinning out of control. The STUC congress in April 1999 took place just days before polling day and a headline-grabbing motion was causing the Labour Party concern. Kept secret at the time, a meeting was set up by the Chancellor, Gordon Brown, high priest of Labour's economic policy and chief architect of PFI in the public services. The meeting's purpose was to defuse the row at the STUC. Scotland's union leaders were all present including the General Secretary of the STUC, Bill Spiers, and the bosses of the major affiliated unions (Unison, GMB and TGWU). In the end, they concocted a mealy-mouthed statement that said, on careful reflection, PFI was not so bad after all! In effect, Scotland's union bosses ate their own words and cheerfully abandoned a policy because it rocked Labour's boat ahead of the election. Of course, every single person at that meeting was a fully paid up member of the Labour Party.

The decade may have ended on a low note of old-fashioned union fixing, but there were real achievements during the 1990s under the stewardship of STUC General Secretary Campbell Christie, who led the organisation through the difficult times of 1986–98. Christie was more pluralist than many of his contemporaries and fought to maintain the STUC's independence from the Labour Party, which it is ostensibly, though the reality is that the Labour-affiliated unions run the show. In 1990 Christie accepted an invitation to join the Guinness board of directors, but the big unions forced Christie into a humiliating climbdown. They did the same when Christie proposed after the 1992 election that SNP leader Alex Salmond address the STUC congress. Undaunted, Christie went on to play a crucial role in the Scottish Constitutional Convention that brokered the deal to deliver a Scottish Parliament and proportional representation.

New Scotland, New Politics?

Scotland under the Tories was a barren land for the trade unions. They were swept out of the corridors of power, and systematically removed from enterprise and health boards (Aitken 2002). Rozanne Foyer, Assistant General Secretary of the STUC, commented on the climate pre-devolution and the change post-devolution: 'In Scotland, we had about five meetings with ministers in twenty years, now we have about five meetings a month with ministers in the Scottish Executive about transport, health, local government and education.' (Murray 2003: 163)

New Labour and Tony Blair enjoyed the longest honeymoon in modern political history following the 1997 general election. Signs of industrial unrest surfaced only after it became clear Labour would win a second term. And as the return of the Tory bogeyman ceased to be credible, union bosses decided it was time to flex their muscles again. A new generation of union bosses came to the fore, at UK level at least: Bob Crow (RMT); Mick Rix (ASLEF); Mark Serwotka (PCS); Billy Hayes (CWU); Dave Prentis (Unison); and Derek Simpson (Amicus). Even old war-horses of the right felt emboldened. GMB leader John Edmonds threatened to withdraw financial support for Labour in Scotland to scupper plans for introducing proportional representation for local council elections. Edmonds, a traditional right-winger, was transformed over the years into a 'troublemaker', by the simple expedient of standing still, politically speaking.

Only 600 or so GMB members in Scotland are members of the Labour Party, yet 99.9 per cent of its 60,000 Scottish members pay a political levy to Labour. A lawful, but dishonest, operation top-slices small sums from union contributions (though not in Northern Ireland where members opt in). Political funds form a conscript army of non-Labour supporters and help the GMB (and others) buy huge influence inside the Labour Party, but under false pretences.

The political levy is about power, not the views of ordinary members. RMT took a Beeching-style axe to its Labour links in 2002. Bob Crow declared the previous affiliation of 56,000 members would be slashed and, overnight, a mighty army of 56,000 levy payers was transformed into a rump of 10,000. One minute 97 per cent of RMT members paid part of their union dues to Labour, the next it was a mere 17 per cent. Such is the essence of the trade union 'rotten boroughs' which affiliate to the Labour Party.

Of course, not one of the 56,000 RMT members involved was asked individually before union bosses used them as canon fodder in the battle over who runs the Labour Party. The RMT cut funding to Labour again in 2003 and threatened to switch its financial support to the Scottish Socialists in Scotland. The simple solution of leaving union members to decide which political party, if any, to support seems to have escaped the RMT leadership.

In 2001, New Labour's election juggernaut pushed aside William Hague, causing the Tories to lose the plot altogether, as they went on to elect Iain Duncan Smith as leader. Labour strategists savoured the prospect of an unprecedented third term, which gave the unions the confidence to increase their attack on the New Labour project.

Meanwhile, in Scotland, the skills of government were proving more difficult for Labour to master. After a rocky start, the Scottish Parliament was dealt a savage blow when Donald Dewar, Scotland's First Minister, died unexpectedly, leaving no obvious successor. Union fixers lost no time going about their usual work. Within hours, Labour's new leader was named in the press, as Gordon Brown and union leaders tried to steamroller Henry McLeish into the job, without an election or debate. Jack McConnell, then Finance Minister, refused to be rolled-over, threw his hat into the ring and forced the issue to an unseemly vote involving Labour's Scottish Executive and Labour MSPs.

In effect, eighty-two people, out of a nation of five million, decided who would become Scotland's next First Minister, a state of affairs much to the liking of union bosses, as it maximised their influence and ignored rank-and-file members. The same 'North Korean' tendencies within Scottish Labour were evident again in 2001 when Jack McConnell was the beneficiary of the lack of a democratic culture in Labour and the trade unions, when he was elected unopposed leader. On both occasions, Labour and union leaderships feared the prospect of proper elections and debate, and used the excuse that running a full Electoral College of Labour affiliates and trade union members would be too difficult and costly. So out went democracy, its price too high!

In many policy areas, Scotland's unions are closer to the Lib Dems, SNP, Greens and Scottish Socialists, but the love-hate relationship with Labour continues, the reason being that despite the well-worn rhetoric about the Scots belonging to one big, happy community, every senior union figure in Scotland is still in the Labour Party. Anyone with a passing interest in equal opportunities knows this situation cannot exist without deep-seated institutional discrimination against non-Labour views.

On election as First Minister, Jack McConnell attempted to build common ground with the trade union movement, offering a 'Memorandum of Understanding' containing new procedures of consultation and dialogue covering economic development, modernising public services, and social partnership. The document acknowledged the STUC's role as 'Scotland's Trade Union Centre' and included the following commitment:

> The Scottish Executive acknowledge that trade unions play an important role in sustaining effective democracy in society, particularly at the workplace, and that the existence of good employment practices are a key contributor to economic competitiveness and social justice; the Scottish Executive will support, as far as practicable, effective trade unionism, fair employment practice, and greater partnership between employers and trade unions. (Scottish Executive/STUC 2003)

These were warm words indeed – recognition after all the harsh years of Thatcherism. And they arose out of events at the 2002 Scottish Labour conference where differences between the Labour and trade union leadership broke out into the open. The trade unions indicated that they were prepared to vote down the entire Policy Forum social policy paper because of PFI/PPP; this caused mayhem among party members and was only narrowly passed because a majority of Constituency Labour Parties backed the leadership. Shortly afterwards the Memorandum was announced by Andy Kerr, Scotland's Finance Minister. UK Labour followed a similar conciliatory tone at the 2003 TUC congress with Douglas Alexander announcing a Public Sector Forum comprising trade unions and government ministers, which was widely interpreted as a reverse for the Blairite New Labour agenda.

Fundamental differences remain on workplace issues and wider policy. In the run-up to the 2003 Scottish Parliament elections, union leaders, disillusioned at the direction of the party, threatened to withdraw organisational support from Labour due to the Iraq war; a threat that, had it transpired, would have significantly handicapped Labour's campaign.

But the question we need to ask is this: do union members share the old-fashioned, undemocratic politics of their leaderships? Kevin Curran succeeded John Edmonds at the GMB in 2003, voted in by 10 per cent of his members on a 15 per cent turnout. Tony Woodley, the TGWU's new leader, enjoyed the support of only 8 per cent of his members on a 20 per cent turnout – neither result suggests that a truly participative union democracy is high up the movement's agenda.

New militants amongst UK union leaders, such as Bob Crow and Mick Rix, are essentially unreconstructed hard leftists (though Rix was unseated in July 2003 by a relatively unknown challenger, Shaun Brady, standing on a moderate ticket). The more moderate left now stands on the ground once occupied by the powerful band of right-wing union barons, with no ideology worth the name, but happy to manipulate the political levy for selfish political ends. In Scotland, especially, this makes a farce of claims that union bosses represent the politics of grass-roots members.

Most of Scotland's union leaders are in the traditional (old right, non-hard left) camp, appointed rather than elected, dominated by the culture of their UK organisations. Scotland's teaching unions are the exception that proves the rule. The EIS and SSTA rule the roost with the EIS in particular hugely influential in Scottish Labour circles. Despite its outwardly independent professional image, many key EIS figures over the years have been Labour Party members, yet the union is widely regarded as oppositional, producer-led and anti-change. Cathy Jamieson, once upon a time a Campaign for Socialism left-winger and firebrand, saw her role as Education

Minister until the 2003 election as solely to avoid any policy pronouncements which might alienate the EIS leadership.

New Labour with its emphasis on individual rights is now the common enemy of the left in all its variants. The long-running fire dispute of 2002–3 rekindled the debate on the modern role of unions. Privately, many union leaders slated the FBU for lodging an over-the-top 40 per cent unachievable pay claim, winding members up to fever pitch and politicising the strike by demanding the return of 'Real Labour', before finally losing control. Yet, publicly, they stifled their criticism as the FBU pursued a pointless and damaging dispute over modern working practices.

The fact is that 99 per cent of union members in Scotland do not belong to any political party and vote the same way as the rest of the population. Yet the combined talents of the STUC and all the individual unions cannot produce one non-Labour figure of any standing; the pro-Labour orthodoxy is stifling, reminiscent of the inflated support once claimed for the Communist Party in the Soviet Union. And ironically, its lack of political diversity has become even worse in the last few years since the demise of our own Communist Party.

Few prominent trade unionists are prepared to speak out publicly against this culture, fearful of having their career prospects ruined. One unattributed full-time official said:

> The reality is that when the chips are down Scotland's union leaders put the Labour Party's interests first. Maybe that's always been the way, but the absence of any non-Labour voices means that all the old checks and balances have gone. What passes for debate now takes place inside a Labour Party straitjacket, with everyone proclaiming their left credentials, yet acting in old-fashioned right-wing ways.

This official went on:

> New thinking is rare and if an idea challenges the ruling elite, it gets crushed without mercy. Michael McGahey was fond of saying the unions are a movement not a monument to the past, but his words of warning are now falling on deaf ears.[2]

So, while the unions remain Labour-only closed shops, the Scottish Parliament is a vibrant, mixed economy of views and representation. Political apartheid on this scale is not sustainable long-term because it is incompatible with the support for equal opportunities enshrined in the Scotland Act. Little wonder the business community is sceptical that the 'social partners' role for the unions is achievable without considerable reform.

FUTURE DIRECTIONS

The STUC has played an impressive role in Scottish politics. As Foyer has said:

> The STUC has been the voice of the working people in Scotland on things like devolution, the poll tax, not just workplace issues. We have a broad social agenda, dealing with most social and political issues. When the Scottish did not have a parliament the STUC was the nearest thing to it, speaking for Scotland. (Murray 2003: 164)

Jim Craigen, a previous Assistant General Secretary, serving under James Jack, has observed the difference between the STUC and Wales TUC:

> The difference between a noun and an adjective can be overplayed, but it still symbolises something more, for the Welsh body is akin to a regional council of the TUC, with little power to initiate anything independently of London. The Scottish TUC, on the other hand, has, since its foundation, been an autonomous body with policies and priorities which echo Scottish needs and a Scottish identity. (Craigen 1989: 154)

Both comments contain an element of truth, but also encapsulate a romanticised view of the STUC's role in Scottish civil society – a role that can easily be overstated if it is not continually challenged and renewed. The issue that needs to be addressed is that representative democracy ceases to be credible when all union leaders and institutions are one-dimensional.

Scottish Labour and the trade union movement have a deeper historic understanding than elsewhere in the UK, but the tensions between the two are just as real. Scotland's trade union leaders and members have other progressive options, including the SNP, Scottish Socialists and Greens, and some are even, shockingly, Tories! Yet the leaderships remain wedded to a Labour-only policy, when the party could only win 34.6 per cent of the first vote in the 2003 Scottish Parliament elections.

The big challenge for today's trade unions, both as employers and as part of civic Scotland, is to embrace the modern democratic politics that underpin the Scottish Parliament and the hopes of devolution. And to begin that road of renewal, they must welcome people from all political faiths and none: only then will the unions represent the views and values of all their members in Scotland, instead of only those from its Labour-dominated past.

NOTES

1. The NUM Scotland – led by Mick McGahey and reflecting the different political dynamic of a still influential CPGB – operated very differently from Scargill vanguardism, and held a strike ballot.
2. Unattributed interview with a trade union official, June 2003.

REFERENCES

Aitken, K. (1997), *The Bairns O'Adam: The Story of the STUC 1897–1997*, Polygon, Edinburgh.

Aitken, K. (2002), 'Scottish Mutuals: Trade Unions and the Business Lobbies', in G. Hassan and C. Warhurst (eds), *Anatomy of the New Scotland: Power, Influence and Change*, Mainstream, Edinburgh, pp. 180–8.

Baslett, P. (1991), 'Unions and Labour in the 1980s and 1990s', in B. Pimlott and C. Cook (eds), *Trade Unions in British Politics: The First 250 Years*, 2nd edn, Longman, Harlow, pp. 307–27.

Craigen, J. (1989), 'The Scottish TUC: Scotland's Assembly of Labour', in I. Donnachie, C. Harvie and I. S. Wood (eds), *Forward! Labour Politics in Scotland 1888-1988*, Polygon, Edinburgh, pp. 130–55.

Crick, M. (1985), *Scargill and the Miners*, Penguin, London.

Foster, J. and Woolston, C. (1986), *The Politics of the UCS Work-In*, Lawrence and Wishart, London.

Minkin, L. (1991), *The Contentious Alliance: Trade Unions and the Labour Party*, Edinburgh University Press, Edinburgh.

Murray, A. (2003), *A New Labour Nightmare: The Return of the Awkward Squad*, Verso, London.

Scottish Executive/Scottish Trades Union Congress (2003), *Memorandum of Understanding*, Scottish Executive, Edinburgh.

Taylor, R. (2003), 'Beyond the Picket Line', *The Guardian*, 10 September 2003.

Woolston, C. and Foster, J. (1988), *Track Record: The Story of the Caterpillar Occupation*, Verso, London.

CHAPTER 14

Socialism, Territory and the National Question

Michael Keating

CLASS, NATION AND SOCIAL DEMOCRACY

Scottish Labour is far from being the only party in the Western world to face the challenge of reconciling class, ideology and territorial demands, while facing competition on all three dimensions. This is a dilemma of contemporary social democracy, founded as it is on a modern, integrated welfare state, that it can no longer take for granted. Yet breaking with the paradigm of the nation-state has proved difficult everywhere.

The modern state is an often precarious construction, the management of its disparate territories a continuous task of statecraft, especially in complex, plurinational and culturally disparate countries like the United Kingdom, Spain, Belgium or Canada, but even in the archetypical centralised state of France. This may now be obvious in Scotland, but it goes against a great deal of modernisation theory in the social sciences, predicated as it is on the idea of progressive national integration and unity. For the classical sociologists, this takes the form of a division of labour and status by function replacing old divisions of birth, culture and territory. Political scientists emphasise the socialisation of individuals into a common identity and citizenship, and the construction of unified systems of representation and bureaucratic administration. There is a strong normative element in these theories, with integration and unification usually presented as part of modernisation and progress, and an essential step in the achievement of democracy. National unity and integration have also been presented as an essential underpinning of the social solidarity on which the welfare state is constructed. Social democracy has been heavily influenced by modernisation theory, with its predictions that older social cleavages would disappear. Marxism was another variant of this, with its predictions about the transition of societies to the politics of class, and their ultimate resolution in socialism.

Recently these assumptions have come into question, largely as a result of the transformation and ideological demystification of the nation-state, which have revealed the limitations of the old integration paradigm and posed a series of difficult questions. Why, for example, if integration is a virtue, should it stop at the boundaries of the nation-state? Why should solidarity be bound by state and nationality? If nationality is the basis for social solidarity, then in plurinational states which nationality should this be? What should be the attitude of social democratic parties to European integration? Does it undermine the state, or create a new level of solidarity and public power? Above all, social democratic parties have had to respond to the re-emergence of territorial politics in a world where class no longer has the same appeal.

THE HISTORICAL TRAJECTORY OF SOCIAL DEMOCRACY

Socialist and social democratic parties have not always been tied to the centralised nation-state. Indeed, they often started out as parties of the periphery, localist in orientation and suspicious of the alien state. During the course of the twentieth century, they became strongly centralist, before adapting to the localist, regional and sub-state nationalisms of the 1980s and 1990s. This adaptation has in many cases been facilitated by the fact that they never entirely lost their pluralistic, decentralist traditions.

Early socialist movements tended to be local in origin, based on local and community struggles against both capital and the state. They also had an ideology of internationalism, at a time when capital tended to be strongly national and often identified closely with the state. Socialism took its ideology from various sources. Marxism was an inspiration to some, with its interpretation of capitalism and emphasis on industrial struggle, but Marxism had little to say about the nature of the state, and the ideas of the later Marx about the possibilities for socialism by constitutional means remained underdeveloped. Others gained inspiration from advanced liberalism, which in the United Kingdom had its spiritual home in the periphery but in most European countries was identified with the capital. Anarchism in Spain, France and elsewhere provided an anti-statist inspiration and left a legacy favourable to decentralisation and pluralism, but not necessarily to any particular form of territorial politics. As they advanced, labour and socialist movements also had to adapt their message to the local political context, often marked by sharp national and ethnic differences.

The result was a considerable differentiation in the paths taken by early socialist movements. In Scotland, Labour adopted strongly home rule positions up until the First World War, inhibiting the rise of a distinct nationalist party before the 1920s. Irish socialism was largely overshadowed by nationalism, to the point that the Labour Party did not put up candidates in the crucial election of 1918, the first under almost universal suffrage. In France, socialism was marked by localist traditions and anarchism but from the late nineteenth century supported the 'left' in the historic republican battles of the period. These pitched Church against State, republic against monarchy, progress against reaction, and centre against periphery. Left-wing forces, including socialists, emerged strongly committed to the 'jacobin' ideology of unity, equality of citizenship, French nationality and centralisation. As always, there were exceptions, leaving an alternative tradition to be picked up by the new left in the late twentieth century.

In Spain, liberals and socialists picked up French jacobin ideas, but in the context of a weak and reactionary state, which could less credibly be presented as the vehicle of progress. Anarchism offered an alternative ideology for both industrial proletariat and the peasantry up until the Civil War. Catalonia and the Basque Country developed nationalist movements, initially under conservative leadership but with very different programmes. Catalan nationalism was led by the modernising bourgeoisie, which demanded home rule, while at the same time calling on the Spanish state to protect it from foreign competition, and to keep its local working class in their place. Basque nationalism was initially reactionary and anti-modern but from the early twentieth century a sector of the industrial bourgeoisie joined it, seeking to co-opt the working class in a programme of nation-building. These circumstances were not propitious for a left-wing nationalism, especially as both Catalonia and the Basque Country had attracted large numbers of incomers from other parts of Spain, which the left-wing parties and trade unions had to accommodate. In Catalonia, indeed, there was in the early twentieth century a virulently anti-Catalan left-wing movement led by Alejandro Lerroux, modelled on French intransigent jacobinism. After the First World War, however, there emerged a left-wing nationalism which was to crystallise into the *Esquerra Republicana de Catalunya* (Catalan Republican Left) under the Second Republic. In the Basque Country, separate trade unions developed for nationalist and non-nationalist workers, which have remained to the present. Like the British Labour Party, then, the Spanish Socialist Party, PSOE (*Partido Socialista Obrero Español*) needed to accommodate both centralist and decentralist demands and adapt itself to distinct traditions. Like Labour, it adopted a formal position in favour of federalism in 1918, but showed little conviction in carrying it through.

Italian socialism faced a sharp division between the industrial north and the agrarian and peasant south, analysed in some detail by Antonio Gramsci (1978). For a long time the prevailing doctrine was that, since the peasantry tended to reaction, the south could only be liberated by a *vento del nord* (wind from the north) under the impulse of the progressive and class-conscious proletariat of the northern regions. This lent itself to a jacobin doctrine of centralisation but also to the northern working class being bought off by concessions from the state, inhibiting an independent socialist movement (the Spanish labour movement had similar tendencies at times). Only after the Second World War did the Socialist and Communist parties make a serious attempt to harness southern agrarian grievances to a common programme for all Italy.

Belgian socialism was stronger in Wallonia, the most industrially developed region, and tended to decry Flemish particularism, which was associated with reaction, Catholicism and rural society. Socialists thus tended strongly to centralisation until the later part of the twentieth century. In central Europe, the Austro-Marxists faced powerful national movements, which threatened serious divisions in the working class, and tended to favour centralisation and state-building. Later, some of them moved towards forms of personal autonomy or non-territorial home rule, in an effort to contain nationalism without fragmenting the state and the working-class movement. Outside the European context, Quebec exhibited an ethnic division of labour as it industrialised, with capital in the hands of an anglophone business class, while the working class was predominantly francophone. This made for an identification of class and ethnic cleavages, while also stemming the emergence of a distinct socialist party. The hold of the Catholic Church further inhibited the expression of socialism. When a left-wing politics did emerge, after the 1950s, it was strongly marked by this experience and was nationalist in tone. A pan-Canadian form of progressive politics, as espoused by Pierre Trudeau, made much less impression.

In some places the divorce between regional nationalism and socialism was formalised by the collaboration of some nationalists during the Second World War. This marked the Breton and Flemish experiences, with repercussions to this day. A contrary example is the reconciliation of minority nationalism and socialism in Spain. Although the Basque Nationalist Party was conservative in ideology and policy and clerical in attitude, it supported the Spanish Republic during the Civil War, given the virulent Spanish nationalism of the right-wing insurrectionists. In turn, the left had, somewhat reluctantly, to concede a Basque home rule statute. Catalan nationalism split, with a conservative faction going along with Francoism, giving the leadership of Catalanism to the left. Under later Francoism the conservative nationalists, also persecuted, were forced into some accommodation with the left, which in turn had to incorporate Catalan home rule into its programme.

SOCIAL DEMOCRACY IN THE TWENTIETH CENTURY

We therefore have a complex picture of socialist, labour and nationalities and regionalist movements in the formative years of the first part of the twentieth century. In some cases, nationality and territorial politics over-whelmed class and left-wing politics, as in Ireland. In other cases, nation-ality was subordinated to class or ideology, as in much of France, Italy or the United Kingdom. Elsewhere, nationality or territory continued to compete with class and ideology as the basis for political mobilisation, as was the case in the minority nations of Spain.

By the middle of the twentieth century, the classic social democratic formula appeared to have reconciled these tensions. There was a broad appeal to class as the foundation of the progressive political coalition. Of course, we know that class politics was never as dominant as it was sometimes portrayed and that class appeals were often a little spurious, as in the case of the French Socialist Party, SFIO (*Section française de l'internationale ouvrière*), whose rhetoric and very name belied the fact that their support among the proletariat was minimal. In their case, or that of the Italian Socialists, class rhetoric served an ideological legitimating function, as well as seeking to ally the professional classes and public service workers to the industrial muscle of the proletariat. In France and Italy, socialism was overshadowed by powerful Communist parties, who were seen as the real representatives of the working class, but also committed to a politics of national unity and working-class solidarity.

A second feature of the social democratic and labour parties was the increasing focus on the conquest of state power as the precondition for advance. The state, no longer seen as intrinsically alien, had become a neutral machine, potentially usable for progressive purposes, even against the economic power of capitalism. Indeed, as capitalism was internationa-lising, labour became increasingly national and defensive of the nation-state.

A third element was a belief in centralisation. This, as we have seen, had its origins in nineteenth-century progressivism and the liberal ideal of equal citizenship. In the twentieth century, it was allied to the interventionist state, able to seize the commanding heights of the economy and to redistribute resources across space and across social classes. Keynesian macro-economic management could be combined with public ownership to provide a stabilisation and steering capacity for the state. The welfare state, an expression quintessentially of national solidarity, similarly required strong centralised control and management.

Centralisation, however, was never enough to achieve national integration and social democratic parties, like others, had to be attentive to territorial management. Hence the fourth element of the formula, a capacity for differentiated treatment of regions and localities, and a series of linkages between centre and periphery. Even in the heyday of class politics, representation was not purely on the basis of social groups, but also of territories. The elaborate mechanisms constructed to allow Scotland to be represented in the centre and the centre to be represented in Scotland are now well documented. They included the political parties as territorial brokers, the decentralised bureaucracy, the ministerial team at the Scottish Office and the Scottish MPs. In other states, elaborate systems of patronage and clientelism allowed peripheral claims to be sublimated into economic demands, which in turn could be satisfied by divisible goods. The French *notable*, Italian *notabile* or Spanish *cacique* were figures from nineteenth-century politics who were able to deliver local votes to the ruling centre in return for a free hand in the distribution of patronage at home (Keating 1988). Canadian politics was heavily dependent on patronage and Quebec could expect its share of government posts. Social democratic parties, as they integrated into national politics, could similarly serve as territorial intermediaries.

Accommodation also took the form of regional policies intended to integrate marginal territories into the national economy. In the Keynesian era, regional policy was an accompaniment to national macro-economic policies intended to ensure full employment. In a booming economy, diversion of investment into needy areas was a zero-sum game that would at the same time satisfy the regions by bringing jobs, the booming areas by relieving congestion, and the national economy by employing otherwise idle resources. While regional policy was not especially associated with social democratic parties, it was enthusiastically taken up by them as a means of reconciling their electorates in the regions with their centralising strategies. It was, as can be seen in Scotland, a way of demonstrating the advantages of centralisation for non-central territories. Labour leaders and socialist politicians were also incorporated into the mass of agencies, committees and associations through which regional planning, intended to apply central policy in the regions, was implemented.

THE NEW TERRITORIAL POLITICS

By the 1970s there were signs of strains in this mode of territorial management. A rising regionalism and minority nationalism challenged parties of the left in the United Kingdom, Spain and Belgium and, to some extent, even in France. In Quebec, the modernising coalition that made possible the Quiet Revolution of the 1960s had split into federalist and secessionist camps, represented by the Liberals and the *Parti Québécois* respectively. On the ground, a series of social struggles took on a territorial form, drawing in actors from various sectors and forging new alliances. Sometimes these were a reaction to economic restructuring, seen as threatening existing sectors and firms and thus employment in both agriculture and industry. In other cases, they were a response to modernising regional policies themselves, which disrupted traditional social and economic networks and displaced old activities and skills. Upper Clyde Shipbuilders or the Breton mobilisation around the strike at the *Joint Français* are just two examples of a phenomenon to be found across the developed world. A critique evolved of centralised regional policy, seen as an instrument in the service of big capital rather than labour, providing subsidised infrastructure and tax incentives and grants. At times this developed into a critique of the state itself, reintroducing Marxist ideas of the state as the handmaiden of the bourgeoisie. In turn these economic struggles linked with others, notably environmental and pacifist movements. While the Scottish left protested at Faslane and the Holy Loch, Occitan militants tried to save the Larzac plateau from further militarisation.

An ideological dimension was provided by the new, libertarian left emerging from 1968 and challenging both the Stalinism of the Communist parties and the establishment in the social democratic and labour leaderships. In France, inspiration was taken from Robert Lafont (1967) and his call for a *révolution régionaliste*, while Michel Rocard's *Parti socialiste unifié* emphasised similar themes, even as Rocard himself emerged as a social democratic centrist. The Spanish left was affected by the spirit of 1968 in the years preceding the transition, especially among the youth, and a similar spirit is visible in Quebec. Irish nationalism, following the outbreak of the Troubles at the same time, could be presented as a popular struggle against oppression. The 1960s also provided the theme of decolonisation as the old empires were wound up and Third World liberation could be presented as something inherently progressive, where minority nationalism at home had been dismissed as backward. Internal colonialism, a theme originating with Gramsci in the early twentieth century and since exported to Latin America, was brought home in the 1960s and featured in the writings of both Lafont and Rocard as well as, in vulgarised form, Michael Hechter's (1975) book on Scotland. Tom Nairn, from the *New Left Review*, sought to convince Marxists of the progressive potential of nationalism, in the British Isles and elsewhere. In Italy, Gramsci's ideas enjoyed something of a revival as the Italian Communist Party shed its Soviet inclinations and began its gradual journey towards social democracy. While the theme of internal colonialism, always a bit forced, died out with the end of empire, it left behind an appreciation of the progressive side of nationalism and a critique of the big imperial states.

As usual, this ideological shift was accompanied by a historical revisionism, which found minority nationalist and regionalist heroes on the side of progress (Keating 2001). If Scotland had its John Maclean and Ireland its James Connolly, Brittany rediscovered its revolutionary past, obscured for two centuries by the received wisdom that it was always a bastion of reaction (Nicolas 2001). Occitan leftists, tired of the portrayal of the nineteenth century cultural revival as anti-republican, remembered the *Félibrige Rouge*, which in turn drew on historical myths of the Cathars as anti-royalists and localists. Basque leftists found progressive potential in the pre-modern systems of autonomy previously derided as reactionary (Lorenzo Espinoza 1995; Sorauren 1998). Regional/national cultures and folklores, often used for conservative purposes in many parts of Europe, were also pressed into the progressive cause. The folk music movement, in particular, re-engaged in the spirit of protest and popular politics that had traditionally underlain the culture. Neo-traditionalism in general shifted from the right to the left (something that still bewilders observers in the Alpine regions were it is still associated with deepest conservatism).

The 1970s and 1980s also saw an expansion of social democratic support into regions previously dominated by conservative interests, often as a result of secularisation or social modernisation. Brittany, formerly a bastion of the Christian Democratic right, swung to the left. Labour became the dominant party in Scotland. Inroads were made into the Christian Democratic hegemony in Flanders. The New Democratic Party sought, with much less success, to advance in Quebec. All this required some adaptation to local conditions and demands, in all their diversity.

Social democratic and labour parties responded to these developments by incorporating decentralisation, regionalism, pluralism and some recognition of plurinationality into their programmes. Yet the conversion was not complete and the tension between centralisation and decentralisation continued. The British Labour Party reverted to its historic home rule stance, but not without considerable internal conflict, and it continues to decry nationalism. As the French left regrouped in the 1970s, decentralisation and regionalism were incorporated into the programme of the new Socialist Party and even the Communists adopted regionalist themes. Decentralisation was one of the earliest initiatives of the Mitterrand government elected in 1981, together with a rather more tolerant attitude to regional languages and cultures. Yet the Socialists were unable make a clear choice for the region and left intact the old *départements*, created by the Revolution and generally regarded as neither tapping cultural identity nor well adapted to modern administrative needs. In fact, the old notables of the *départements*, together with the big-city mayors, emerged as the main winners from the process. Some moves were made to give Corsica a distinct status, but a proposal to recognise the existence of a 'Corsican people' was struck down by the Constitutional Court.

In Spain, the transition saw the granting of home rule to the nationalities and regions, with the support of the Socialist Party, itself in power from 1982. Yet the Socialists could not recognise the historic rights of the Basque Country, or the special status of the historical nationalities in general, and supported the LOAPA (*Ley de Armonización del Proceso Autonómico* – law to harmonise the devolution process) which sought to reduce the historic nationalities to the same status as other regions. Regions were finally established in Italy in the 1970s as a result of the centre-left coalition formula, bringing the Socialists in, but they were not endowed with great powers. In both France and Italy the Socialist and Communist left respectively started to use the limited powers of regional government to some effect, in the process convincing themselves of the merits of decentralisation, especially when they could use the regions as a platform to oppose central governments dominated by their opponents.

European Integration, Globalisation and the New Regionalism

The 1990s saw a further advance in regionalism and peripheral nationalism, responding to the new political economy and to the opening up of national states and markets to global and European influences. This forced the left to rethink radically its attitude to the state and the constellation of political authority. States in Europe and elsewhere are being transformed, losing power upwards to global and European institutions, downwards to regions and localities, and outwards to the market and civil society. One response to this on the part of the left is to defend the old centralised state model as the only bulwark against rampant global capitalism, and this stance was widely visible in the 1980s and 1990s. A whole genre of books in France draws attention to the 'end of territory' (Badie 1995) or the 'end of the nation-state' (Guéhenno 1995). Indeed the French version of Guéhenno's book gives the title as 'the end of democracy' as though the two were synonymous (Guéhenno 1993). Jean-Pierre Chevènement, once a prominent Socialist, staged his third resignation from the government on the issue of home rule for Corsica and went on to stand for the presidency on a platform of total opposition to European integration, globalisation, multiculturalism and regional devolution.

More measured judgements recognise that the nation-state formula may be a thing of the past, but that territory remains a vital element in political life and in government; it is just that it is changing scale. There is a large literature on local and regional economic restructuring, showing how the social construction of territories is a key feature in their adaptation to global and European markets (Keating et al. 2003). Territories are not so much being destroyed as reconfigured, above and below the nation-state. Old-style regional policies in which the state can redistribute investment across the territory are no longer viable in a world of mobile capital. Growth is less a matter of getting help from the centre and more of exploiting endogenous capacity. There are neo-liberal versions of these theories, purporting to show that regions are in a dog-eat-dog competition with each other for investment, technology and innovation, and must adapt to global markets by deregulation, cost-cutting and abandoning social protection (Ohmae 1995); these have become very influential among management consultants. In other cases, we are seeing a 'bourgeois regionalism' (Harvie 1994) in which regional business interests in partnership with government invest heavily in the infrastructure of development, including science and technology, as in Flanders, Quebec or some of the German Länder. There is also, however, a social democratic regionalism, with a search for a new social compromise at the territorial level, a way of reconciling growth in the new competitive conditions with social solidarity and environmental renewal.

Adaptation to the new regional economics is helped by the widespread abandonment of large-scale planning and nationalisation as an instrument of policy. Social democrats now accept the market economy but are coming to recognise that markets are different in different places, are socially constructed and distinguished by a range of factors including culture and politics. The further move to the right represented by the Third Way or New Centre can also open up space for differentiation, experimentation and flexibility. The New Public Administration, another favourite of Third Way politicians, emphasises debureaucratisation and reducing the role of the state, which again might favour a more decentralised style. On the other hand, the emphasis by New Labour on managerialism, technical criteria of success and centralised control militates against this.

There is some evidence, in places like Quebec, Catalonia, Flanders and Scotland, that social solidarity may also be reconfiguring at new territorial levels, although this aspect of the new territorial politics is less well researched than is the economic restructuring. To the extent that this is true, social democratic parties will be obliged to reconsider their strategies, as indeed they are doing. Nationalist parties, for their part, are obliged to consider the reverse implications. If they are to build a nation at a new territorial level, they must now consider how it will operate in global markets, and how it can sustain social solidarity in the face of global competitive pressures. One response is to move right and promote a tax-cutting agenda, as the SNP has done in 2003, although this comes at the cost of social cohesion. All of this provides a new context for the competition between social democratic parties and their territorial competitors as we see in Scotland as in other stateless nations and regions.

Europe provides another key factor. Social democratic parties have had the same ambivalent mixture of attitudes to European integration as they have to regional and national devolution. Some have favoured it (in France, Italy and Spain) while others have been cooler (in the United Kingdom and Scandinavia) but most are divided. They like Europe as an expression of internationalism and peace and some are ideologically inclined to European federalism. On the other hand, they are suspicious of the loss of power, the weakening of the state, the opening of markets to competition and the neo-liberal character that some attribute to the enterprise. One way out was to declare oneself in favour of Europe but of another type, more democratic, less bureaucratic, more social and less economic, a Europe of the people and not of the banks. By the 1990s, social democratic parties recognised that there is only one Europe on offer and had committed themselves to working with and within it; this included post-Communist parties like the Italian *Democratici di sinistra* (Left Democrats). They also appreciated that Europe, while it is organised on capitalist lines, does have a commitment to social protection; indeed this is one of the things that so infuriated Margaret Thatcher.

There is a strong territorial dimension to this, as minority nationalists and regionalists have seen in Europe a space for independence or, more commonly, new forms of autonomy transcending the old categories of statehood altogether. Social democrats have also discovered the link between supra-state integration and sub-state devolution and have entered into the new politics of the Europe of the Regions. This is a vague term, not referring to any specific set of political demands, but focusing on the reconfiguration of territory at all levels and the need for progressive politics to be aware of the articulation among them all. For social democrats the Europe of the Regions theme has an additional advantage, that it is tied to European regional policy as an expression of pan-European solidarity. With regular meetings and exchanges through European institutions, we can see the emergence of a European territorial social democracy, exploring the possibilities of the new complex and multi-level order. Outside Europe, such possibilities are scarce. Quebec social democrats do not have a transnational order to soften the impact of continental economic integration and have few homologues within the North American space for mutual support.

European social democracy is thus adapting to a new territorial politics. In some ways this represents a return to the origins, of locality, region and nationality, but it is new in its recognition of the new political economy and transnational integration. There are still conflicts and contradictions. The Italian left faces a stridently right-wing regionalist movement in the *Lega Nord*, which has gone the gamut of positions from federalism, to separatism, to Italian nationalism and devolution (the word is used in Italian). The racism, xenophobia and general extremism of the Lega have served to discredit regionalism and minority nationalism in Italy widely, although the Lega have long been disowned by other territorial parties in Europe. Nor has the Italian left made the complete ideological adaptation to the decentralised and pluralist state. It supports federalism but interprets this to mean administrative decentralisation. The French left are still caught between their centralist and decentralist instincts but were able during the Jospin government to bring forward proposals for Corsica that are radical by French, if not UK standards. Spanish socialists are divided between the centre, who broadly support the constitutional status quo, and their Catalan wing, who have brought out plans for a multinational confederation to compete with those of the Catalan nationalists of *Convergència i Unió*. Spanish socialists have also refused to accept the legitimacy of Basque proposals for reopening the constitution on the grounds that they violate the unity of Spain. The Canadian left largely opposed recognition of special status for Quebec in the 1980s and 1990s, although the leadership of the New Democratic Party was generally more supportive. For its part the Quebec left declined to support the opposition of the Canadian left to North American free trade. Flemish socialists face a dilemma over the proposals of other Flemish parties to decentralise social security to the communities, with a loss of pan-Belgian solidarity.

Social democracy has come a long way over the territorial question but, as in Scotland, it still faces its historic tensions. The old world of centralised state management has disappeared, certainly across the large states of Europe, and an intermediary layer of politics and government has emerged in conjunction with supranational integration. Neither right nor left has adapted fully to this – British Conservatives, for example, are torn between an economic globalism and a strident insular nationalism in politics. Social Democratic parties likewise are still searching for a new formula. Scottish Labour, as we noted at the beginning, is not alone.

REFERENCES

Gramsci, A. (1978), 'Operai e contadini', from *l'Ordine Nuovo*, 3 January 1920, reprinted in V. Lo Curto (ed.), *La questione meridionale*, D'Anna, Florence.

Guéhenno, J. M. (1993), *La fin de la démocratie*, Flammarion, Paris.

Guéhenno, J. M. (1995), *The End of the Nation-State*, University of Minnesota Press, Minneapolis.

Harvie, C. (1994), *The Rise of Regional Europe*, Routledge, London.

Hechter, M. (1975), *Internal Colonialism. The Celtic Fringe in British National Development, 1536–1966*, Routledge and Kegan Paul, London.

Keating, M. (1988), *State and Regional Nationalism. Territorial Politics and the European State*, Harvester-Wheatsheaf, London.

Keating, M. (2001), *Plurinational Democracy. Stateless Nations in a Post-Sovereignty Era*, Oxford University Press, Oxford.

Keating, M., Loughlin, J. and Deschouwer, K. (2003), *Culture, Institutions and Economic Development. A Study of Eight European Regions*, Edward Elgar, Cheltenham.

Lafont, R. (1967), *La révolution régionaliste*, Gallimard, Paris.

Lorenzo Espinoza, J. M. (1995), *Historia de Euska Herria, III: el nacimiento de la nación*, Txalaparte, Tafalla.

Nicolas, M. (2001), *Bretagne. Un destin européen*, Presses universitaires de Rennes, Rennes.

Ohmae, K. (1995), *The End of the Nation State. The Rise of Regional Economies*, The Free Press, New York.

Sorauren, M. (1998), *Historia de Navarra, el estado vasco*, Pamiela, Pamplona.

Index

Abercrombie, Sir Patrick, 30
administrative devolution, 56–9
Airlie, Jimmy, 220
Alexander, Douglas, 167, 188, 206, 229
Alexander, Wendy, 48, 62, 129–30,
    135, 139, 188, 207
Allison, Jimmy, 44
Amalgamated Society of Engineers, 53
anarchism, 234, 235
Ashdown, Paddy, 128, 212
Asquith, Herbert Henry, 53
Attlee, Clement, 34
Austro-Marxists, 236

Baillie, Jackie, 121n, 142, 176
Baker, Richard, 143
Baldwin, Oliver, 37
Baldwin, Stanley, 155
Balfour, Arthur, 52
Barbour, Mary, 105
Barnett, Joel, 157
Barnett Formula, 59, 157
Barr, Rev. James, 26, 146, 147, 157
Basque Country, 235, 236, 240, 241
Beckett, Margaret, 8
Belgian socialism, 236, 240, 244
Benn, Tony, 8, 58
Bennites, 196–7
Bevan, Aneurin, 147, 150
Beveridge Report (1942), 30, 35
biographies, 3
Blair, Tony, 48, 63, 64, 188, 203
    and devolution, 47, 48, 127–8
    and Gordon Brown, 202, 203, 209–
      15
    Scottish Labour members' views, 8
    and trade unions, 223–5

Blunkett, David, 8
Bolton, George, 220
Boyack, Jimmy, 63
Boyack, Sarah, 130
Boyson, Rhodes, 197
Brady, Shaun, 229
Brankin, Rhona, 121n
Britishness, reassertion, 166–8, 206
Brittany, 239, 240
Brown, Gordon, 64, 154, 166, 185,
    188
    background, 195
    biography, 3
    devolution, 41, 60, 128, 167, 196,
      199
    early career, 196–7
    parliamentary career, 197, 201; as
      Chancellor, 205–9
    political thought, 195–218
    promotion of Britishness, 167, 206
    rector of Edinburgh University, 58
    and Scottish Labour, 8, 207
    and Tony Blair, 202, 203–4, 209–
      15
Brown, Prof. Alice, 131
Buchanan, George, 26, 27, 146
Burns, Thomas, 29
Burns, Tom, 58
by-elections
    Glasgow, Govan (1973), 150
    Glasgow, Govan (1988), 46, 131,
      172n
    Glasgow, Hillhead (1982), 44
    Hamilton (1967), 40, 150
    Mid-Lanark (1888), 1
    North Lanark (1929), 108
    Paisley (1948), 37

Callaghan, Jim, 41, 42
Cameron, James (journalist), 57
Cameron, Jim (Militant supporter), 43–4
Campaign for a Scottish Assembly, 46
Campaign for Socialism, 187
Canavan, Dennis, 90, 132–3, 134
Catalonia, 235–6, 244
Caterpillar factory, occupation, 223
centralisation, 36–7
   regional policies and, 238, 240–1
   social democracy and, 237–8, 240
Chevènement, Jean-Pierre, 241
Chisholm, Malcolm, 42, 135, 186
Christie, Campbell, 46, 226
Churchill, Winston, 35, 53
Clarion Clubs, 53
Clark, Alan, 197
Clark, Lynda, 12
class, social
   Scottish Labour and, 21
   social democracy and, 237
   see also working-class interests
Clinton, Bill, 202, 210
Clyde Valley Plan, 30
Clydeside, Red, 9, 54, 148
co-operative movement, 24
coalition government
   Holyrood, 94–5, 137–8, 140, 143
   local government, 143–4
colonialism, internal, 239, 240
communism/Communist Party, 28, 57, 222
   and trade unions, 220, 221
Community Charge (poll tax), 45, 61, 164, 172n
Compass, 190n
Connarty, Michael, 132
Conservative collectivism, 55
Conservative Party
   before 1914, 22
   decline, 45, 48
   see also Unionists
Constitutional Convention, 46–7, 61, 63, 128, 129, 144, 165, 172n
   women and, 115
Cook, Robin, 58, 60, 154, 166, 200
   biography, 3

devolution, 42, 165
   Scottish Labour members' views, 8
corporatism, 28, 31, 35
corruption in local government, 4, 36
Craigen, Jim, 231
Campaign for Socialism, 187
Crawfurd, Helen, 105
Crosland, Tony, 59, 210
Crow, Bob, 227, 229
Crowther Commission *see* Kilbrandon Commission
Crowther-Hunt, Lord (Norman Hunt), 151, 153
Curran, Kevin, 229
Curran, Margaret, 121n

Daily Record, 38, 44
Dalyell, Tam
   biography, 3
   devolution, 42, 130, 147, 151, 152, 153, 157, 165
Davidson, Ian, 132
Deacon, Susan, 129, 133, 141–2
depression, economic, 26, 27
devolution, 10, 60, 61, 62–3
   administrative, 56–9
   Gordon Brown, 198–200, 206
   Labour Party and, 40–1, 42, 150–2, 156–8, 176–7, 178
   proposals/campaign (1987–97), 45–8
   referendum (1979), 41–2
   referendum (1997), 47, 48
   Scottish Labour and, 128–30, 142–4, 163–70
   women's representation and, 112–15
   see also home rule; Scottish Parliament
Dewar, Donald, 45, 58, 133, 135, 142, 154, 184, 185
   death, 138
   and devolution, 46, 48, 128, 129, 165
   as First Minister, 138, 142
   Gordon Brown tribute, 206–7
   and nationalism, 147–8
   and Scottish Parliament candidate selection, 135–6
   as Secretary of State, 48

Din, Anwari, 133
doctrine, Scottish Labour Party, 13–14
Dollan, Agnes, 105
Dollan, Sir Patrick, 34, 36, 56
Drucker, Henry, 8, 13, 196, 199
Duncan Smith, Iain, 157, 227

economic issues
    pre-1914, 51–3
    World War I, 24, 25
    inter-war years, 26–7, 28, 29, 35,
        53, 54–6
    World War II, 30–1
    post-1945, 39, 56, 57–64
    Gordon Brown, 201–2, 205–6, 207,
        208–9
Edmonds, John, 227
education, Scottish, 147
Education (Scotland) Act (1918), 53,
    147
Educational Institute of Scotland
    (EIS), 38, 229
Elder, Murray, 48, 132, 135
elections
    turn-out, 87–8, 90, 91, 97–8
    see also by-elections; general
        elections; Scottish Parliament
        elections
electoral system
    first-past-the-post, 5
    proportional representation, 95–7,
        225; gender balance in, 114
    reform, 95–7, 138
Elgar, William, 35
Elliot, Walter, 35, 55, 56
emigration, post-World War II, 57
ethos, Scottish Labour Party, 13–14
European Community membership, 59
European integration, 241–2, 243
European Parliament, women in, 110
Ewing, Winifred, 40, 150

Fabian Society, 23, 52
Fair is Efficient (Brown), 204
Fife council, 16n
financial services, 61
Findlay, Moira, 121n
Fitzpatrick, Brian, 136

Foot, Michael, 43, 44, 128, 196
Forsyth, Michael, 61
Forward, 24, 52
Foyer, Rozanne, 226, 231
France, socialism, 235, 237, 239, 240–
    1, 244
Freeman, Jeanne, 133
funding
    formula for Scotland, 154–5, 156,
        157
    Scottish Labour Party, 179–80
Fyfe, Maria, 132

Gaitskell, Hugh, 38
Galbraith, Sam, 134, 135, 139
Gallacher, Willie, 57, 149
Galloway, George, 36, 45, 196
Gartcosh, 223
Geddes, Patrick, 53, 56
General, Municipal, Boilermakers and
    Allied Trades Union (GMB),
    227
general elections
    1900, 52
    1906, 52
    1922, 25
    1923, 2
    1929, 2
    1931, 27, 34
    1935, 27
    1945, 34
    1951, 37
    1955, 37
    1959, 2
    1964, 2, 39
    1966, 39
    1970, 40, 150
    1974 (Feb.), 40, 42–3, 151
    1974 (Oct.), 40–1, 152
    1979, 42, 45, 152
    1983, 45, 60
    1987, 45, 61, 165, 222
    1992, 45, 61, 166
    1997, 48, 98
    2001, 99
    Scottish Labour Party share of vote
        (1918–2001), 2, 3
General Strike, 54

Gilmour, Sir John, 55
Gladstone, William Ewart, 157
Glasgow, Govan, 46, 131, 150, 151, 172n
Glasgow, Hillhead, 44, 45
Glasgow Women's Housing Association, 105
Glen, Marilyn, 121n
globalisation, 241–2
GMB Union, 227
Godman, Norman, 132
Goschen, George, 154
Goschen Formula (Proportion), 155
Government of National Emergency, 27
Graham, Sir James, 154
Gramsci, Antonio, 236, 239–40
Grant, Ted, 43
Gray, Iain, 12, 90
Grierson, John, 56

Hague, William, 157, 227
Haldane, R. B., Viscount, 54
Hamilton, by-election (1967), 40, 150
Hardie, Agnes, 107, 108
Hardie, Keir, 1, 21, 52, 106
  biography, 3
  nationalism, 146, 147
Harrison, Doug, 220
Hayes, Billy, 227
Healey, Denis, 59, 197
health service, World War II, 30
Heath, Edward, 42–3, 220
Herbison, Margaret (Peggy), 57, 108
Holloway, Richard, bishop, 133
Home Robertson, John, 134
home rule
  inter-war years, 28–9
  Labour Party attitudes, 38, 40–1, 146, 147–8
  MacCormick, John and, 36
  see also devolution
housing
  World War I, 25
  inter-war years, 26, 27, 28, 35, 54, 56
  World War II, 30
  post-1945, 56

Housing Act 1924 (Wheatley), 26
Hughes, Janis, 134
Hunt, Norman (Lord Crowther-Hunt), 151, 153
Hutton, Sadie, 151

ideology, 21, 25, 28, 32
Independent Labour Party (ILP), 1, 22, 23, 24, 34, 52
  disaffiliation, 27, 34
  women in, 108
individualism, 98
industrial heritage, 51–2
Industrial Workers of the World (Wobblies), 53
industry
  pre-1914, 51–3
  World War I, 24, 25, 54
  inter-war years, 54–6
  World War II, 30, 31
  post-1945, 38, 39, 56, 57–64
Ingram, Adam, 42
Ireland, 53, 55, 62
  home rule, 154
  socialism/nationalism, 235, 237, 239
Italy
  Lega, 244
  socialism, 235–6, 237, 239–40, 241, 244

jacobinism, 235, 236
Jamieson, Cathy, 141, 229–30
Jenkins, Roy, 44, 45, 210
John Smith: Life and Soul of the Party (Brown and Naughtie, eds), 202
John Smith House, 127
Johnston, Douglas, 37
Johnston, Tom, 23–4, 26, 27, 29, 54, 56, 154
  biographies, 3
  and nationalism, 147–8
  as Secretary of State, 29–31, 35–6, 56

Kelly, Dr Michael, 60
Kennedy, Charles, 45
Kerr, Andy, 140, 229

Kilbrandon Commission, 40, 58, 150, 163, 172n
Kinnock, Neil, 42, 128, 197, 223
Kirkwood, David, 26, 27, 54
Kitson, Alex, 40

Labour Co-ordinating Committee (LCC), 43, 44, 46, 54, 187
Women's Network, 116
Labour governments
1924, 25
1929–31, 26–27
1945–51, 34–5, 36, 37, 57
1964–70, 39–40
Labour Party
devolution, 164–5, 166–8
image (1992–2001), 72–9, 82
membership, 5–6
nationalism, 161–2
reaction to Thatcher, 43
Scottish Labour contribution, 15
women in, 106, 110–12, 114–15, 117
see also New Labour; Scottish Labour Party
Labour Renewal Network, 99, 187
Labour Representation Committee, 1
Labour Women's Action Committee (LWAC), 114, 116
Labour Women's Network, 121n
labourism, politics of, 211
Lafont, Robert, 239
Lamont, Johann, 121n
Lanark see Mid-Lanark; North Lanark
Lazarowicz, Mark, 133
Lee, Jennie, 108
Let Scotland Prosper (1958 report), 162–3
Liberal Democrats, 45
coalition with Scottish Labour, 94–5, 137–8, 140, 143–4
Scottish Parliament elections, 90
Liberal Party
pre-1914, 22, 52
inter-war years, 25, 53
Liberal–SDP Alliance, 45
1979 general election, 45
liberalism, 234
New, 22

Liddell, Helen, 38, 129
Lindsay, Isobel, 133
Lithgow, Sir William, 57
Lloyd George, David, 54
local government
before 1914, 22
coalition politics, 143–4
corruption in, 4, 36
proportional representation, 95–7
voting reform, 138
women in, 110, 119

Mabon, Dickson, 45
McAllion, John, 132, 133, 135, 141, 186
McCabe, Tom, 139
McConnell, Jack, 48–9, 129–30, 139, 166, 180, 184, 185–6, 188, 228
devolution, 168
as First Minister, 63, 129, 138, 139, 141, 170, 228
and New Labour, 12
as Scottish General Secretary, 48, 129, 179, 188
Scottishness, 168–9
selection for Holyrood, 133–4
and trade unions, 228
women's representation, 115
MacCormick, John, 36–7, 162
MacCormick, Neil, 58
McCrae, Rosina, 121n
MacDiarmid, Hugh, 54, 57
MacDonald, Ramsay, 21, 26–7, 53, 54, 154
biography, 3
nationalism, 146, 147
MacDonnell, Sir Anthony, 55
McGahey, Mick, 220
MacGuiness, James, 55
Macintosh, John P., 38
McKenna, Rosemary, 131
Mackenzie, R.F., 57
McLean, Bob, 134
Maclean, John, 25, 55
McLeish, Henry, 135, 143, 180, 184, 207, 228
as First Minister, 138, 169
resignation scandal, 4–5, 16, 139

MacLennan, Robert, 45
McLetchie, David, 12, 90
McMaster, Gordon, 131
Macmurray, John, 210
Maginnis, Elizabeth, 133
Major, John, 48, 61
Mann, Jean, 57, 108
Marshall, Willie, 34, 40
Marxism, socialism and, 233, 234
Maughan, Doug, 133
Maxton, James, 26, 27, 56, 149
    biographies, 3, 200–1
Maxton, John, 179
Mid-Lanark, by-election (1888), 1
Middleton, George, 57
Militant Tendency, 43–4, 221
Milne, James, 220
Miners Federation of Great Britain
    (MFGB), 53
miners' strike (1984–5), 222
Moffat, Abe, 57
Motherwell and Wishaw Constituency
    Labour Party, 180

National Covenant, 37
National Executive Committee
    (NEC), Scottish Advisory
    Committee, 34
National Party of Scotland, 29
    see also Scottish National Party
nationalisation, 31, 36–7
nationalism, 160–1
    British, 161–2
    cultural, 147–8, 149
    Scottish Labour and, 146–50, 160–
    75
    socialism and, 234–45
Naughtie, James, 202
The Network, 131, 187
New Centre, 242
New Labour, 11, 14, 60–4, 93
    attachment to USA, 210–11
    Brown/Blair and, 204–5, 210–15
    and devolution, 128–9
    image of, 72–9, 82
    Scottish Labour and, 7–8, 11–12,
    63–4, 69, 74–6, 93–4
    and trade unions, 223–6, 227, 230

New Scotland, New Britain (Brown
    and Alexander), 206
new towns, 30, 56
North Lanark, by-election (1929),
    108
North Sea oilfields, 58–9, 150, 153

O'Brien, Gerry, 116
oilfields, North Sea, 58–9, 150, 153

Paisley, by-election (1948), 37
Parliament, Holyrood *see* Scottish
    Parliament
Parliament, Westminster *see*
    Westminster Parliament
Peacock, Peter, 135–6
Pentlands question, 12
policy forums, 99–100, 109, 183–4
*The Politics of Nationalism and
    Devolution* (Brown and Drucker),
    199
poll tax (Community Charge), 45, 61,
    164, 172n
Pollock, John, 40
pragmatism, 32
Prentis, Dave, 227
Prescott, John, 8
press, attitude to Scottish Labour, 38
private finance initiative (PFI), 225–
    6, 229
privatisations, 62
Progressivism, 22
proportional representation
    local government, 95–7
    Scottish Parliament, 96, 225;
    gender balance and, 114
public private partnership (PPP), 229
public service reform, 101

Quebec, 236, 239, 240, 244
Quinn, Esther, 121n
Quinn, Lesley, 109

Rail, Maritime and Transport (RMT)
    Union, 227
The Real Rulers of Scotland (Burns), 29
rearmament, inter–war years, 28–9, 55
Red Clydeside, 9, 54, 148

The Red Paper on Scotland, 58, 197–9
Reform Act (1888), 52
regional policies, 238, 240–1, 242
regionalism, 242–4
Reich, Robert, 210
Reid, Jimmy, 60, 220
Reid, John, 142, 179
Reinventing the Left (Miliband, ed), 204
religion, politics and, 38, 55
Renewal, 187
Renfrewshire council, 16n
rent strike, Glasgow (1915), 24
    women and, 105
Rifkind, Malcolm, 12, 58, 61, 165
Rix, Mick, 227, 229
RMT Union, 227
Roberton, Esther, 133
Robertson, George, 47, 129
Robertson, John, 41
Rocard, Michel, 239
Ross, Ernie, 131
Ross, Jim, 62
Ross, Willie, 39, 40, 128, 151, 154
Rowley, Alex, 207
Royal Commission on the
    Constitution (Kilbrandon), 40,
    58, 150, 163, 172n
Ruskin Society, 52

scandals, 4, 36
Scargill, Arthur, 222
Scotland: The Real Divide (Brown and
    Cook, eds), 200
Scotland Act (1978), 152, 1163
Scotland Act (1998), 156
Scotland and Wales Bill (1977), 156
Scott, Paul, 62
Scottish Advisory Council, 1, 176
Scottish Co-operative Women's
    Guild, 105, 107
Scottish Constitutional Convention,
    46–7, 61, 63, 128, 129, 144, 165,
    172n
    women and, 115
Scottish Convention, 36, 37, 162
Scottish Council of Development and
    Industry, 35

Scottish Council of State, 35
Scottish Development Agency, 59
Scottish Home Rule Association, 52–
    3
Scottish Home Rule Bills (1924 and
    1928), 146
Scottish Labour Action (SLA), 46,
    129, 165–6, 172n, 176, 184, 187,
    188–9
Scottish Labour Party
    pre-1914, 22–4, 52–3
    World War I, 24–6
    inter-war years, 2, 26–9, 53–6
    World War II, 29–32
    post-1945, 2, 34–50, 56–8
    autonomy and organisation, 176–
        91
    and British politics, 146–59, 161,
        169–70
    defactionalisation, 188
    and devolution, 128–30, 142–4,
        146, 147–8, 152, 163–70
    doctrine and ethos, 13–14
    funding, 179–80
    Hardie, Keir, 1, 52
    headquarters, 127, 129
    hegemonic instincts, 5
    labour culture and, 8–15
    leadership, 184–6, 207
    membership, 4, 5–8, 143, 180–3;
        influence of, 99–100, 183–4,
        185–6
    nationalism and, 146–50, 160–75
    policy making in, 183–4
    regional variations/heartlands, 9,
        86–103
    renewal, 101–2, 104–23
    in Scottish Parliament, 48–9, 136–
        42, 169
    Scottishness, 10–11
    support for, 13, 69–71, 79–82, 87–
        9, 91–5, 109
    women and, 102, 104–23, 143
Scottish Labour Party (Sillars), 41,
    152
Scottish Labour Women's Caucus,
    121n, 187
Scottish Militant Labour, 44

Scottish National Party (SNP)
  inter-war years, 28, 29
  post-1945, 40–1, 58–9, 150–1, 152–
    3
  in Scottish parliament, 137
  and devolution campaign, 46
  support for, 79–82
Scottish Office, 55
Scottish Parliament, 138–44
  candidate selection, 130–6, 142–3
  coalition politics, 94–5, 137–8, 140,
    143–4
  committee system, 140–1
  elections: 1999, 136; 2003, 12, 63,
    87–8, 98
  electoral system, 95, 96, 114, 225
  membership, 63, 136–7, 141, 143
  national distinctiveness, 137–8,
    169–70
  tax discretion, 47
  trade unions and, 226, 228, 231
  and Westminster, 137–8, 142, 169–
    70
  women in, 104, 109, 110, 113–15,
    119–20
Scottish Self-Government Committee,
    29
Scottish Socialist Alliance, 44
Scottish Socialist Party, 44, 56, 140
Scottish Trades Union Congress
    (STUC), 46, 219, 223, 226, 228,
    231
Scottish Unionist Association, 36
Scottish Women's Committee, 116,
    117
Scottish Workers' Parliamentary
    Committee, 1
Secretary of State for Scotland, office
    of, 29, 49, 64, 152, 154, 158,
    185
Serwotka, Mark, 227
Sewel, Lord John, 135
Shaw, Clarice McNab, 106, 108
Sheppard, Tommy, 133, 176
Sheridan, Tommy, 44, 140, 149
Shinwell, Manny, biography, 3
Signposts for Scotland (1963 report),
    163

Silicon Glen, 61
Sillars, Jim, 41, 46, 89, 196
Simpson, Derek, 227
Smart, Ian, 134
Smith, John, 47, 58, 61, 64, 112, 166,
    202, 223
  biography, 3
  and devolution, 127–8, 152
  Gordon Brown on, 202–3
Smith, Nigel, 131
social democracy
  historical trajectory, 234–7
  and nation-state, 233–4, 237, 241–2
  twentieth century, 237–44
Social Democratic Party (SDP), 44–5,
    60
  Liberal–SDP Alliance, 45
social issues
  World War I, 24, 25
  inter-war years, 26–7, 28
  World War II, 30
  post-1945, 39, 59
  women, 107, 117, 141
socialism, 21
  Christian, 210
  Gordon Brown, 198, 203, 204
  gradualist, 25, 28
  historical development, 234–7
  nationalism and, 234–45
  Scottish, 148–50; pre 1914, 22–3;
    World War I, 24–5; inter-war
    years, 26
Socialist International Women, 110
Socialist Labour Party, 53
Socialist Workers' Party (SWP), 221
Spain, socialism, 235, 236, 239, 241,
    244
Special Areas Act (1934), 55
Spiers, Bill, 226
Steel, David, 58
Stephen, Nicol, 90
Stevenson, Ronnie, 43
Straw, Jack, 8

Tartan Tax, 47
territorial politics, 237–44
Thatcher, Margaret, 43, 59, 60–1,
    130, 221

Third Way politics, 242
Thompson, Sir Clive, 224
Tindall, Frank, 56
Toothill Report (1961), 57–8
Tory Party *see* Conservative Party;
   Unionists
trade unions
   pre-1914, 23, 53
   World War I, 24
   and Labour movement, 219–32
   Scottish Labour funding, 180
   and Scottish Parliament, 226, 228,
   231
Tynan, Bill, 133

unemployment
   inter-war years, 26–7, 28
   post-1945, 38
unionism, 154
   Gordon Brown, 198, 206
   Labour Party, 154
Unionists
   nineteenth century, 52
   inter-war years, 55
   post-1945, 36, 37–8
   decline, 37–8, 39
   see also Conservative Party
United States, New Labour and, 210–
   11
Upper Clyde Shipbuilders, 220, 239

Values, Visions and Voices (Brown and
   Wright, eds), 203

Wallace, Jim, 137
Watson, Mike, 140
welfare issues
   World War I, 25
   inter-war years, 27, 28
   World War II, 30
welfare state, creation of, 34–5
Welsh, Ian, 133

West Lothian Question, 147, 157
West of Scotland Labour question, 5
Westminster Parliament, 153–4
   funding for Scotland, 154–5, 156,
   157
   Scottish representation, 147, 155–8
Westwood, Joseph, 36
Wheatley, John, 23, 26, 54, 107, 154,
   201
   Housing Act, 26
Where There is Greed (Brown), 201
White, Rev. John, 55
Wilkie, George, 53
Wilson, Andrew, 87
Wilson, Brian, 42
Wilson, Harold, 39, 40, 58, 150, 151
Wobblies, 53
women
   50:50 campaign, 113
   Scottish Labour, 102, 104–23, 143
   Scottish Parliament, 104, 109, 110,
      113–15, 119–20; selection as
      candidates, 134
   Westminster Parliament, 108–9,
      112
Women's Labour League, 105, 106
Women's Labour Party, 105
Woodburn, Arthur, 34, 162
Woodley, Tony, 229
Workers' Revolutionary Party (WRP),
   221
working-class interests, 21, 23, 24–5,
   26, 27, 28
World War I, 24–6
World War II, 29–32
Wright, Kenyon, 63
Wright, Tony, 203
Wyper, Hugh, 220

Young, Alf, 196
Young Scots' Society, 52
Younger, George, 60, 61

The Scottish Labour History Society

The aim of the Society is to promote the study, discussion, publication, exhibition, filming, recording etc. of labour history – that is, the history of the working class, especially in Scotland.

Since the Society's formation in 1961, these aims have been carried out through conferences, publications, exhibitions and special projects.

The Society's *Journal* is published annually and sent free to members. Volumes 1 to 30 of the *Journal* will shortly be available on CDROM and our new website can be visited at: www.SLHS.org.uk

The Society has undertaken several projects – to preserve records of working-class movements in Scotland, tape record recollections of labour activists, promote the making of film, video and TV programmes (such as the 1987 Channel 4 series *Pioneers of Socialism*) and photograph trade union banners.

The Society is an independent organisation, but has always enjoyed strong practical, moral and some financial support from the broad trade union, labour and cooperative movement.

The Society warmly welcomes new members. The annual subscription is £10 (waged), £4 (unwaged), £15 (organisation) or £20 (overseas). Fees are payable to Scottish Labour History Society and should be sent to the Treasurer, Jim Cranstoun, 10 Fountainhall Road, Edinburgh EH9 2NN.

Sectarianism in Scotland

Steve Bruce, Tony Glendinning, Iain Paterson and Michael Rosie

'This is a subject which has generated much impassioned commentary, not a little emoting and much high-profile assertion, but there has been scant academic analysis. The gap is there for all to see. This book fills it.'
Harry Reid, author of *Outside Verdict: An Old Kirk in a New Scotland*

Is Scotland a sectarian society?

Scotland is divided not by religion as much as by arguments about the enduring importance of religious divisions. The 'curse' of Sectarianism is debated in the Parliament, the General Assembly and in the media. What we have not had until now is a serious assessment of the evidence.

This book tests the rhetoric with historical and social scientific data, describing and explaining the changing pattern of relations between Catholics and Protestants over the 20th century. It concludes that Catholic integration in Scotland has been far more successful than most commentators would have us believe. While there were once deep social, political, economic and cultural divisions, these have now all but disappeared. In Scotland's increasingly secular society, religious identity has steeply declined in social significance.

The book is informed by both a considerable body of evidence from new historical research and major social surveys, and by the authors' understanding of what the mixing of religion and politics looks like elsewhere – in America, Australia and New Zealand, as well as in Ulster.

Presenting a reasoned argument and up-to-date information, the book aims to contribute to a better-informed view of sectarianism in Scotland.

Steve Bruce is Professor of Sociology at the University of Aberdeen
Tony Glendinning is Senior Lecturer in Sociology at the University of Aberdeen
Iain Paterson is a Senior Research Officer at Glasgow City Council
Michael Rosie is Lecturer in Sociology at the University of Edinburgh

June 2004 224pp Paperback 0 7486 1911 9 £11.99

Order from Marston Book Services, PO Box 269, Abingdon, Oxon OX14 4YN
Tel 01235 465500 • Fax 01235 465555 • E: direct.order@marston.co.uk

Visit our website **www.eup.ed.ac.uk**

All details correct at time of printing but subject to change without notice

SECOND EDITION
The Scotsman Guide to Scottish Politics
Edited by Matthew Spicer

The second edition of *The Scotsman Guide to Scottish Politics* gives you a completely revised, updated and easy-to-use guide to all the information you need to follow Scottish politics, both at Holyrood and at Westminster.

A series of specially commissioned short essays from a range of eminent politicians, academics and Scotsman writers provides the context:

- Jason Allardyce on the 2003 Scottish Parliament Election
- John Curtice's analysis of Scottish voting patterns
- Susan Deacon MSP on the role of women in politics
- Joyce McMillan on Government and the Arts
- George Kerevan reviews systems of Proportional Representation
- Fraser Nelson on the ancient office of Secretary of State for Scotland
- Robert McNeil takes a sideways look at the new Parliament building

The core of the book is an invaluable directory of political facts and figures – results from the Scottish Election of 2003, biographies of all MSPs, the Scottish results of the General Election of 2001, biographies of Scottish MPs and Scottish MEPs, and an appendix of further useful information about the Scotland Office, the Scottish Executive, access to the Parliament, Scottish Parliament Committees, Scottish constituencies and their representatives, Scottish political parties, and useful addresses and numbers.

Key Features
- Completely revised and updated
- Includes essays from a range of journalists, academics and politicians
- Gives a full listing of results from the 2003 Scottish Election

Matthew Spicer is a journalist, producer and former Editor, Television Current Affairs, at BBC Scotland

February 2004   384pp   Paperback   0 7486 1924 0   £12.99

Order from Marston Book Services, PO Box 269, Abingdon, Oxon OX14 4YN
Tel 01235 465500   •   Fax 01235 465555   •   E: direct.order@marston.co.uk

Visit our website **www.eup.ed.ac.uk**

All details correct at time of printing but subject to change without notice

Living in Scotland
Social and Economic Change since 1980

Lindsay Paterson, Frank Bechhofer and David McCrone

Living in Scotland gives an account of the key social changes in Scottish society, describing how it has been transformed over the last two to three decades. Drawing on a uniquely wide range of data from government statistics, social surveys and over-time data sources, the book tells the story of society in Scotland during the approach and arrival of the new century.

The authors analyse the large-scale changes which have profoundly altered Scottish society affecting the country's demography, patterns of work and employment, the distributions of income, wealth and poverty, social class and social mobility, educational opportunities, and patterns of consumption and lifestyle.

While Scotland shares many of these social trends with similar western societies, its reaction to them is shaped by its own history and culture. The authors argue that Scotland is now a more affluent, comfortable and pleasant place to live in than just two or three decades ago, but that it remains seriously divided and stratified. A significant minority of its people remain disadvantaged and relatively deprived. This represents the major political and cultural challenge for the new Scotland.

Living in Scotland is written by three of the country's foremost sociologists. Together, they build a picture of a changing Scotland at the beginning of the 21st century.

Key Features
- A CD-ROM of all the key tables is provided with the book
- Builds a picture of the changing society of Scotland over the second half of the twentieth century
- Uses a uniquely wide range of statistical data sources which are set in context and explained in non-technical ways

June 2004   224pp   Paperback   0 7486 1785 X   £16.99

Order from Marston Book Services, PO Box 269, Abingdon, Oxon OX14 4YN
Tel 01235 465500   •   Fax 01235 465555   •   E: direct.order@marston.co.uk

Visit our website www.eup.ed.ac.uk

All details correct at time of printing but subject to change without notice

Being English in Scotland

Murray Watson

'This book is a truly ground breaking achievement. Despite their importance, English migrants to Scotland have received little attention from scholars. Now, for the first time, we have a thorough examination of their place in modern Scottish society which is at once provocative and immensely stimulating. *Being English in Scotland* deserves a wide readership.'   Tom Devine, author of *The Scottish Nation*

Boldly venturing into new territory, *Being English in Scotland* reveals how a massive increase of English settlers has unobtrusively formed Scotland's most significant migrant community in modern times. The history of relations between England and Scotland is always passionate and often controversial. What is extraordinary is that the pervasive spread and influence of English migration north of the Border has been largely ignored until now.

Using a range of different sources including oral history contributions from English people living all over Scotland, Murray Watson explores how the English merged into and contributed to Scottish society in the second half of the twentieth century. Many of the myths surrounding the English in Scotland are dispelled and what emerges instead is that the migratory experience has been extremely complex and multi-faceted in nature. The near-invisible absorption of so many English-born migrants has far-reaching implications for the host communities at a local, regional and national level, as well as influencing Scotland's economy, its demography, culture and society.

At a political and constitutional level, after a number of false starts, Scotland has gained some measure of devolved autonomy. And here, English migrants have shown a range of fascinating responses in the reconstruction of their own identities. In leaving behind the undoubted insecurities and uncertainties about what it means to be English, their reactions to moving to a country with strong traditions of national feeling has been intriguing and surprising.

The first comprehensive exploration of the complex process of English migration into Scotland, *Being English in Scotland* challenges us with as many questions as answers.

October 2003   224pp   Paperback   0 7486 1859 7   £12.99

Order from Marston Book Services, PO Box 269, Abingdon, Oxon OX14 4YN
Tel 01235 465500 • Fax 01235 465555 • E: direct.order@marston.co.uk

Visit our website **www.eup.ed.ac.uk**

All details correct at time of printing but subject to change without notice